INFORMATION SYSTEMS PROVISION

The McGraw-Hill Information Systems, Management and Strategy Series

Series Coordinator
Dr Nimal Jayaratna
Heriot-Watt University
Edinburgh

Series Board

Professor Trevor Wood-Harper, Salford University
Professor Bob Galliers, Warwick Business School
Dr Steve Smithson, London School of Economics
Mr Bob Wood, Salford University
Dr Patrik Holt, Heriot-Watt University
Professor Frank Stowell, University of Paisley
Dr Daune West, University of Paisley
Dr Ray Miles, North East Wales Institute
Professor Hans-Erik Nissen, Lund University
Professor Jean-Michael Larrasquet, Université de Pau et des Pays L'Adour
Professor Tom Wilson, University of Sheffield

Further Titles in this Series

Client-Led Design: A Systemic Approach to Information Systems Definition
Frank A. Stowell and Daune West

Information Management
Andrew Mortimer

Understanding and Evaluating
Methodologies: NIMSAD A Systemic
Framework
Nimal Jayaratna

INFORMATION SYSTEMS PROVISION

The Contribution of Soft Systems Methodology

Frank Stowell

McGRAW-HILL BOOK COMPANY

London • New York • St Louis • San Francisco • Auckland • Bogotá
Caracas • Lisbon • Madrid • Mexico • Milan • Hamburg • Montreal
New Delhi • Panama • Paris • San Juan • São Paulo
Singapore • Sydney • Tokyo • Toronto

Published by
McGRAW-HILL Book Company Europe
Shoppenhangers Road, Maidenhead, Berkshire, SL6 2QL, England
Telephone 01628 23432
Fax 01628 770224

British Library Cataloguing in Publication Data
Information Systems Provision:
Contribution of Soft Systems Methodology.
– (McGraw-Hill Information Systems,
Management & Strategy Series)
I. Stowell, Frank A. II. Series
004.2
ISBN 0–07–707716–4

Library of Congress Cataloging-in-Publication Data
Stowell, Frank A.
Information systems provision : the contribution of soft systems
methodology / Frank Stowell.
p.   cm. – (McGraw-Hill information systems, management
and strategy series)
Includes bibliographical references and index.
ISBN 0–07–707716–4
1. Management information systems.   2. Computer software-Development.
3. System design.   I. Title.   II. Series.
T58.64.S75 1994
004.2'1–dc20
94–40924
CIP

12345 CUP 98765

Typeset by Datix International Limited, Bungay, Suffolk
and printed and bound in Great Britain at the University Press, Cambridge

CONTENTS

PREFACE

This text comprises contributions from nine authors whose work in information systems (IS) has been influenced by soft systems thinking. The test does not seek to establish a case for soft systems thinking as there are many published papers which have competently dealt with this argument over the past twenty years. Rather, the text seeks to provide both a history of the development of soft systems thinking within IS and a range of different examples where this kind of thinking has been used as part of the process of IS provision.

While the application of soft systems methodology (SSM) is evident throughout the text, the more important message is the way in which the thinking which underpins SSM has influenced modern information systems provision (ISP). It will soon become evident to the reader that while the authors have been influenced by SSM as a useful methodology in its own right, the stimulation for their work owes as much to Checkland's contribution to systems thinking as to SSM. Each chapter provides an illustration of the influence of soft systems ideas upon a particular IS concern and, in many instances, an account of the practical application of these ideas.

The trend in the use of soft systems ideas to ISP reflects the change in emphasis of information technology (IT) design. There is a clear move away from treating an organization as something to be computerized towards thinking about it as comprising an information system that can be supported by information technology. Information is, *de facto*, subjective and the design of a technology-supported information system must encompass this recognition. Many of the popular design methodologies used today have their origins in the 1970s and 1980s when computers were incorporated within an enterprise to do a specific processing task. Ideas about providing a network of flexible technologies to aid decision making were in their infancy, with the accent upon reliable and cost-effective computer processing.

As IT becomes increasingly 'transparent' to its user (i.e. the users of IT are not overawed by the technology) the considerations about the definition of management information systems also become more pronounced. Information itself is viewed by managers as an essential resource which needs to be managed and exploited to benefit the operation of the enterprise. Decision makers within an enterprise are more concerned with how technology can aid them in their duties than with the technology itself.

The demands by managers for a variety of decision support aids and the advent of the whole enterprise information system have caused IS professionals to question the flexibility of the design methodologies to satisfy these demands. Moreover, the number of recent computer system 'failures' has brought about a re-evaluation of the way in which large technology-supported information systems are developed.

This text attempts to highlight the shift in thinking about IS provision and offers some practical illustrations on how this has been accomplished. We feel that the book will be a valuable aid for modern managers, many of whom will possess a level of technological expertise gained either as part of their management education or from practical experience. The text provides examples where soft systems thinking and tools have been used in strategic information systems, systems analysis, information system requirements analysis (ISRA) and data modelling. It will provide illustrations that may be useful to managers who take responsibility for the introduction of small IT installations and those who have the responsibility for overseeing the development of whole enterprise information systems.

The text is also useful for the student who is seeking examples of the kinds of problems that are being addressed using soft systems ideas and the breadth of skills that the modern IS professional needs to possess. For example, the modern IS professional is concerned with understanding what problems or opportunities exist for an enterprise, its mission, and company strategies, as well as an in-depth understanding of how IT might be used to support all levels of organizational decision making. In this text we illustrate approaches to the process of IS provision at varying levels of concern.

The contributions include examples of soft systems thinking in the IS development process, strategic IT, and data modelling. These are grouped together into: (a) the evolution and use of soft systems methodology in information systems development; (b) strategic information systems; (c) information systems analysis; and (d) specific applications of soft systems thinking to knowledge elicitation, object-oriented analysis and data modelling.

Chapter 1 provides an account of the evolution of soft systems thinking and the development of soft systems methodology through to its current form. The chapter is written by Peter Checkland who provides the reader with a record of the development of SSM and some insightful comments about its use within information system development. The chapter provides a description of the way in which 'soft' systems thinking at Lancaster evolved out of the recognition of the deficiency of the methods of hard systems engineering to cope with difficult-to-define problems characteristically found in organizations. Checkland gives an account of the thinking that provided the basis of

SSM and describes how the methodology evolved over time through a programme of action research.

Chapter 2, written by John Mingers, carefully recounts a history of the use of SSM in information systems development. The chapter provides a useful chronology of the use of SSM in the information systems design process as well as giving an overview of some of the various ways in which it is being used. This chapter complements Checkland's chapter by providing an account of the way that both SSM and the ideas that underpin SSM are being used in information system provision. Mingers' chapter supplies the context for several of the chapters that follow and provides a link between SSM and ISP.

Chapters 3 and 4 are dedicated to the use of SSM as a way of integrating information technology into a business. In Chapter 3, Bob Galliers describes his specific application of soft systems ideas to the development of strategic information systems. The chapter includes a critical review of developments in information systems strategy thinking and practice. Two success factors Galliers suggests are the integration of an organization's information systems strategy with its business strategy and the identification of the organizational changes associated with gaining advantage from IT. In this chapter considerations that help to integrate the two strategies are discussed, as well as a critical analysis of key points arising from the business re-engineering literature. Galliers provides a summary of his development of SSM, which he uses to help in the identification of key information needs and flows and changes to the business processes. The following chapter, by Richard Ormerod, complements Galliers' discussion by providing practical examples of the way in which SSM was used in a number of business organizations and an account of the lessons learned. Ormerod's experience of the use of soft systems ideas includes examples from the coal industry, retailing, health care and the national grid. It is interesting to consider Ormerod's account of projects in which SSM was used and in which SSM was not used. In the latter case Ormerod conjectures upon the difference that SSM may have made to these studies, and hence provides the reader with some interesting observations about SSM from the practice.

Chapters 5 and 6 provide the reader with two examples of the influence of soft systems thinking on information systems analysis. David Avison and Trevor Wood–Harper describe the use of Multiview and the lessons they have learned through its application. The development of Multiview is an attempt to address the subject of problem definition because of its importance to the final IS design. The lessons that have been learned from the practice of Multiview provide the reader with a valuable insight into the difficulties of modern IS definition. In the following chapter Frank Stowell describes the way in which 'soft' systems thinking has contributed to the concept of client-led design.

Client-led design is defined as an attempt to demystify technology and provide the client with greater control over the definition and specification of business information systems. By providing clients with a means of expressing their information needs, the IS requirements for the whole enterprise can be more readily appreciated by all those involved. The idea behind the approach is to provide clients with simple but powerful ideas that will allow them, firstly, to express their information system requirements and then participate in the whole design process. The practice of client-led design is an attempt to capitalize upon the lessons learned from other participatory approaches and to recognize both the potential that modern IT offers and the growing awareness of technological developments that employees possess.

Chapter 7 provides an account by Daune West in which she describes a method of 'knowledge elicitation' which draws upon the ideas of Vickers and Checkland. The method of inquiry, called the appreciative inquiry method (AIM), is described and the way that it might help in the elicitation of expertise that calls upon hard facts and heuristic judgement is illustrated. AIM is the result of an on-going action research programme concerned with the exploration of interpretivist ideas as a basis of allowing 'experts' to express their expertise unencumbered, as far as possible, by the method of inquiry itself.

In Chapter 8 the author deals with the difficulty of reconciling hard computing with 'soft', more subjective thinking, associated with information systems. The author, John Gammack, suggests that the use of object-oriented design embedded within a symbiotic human centred approach may be one possible way of effecting this reconciliation. This chapter highlights some aspects of the issues currently being explored by researchers and practitioners as they attempt to exploit both 'soft' and 'hard' systems thinking in their re-evaluation of information system design methodologies. Gammack describes the use of intelligent decision making in online management systems (IDIOMS) which is an object-oriented GUI that has been developed to operate under the X-windows system. One of the key concepts implemented in IDIOMS is the human-centred principle of users-as-designers. Gammack, like Stowell, suggests that shifting the onus of detailed design onto the user will introduce flexibility in the design process, and promote user empowerment.

In Chapter 9 Paul Lewis elaborates upon his thinking about systems theory in the field of information systems in general and data modelling in particular. Taking up a theme from his book on IS, Lewis describes the way in which he has used 'soft' systems thinking in the hitherto 'hard' area of data modelling. Lewis suggests that the objectivity associated with traditional database design may not be quite as objective as some practitioners think it to be and perhaps as a consequence may lead to a design bias. Lewis's chapter provides a useful account of how the idea of appreciation and the formal definitions of relevant systems used in SSM together might provide the possibility of creating an alternative form of interpretative data model. The chapter serves to raise awareness of some of the problems facing data analysis and also discusses the contribution that soft systems ideas might make to this aspect of ISP.

To conclude, in producing this text the authors aim to provide and discuss ideas and experiences relevant to the use of soft systems thinking in the provision of computer-supported information systems. We hope that you find the book an enjoyable and informative read.

Frank Stowell
Hampshire, England

ACKNOWLEDGEMENTS

This text could not have been produced without the efforts of a very busy group of academics—the chapter authors—whose efforts and cooperation I wish to acknowledge. Particular thanks go to John Mingers whose forum for an Information Systems debate at the University of Warwick sowed the seeds for the text, and to Peter Checkland whose work has been the inspiration for the chapters herein.

Frank Stowell

SOFT SYSTEMS METHODOLOGY AND ITS RELEVANCE TO THE DEVELOPMENT OF INFORMATION SYSTEMS

Peter Checkland
Management School, University of Lancaster

INTRODUCTION

The first systems department in a UK university was founded by Gwilym Jenkins at Lancaster in the mid-1960s, the multinational company ICI having given the university a grant for that purpose. It was a postgraduate department, one of a number which the then new University of Lancaster created in the management area, and it was known as 'The Department of Systems Engineering'. The university had suggested 'Systems Analysis' but Jenkins argued against this on two grounds: 'Systems Analysis' would be taken to mean *computer* systems analysis, but his aims were broader than that and his aspirations were higher; in any case analysis is never enough: beyond analysis it is necessary to create something—to make something happen, to 'engineer' something.

After a few years, accepting that the outside world would never interpret the word 'engineering' in this broad sense, the department dropped the word from its name and became simply 'The Department of Systems'. Some years later this was changed again to 'Systems and Information Management', and that title remained until 1993 when the members of the department merged with their colleagues in 'Operational Research and Operations Management' to form a new 'Department of Management Science'.

The changes in the name of the Department of Systems accurately reflect its intellectual history. Its initial expertise was in what would now be called 'hard' systems engineering, and the present author joined in 1969 with the research task of exploring the broad sense of the word 'engineering': could systems engineering methods be extended to tackle management as well as technical problems? Later, when this had led to the development of soft systems methodology (SSM), work in that field led naturally to much involvement in studies aimed at the creation of appropriate information systems (IS) in organizations—hence the addition of 'Information Management' to the department's name. (The final merger with OR and OM signals the importance of a significant development in management science in the 1990s: the emergence of 'soft OR', with its emphasis on problem structuring rather than the use of classical OR techniques. This is a development in which SSM has played a part.)

This chapter will review briefly the intellectual history which these name changes reflect, showing how work on information systems became significant; it will (a) set out the state of SSM as that methodology is perceived in the 1990s by those who developed it, (b) discuss its role in IS development and (c) indicate themes for further development.

SSM DEVELOPMENT
THE RESEARCH PROCESS AND ITS OUTCOME
It was accepted from the beginning at Lancaster that research into whether or not the application of systems engineering methods could be extended to cover management problems, broadly defined—and if so, how—could be conducted only by carrying out systems studies in real-world situations. This indicated some kind of 'action research' approach, using as the research object the process of change in a real problem situation. In all such situations concerned people struggle to bring about what will be seen as 'improvement'.

This action research mode was adopted, but the literature of action research (see, for example, Blum, 1955; Foster, 1972; Clark, 1972; Susman and Evered, 1978; Hult and Lennung, 1980; Gilmore *et al.*, 1985) was felt to be seriously deficient in one important respect. If descriptions of action research were to be more than merely anecdotal accounts of what had happened, it seemed an essential requirement that the researcher declare in advance the intellectual framework within which knowledge in the research situation will be defined. In other words, the researcher must set out the *epistemology* in terms of which research findings will be expressed. This is essential if others are to be able critically to appraise the work. Indeed, it is what makes accounts of action research potentially more than the equivalent of 'a letter home to mum'. Accounts of action research without even the ghost of an analytical framework are no more than anecdotes. The version of action research adopted in the development of SSM is that illustrated in Figures 1.1–1.3 (Checkland, 1991). In terms of its concepts, SSM itself is

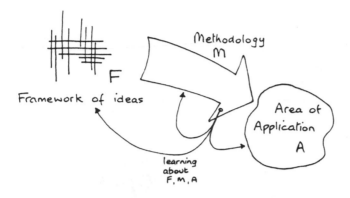

Figure 1.1   The elements of any piece of research (adapted from Checkland in Nissen et al., 1991, p. 400)

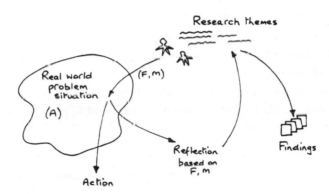

Figure 1.2   The cycle of action research, using the nomenclature of Figure 1.1 (adapted from Checkland in Nissen et al., 1991, p. 401)

the methodology M, based on a framework of systems ideas F, used to tackle the area of application A, defined as 'real-world problem situations'. Since the cycle of action research as described has been operated for 20 years, SSM itself has continually evolved over that period. There is now a relatively stable mature form of it (Checkland and Scholes, 1990, Chs. 2 and 10), though the secondary literature is often found to be addressing the SSM of yesteryear (Checkland, 1993).

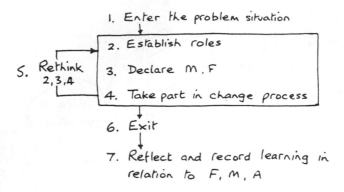

1. Enter the problem situation
2. Establish roles
3. Declare M, F
4. Take part in change process
5. Rethink 2,3,4
6. Exit
7. Reflect and record learning in relation to F, M, A

Figure 1.3   A process for action research (adapted from Checkland in Nissen *et al.*, 1991, p. 402)

The progress of the action research programme on SSM can be understood—with hindsight, since doing research is always a messier business than providing *post-hoc* accounts—in terms of the cycle shown in Figure 1.4. Systems engineering methodology was taken as a given; attempts were made to apply it to ill-defined, 'messy' problem situations. The methodology was found to be inadequate for the complexity of the situations addressed, and learning from this experience led to the reformulation of the methodology as SSM. SSM was found to be relevant to problems of creating appropriate information systems.

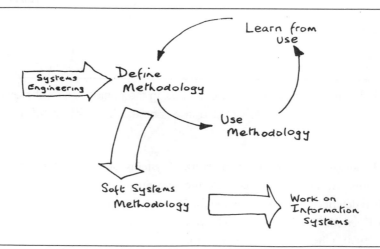

Figure 1.4   The evolution of SSM from systems engineering

The kind of problem situations tackled during this development, both in industry and the public services, is exemplified in the books which describe SSM's development at Lancaster: *Systems Thinking Systems Practice* (Checkland, 1981), *Systems: Concepts, Methodologies and Applications* (Wilson, 1990) and *Soft Systems Methodology in Action* (Checkland and Scholes, 1990). Typical early examples included: working in what was then the British Aircraft Corporation to help improve management of the Anglo-French Concorde Project; helping three people who ran a privately-funded community centre in Liverpool to redefine its role; working with the managing director of a small carpet manufacture who claimed only to live from day to day: 'I want you to make me plan', he said.

A number of such problems were tackled each year. The research activity often included the involvement of mature postgraduates taking the department's Masters Course, their 5-month projects constituting a serious part of the research programme. This institutional arrangement enabled rapid feedback of learning to be achieved as well as the rapid development of a shared language among those taking part in the programme. The Masters based work was then supplemented by other studies carried out at various levels over various time-scales by a university-owned consultancy company, ISCOL Ltd. The outcome of the research was a structured process of inquiry which has been neatly summarized by von Bulow (1989; the words in brackets have been added by the present author):

> SSM is a methodology that aims to bring about improvement in areas of social concern by activating in the people involved in the situation a learning cycle which is ideally never-ending. The learning takes place through the iterative process of using systems concepts to reflect upon and debate perceptions of the real world, taking action in the real world, and again reflecting on the happenings using systems concepts. The reflection and debate is structured by a number of systemic models. These are conceived as holistic ideal types [relevant to] certain aspects of the problem situation rather than as accounts of it. It is taken as given that no objective and complete account of a problem situation can be provided.

The last sentence of this extract is important. For a systems engineer seeking, say, to improve the productivity of a chemical plant, there *will* be available what those concerned are prepared to accept as 'an objective and complete account' of the problem situation—and a testable one at that. In ill-structured problem situations, where *what to do*, as well as how to do it, is part of the problem, SSM becomes an inquiry system based on building models of purposeful activity (from declared explicit points of view) and using them to structure debate about the situation. The purpose of the debate is to enable accommodations to be achieved which allow motivated action to be taken to bring about improvement in the process, as illustrated in Figure 1.5.

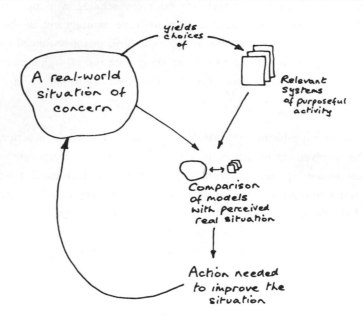

Figure 1.5   The basic process of soft systems methodology (from Checkland and Scholes, 1990, p. 7)

In recent years the stream of activity based on model building is supplemented and informed by a second stream of 'cultural' analysis which currently comprises examination of three things: the intervention itself; the 'social system' of the problem situation; and its politics. This yields the process shown in Figure 1.6, which is a model of SSM as an ideal type that can be used to make sense of any use of the approach.

In arriving experientially at the process of Figure 1.6, several key moments can be identified at which the thinking moved forward. They are discussed in the next section.

FOUR STEPS IN THINKING
Looking back over the period of SSM's development it is possible with hindsight to identify four important steps in the thinking: four key thoughts derived from experience which, we can now see, dictated the emerging form of the approach and the direction future development would take.

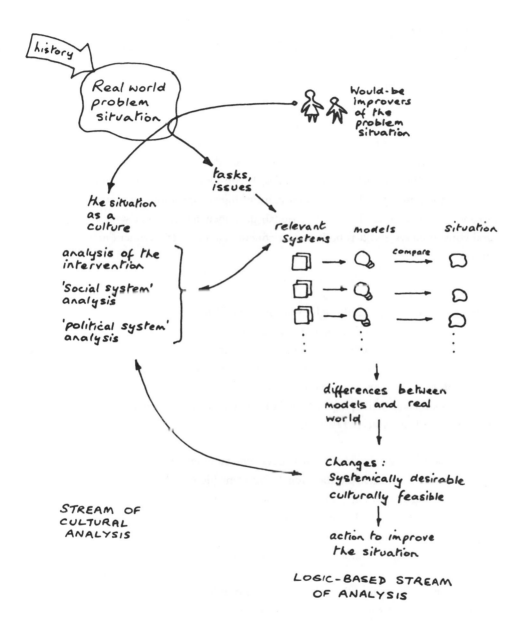

Figure 1.6   The process of soft systems methodology as an inquiring system
(from Checkland and Scholes, 1990, p. 29)

1. Purposeful activity

The first crucial thought which moved the development of SSM forward came when systems engineering, with its straightforward assumptions about 'the system' in question and its objectives, was failing in the face of the complexity of management problem situations. The thought is that all such problem situations, despite all their idiosyncrasies, have at least one thing in common: they all contain people who, in the face of ambiguity, uncertainty, disagreement and conflict are trying to take [*purposeful action.*] This suggested that it might be useful to take a set of activities, linked and structured so that together they constitute a purposeful whole as a new kind of system. Such systems were called 'human activity systems', and ways of modelling them were duly developed (Checkland, 1981; Checkland and Scholes, 1990). Figure 1.7 shows a model of such a system. It consists of a set of activities constituting an operations subsystem, linked by arrows which represent logical (functional) dependencies, together with a monitoring and control subsystem. It is built from a concise statement of its function: a 'root definition'.

2. Weltanschauungen

The second determining thought was the immediate result of trying to establish a method of building models of purposeful activity systems. Since any purposeful or intentional action in real life can be perceived in many different ways—one observer's 'terrorism' being another's 'freedom fighting'—every model of a notional purposeful whole, if it is to be coherent, will have to be built according to a declared world view or *Weltanschauung*. What purposeful wholes might relate, for example, to the Anglo-French Concorde project? Is its aim:

- to create the world's first supersonic passenger aircraft?
- to help persuade the French President (de Gaulle at the time) from vetoing British entry to the European Common Market?
- to keep the Europeans ahead of the Americans in at least one advanced technology?
- to help sustain a European precision engineering industry?

A case can be made for all of these (and many other) perceptions being relevant to exploration of the Concorde project.

This thought led inexorably—it now seems—to the third of these climacteric moments in the development of SSM.

3. Learning with holons

The third of these crucial pieces of learning was more complex than the first two, but

Root Definition of a Relevant System :

> A professionally-staffed system in a manufacturing company which, in the light of market forecasts and raw material availability makes production plans for a defined period

CATWOE Analysis :

Customer — People in Production function

Actors — Professional Planners

Transformation Process — Data → Organised data (information) in a Production Plan

Weltanschauung — Planning can be satisfactorily delegated to professional planners

Owner — The Company

Environmental Constraints — Production - Planning split ; availability of data

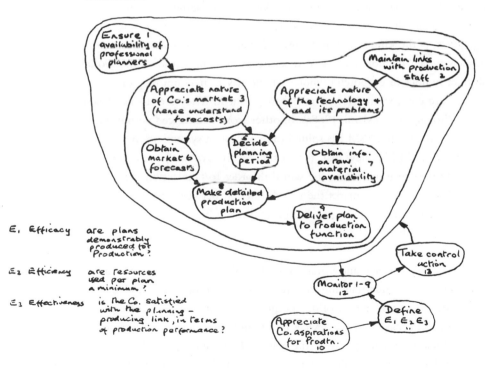

Figure 1.7 The roof definition, CATWOE analysis and conceptual model, as used in SSM

follows from them. We had learned that every 'real-world problem' is best thought of as a problem *situation*. In such a situation accommodations between conflicting views and interests are sought—accommodations which allow purposeful action to bring about 'improvements'. (Just occasionally the accommodations become a consensus.) We were finding that such situations can be explored, and facilitation of the move towards action achieved, by the explicit use of systems thinking. This entailed richly picturing the problem situation, selecting some likely-to-be relevant purposeful wholes (including both different wholes and different perceptions of a given whole) and building models of them according to declared world views. The process then necessarily entailed *debating* the nature of the perceived problem situation, in pursuit of accommodations allowing action to ensue. The debate was carried by a 'comparison stage' which consisted of using the models to pose questions concerning the situation, the eventual outcome of this debate being the identification of changes that were both arguably desirable and culturally feasible. (The 'cultural' stream of analysis, carried out in parallel with the stream based on modelling, both informed choice of 'relevant' purposeful wholes to model and enabled judgement of cultural feasibility to be made.) Two connected concepts follow from this and constitute the next step in the learning. Firstly, the approach as a whole is not, like systems engineering, an arrowlike progress towards goals which from the outset are taken to be desirable. Rather *it is itself a learning system*, of the kind shown in Figure 1.5. Secondly, the learning system makes use of models which do not purport to describe purposeful action in the world. They are abstract notions of purposeful wholes which may or may not map onto perceived reality but are considered relevant to debate about it. They are, to use Koestler's useful word, 'holons' (Checkland, 1988a). In other words, compared with its starting point in systems engineering, SSM has shifted the concept of systemicity from assuming that it lies in the world (the view that 'the world contains systems') to assuming that it can lie in the process of inquiry into the world in order to take action. This shift of assumptions about systemicity marks the real distinction between 'hard' ('the world contains systems') and 'soft' ('learning about the world can be organized systemically') systems thinking (Checkland, 1983).

This is all very abstract, and it may be useful to emphasize that a true understanding of SSM starts from understanding the crucial difference between models which strive to be *of* part of the perceived world, and models *relevant to* debate and argument about it. The models in SSM are only devices (epistemological devices, in fact) to enable coherent exploration of perceptions of the real world to take place. Thus, to tackle management problems in the prison service it might be useful to structure debate by using such models as 'a rehabilitation system', 'a punishment system', 'a system to protect society', a 'system to train criminals' (the 'college of crime' concept) and 'a human storage system'.

4. Activity models and information systems

The fourth determining step in the development of SSM lay in the early realization that a model of a purposeful holon could be examined to answer some questions about data and/or information support for the activity. Thus, for activities in a model it is possible to ask what you would have to know in order to be able to do each activity and what you would know as a result of doing it. Take, for example, the activity in a possible model relevant to manufacturing: 'obtain raw material'. Doing this activity would entail having data available in the form of a specification for the raw material, a list of suppliers and prices, possibly data on their reliability and service levels. Carrying out the activity would augment knowledge of their service level and reliability. Thus any activity model can be linked through this kind of analysis to an associated set of information/data items. These are the notional information/data items which are required to enable or help the purposeful activity to occur, and which are generated as a result of doing it. Since information and data support for purposeful action will be a feature of any real-world problem situations, it is not surprising that information studies are common among uses of SSM.

SSM IN THE 1990S: MODES 1 AND 2

In describing and teaching SSM an obvious strategy is to declare that it is a process with a number of stages that can be described in sequence, as in Figure 1.8.

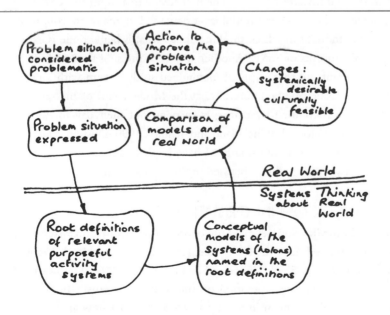

Figure 1.8   The early account of SSM in terms of seven stages (from Checkland and Scholes, 1990, p. 27)

This is not entirely wrong. It is how SSM was developed, and it is one way in which SSM can be used: to do so is to make a particular strategic choice. In general, though, thinking of SSM as a seven-stage process is how neophytes regard it. More sophisticated users, who have internalized the mosaic of activities in Figure 1.8, tend to use it much more flexibly This flexibility takes two forms: (1) starting anywhere in Figure 1.8 and moving in any direction; (2) using SSM not as a prescriptive process to follow stage by stage but as a set of processes used to *make sense of* real-world problem-tackling activity.

These developments have led to formulation of a simple means of consciously thinking about the mode in which SSM is used, which is especially useful in the early stages of a study since a methodology (unlike a method) always needs to be tailored to both the user and the situation addressed. Two 'ideal type' models of SSM can be used to define a spectrum within which any actual use may be placed. At one extreme, 'Mode 1' takes SSM as a seven-stage process to be articulated in sequence; at the other end of the spectrum, 'Mode 2', in its most extreme form, would consist of users making sense of a problem-solving activity by trying to describe it to themselves using the epistemology that defines SSM. Actual uses will fall between these extremes, and the ten studies in the 1990 book are placed at different points in this spectrum (see Checkland and Scholes, 1990, Ch. 10). On the whole, increasing sophistication will lead to a shift away from Mode 1 and towards Mode 2. The best advice to a sophisticate is: 'Remain problem-oriented (rather than methodology-oriented) but maintain continually a meta-level strand of thought in which thinking about what is being done is expressed in the language and concepts of SSM.' Another way of expressing the Mode 1–Mode 2 difference is to point out that a special highlighted study, set up with a project team, is most likely to reside, methodologically, at the Mode 1 end of the spectrum. On the other hand, the SSM used by managers carrying out their day-to-day tasks is more likely to be nearer Mode 2. (Checkland and Scholes, 1990, illustrates both types of SSM use.) These different ways of using SSM have implications for SSM in work on information systems, which will be discussed in the final section.

SSM IN WORK ON INFORMATION SYSTEMS

As an arena for the development and use of SSM, the information systems field has been especially emphasized since the 1980s (see, for example, Checkland, 1988b; Checkland and Scholes, 1990, pp. 53–8; Checkland and Holwell, 1990, 1993; Lewis, 1991, 1992, 1993; *Systemist*, 1992 (special edition on information systems)). In fact, information-related work has always been important in SSM. At what now appears to be the crucial moment in the development of SSM—which occurred on a hot summer's afternoon in a dusty office in Belfast Ropeworks—Checkland and Griffin abandoned the attempt to build systems engineering-type models *of* the Ropeworks' operations and instead built a notional 'ideal type' model of an information-processing holon, one that did not describe anything observable in the company but was simply *relevant to* exploring the Ropeworks' confused order-processing system (Checkland and Griffin, 1970).

The model in question was not thought of as an activity model; that generalization came later; rather it was conceived as a structured set of key decisions that would recur in any order-processing system in a manufacturing company with a range of products: Do we accept this order? Can we supply from stock? etc. Once the model was built it was used to work out what information would have to be available if the decisions were to be taken sensibly—this analysis leading eventually to the design and implementation of a new order-processing system in the company and a new subfunction to implement it, which was then managed by an ex-Lancaster Masters student who carried out a later study in the Ropeworks!

In this way conceptual modelling emerged in the development of SSM, and thus was initiated the stream of work that led to the use of purposeful activity models to define a particular kind of information—namely, that necessary in principle to enable an activity to occur. This led to broader consideration being given to 'information requirements analysis' and information strategy in SSM work. The basic stance adopted in the Lancaster work may be summarized as follows:

(1) It is necessary to make a sharp distinction between 'data' and 'information'. The former are the 'givens'—the myriad facts that situations present us with, some of which are noticed as significant according to the 'appreciative settings' of the people concerned (Vickers, 1965; Checkland and Casar, 1986). These have more specific meaning attributed to them in a particular context of time and place (Holwell, 1990). This process of meaning attribution turns data into something else, which we may call 'information'. Thus, since meaning attribution is a uniquely *human* act, what are now normally called 'information systems' are really 'data manipulation' systems. (The 1960s language of 'data-processing systems' was in fact much more accurate than the current phrase 'information systems', but the earlier language probably cannot now be rescued and restored since politically it would be seen as undermining the management aspirations of computer professionals!)

(2) Since holons, which are models of human activity systems built on the basis of different world views, can be used to structure coherent debate about the meanings relevant to the people in a particular situation, SSM in principle provides a vehicle for deciding *which* 'information systems' should be designed and implemented in a particular situation.

(3) Information analysis of purposeful activity models can thus lead to useful discussion of both information requirements and, on a broader scale, information strategy in an organization. Work of this kind now goes on steadily: see, for example, Checkland and Holwell (1993); and in the summer of 1993 in a large teaching hospital, a dozen working groups of health professionals have built models relevant to their day-to-day responsibilities and defined the information required to support this activity. This has been part of a large participative project to define the hospital's information strategy.

Experience of this kind has convinced the Lancaster researchers that the standard methods of information system design, viewed from an SSM perspective, leap much too quickly to considerations dominated by technology and data. This makes SSM a rather natural precursor to conventional design methods, given its emphasis on learning one's way to seeing how a particular group of people in a particular situation perceive and construe their world. Looking to the future, from the work on IS done so far as part of the development of SSM, we can expect two main themes to be pursued. One concerns attempts to treat SSM as providing a way in to detailed design work on information systems. This involves linking SSM to well-established design methods, and is exemplified by attempts sponsored by the the UK Government's Central Computer and Telecommunications Agency to graft a rather mechanical version of SSM onto SSADM (CCTA, 1989, 1991). This approach necessarily accepts a model of IS development based on: 'design the system and then implement it'—a concept that is being somewhat eroded by such developments as prototyping and 'end user computing'. There are also problems in making the link between SSM's information-oriented approach and the data-oriented approach of detailed design methods (Checkland, 1992; Miles, 1988). Nevertheless, this is potentially a rich vein worth mining.

The other main theme for current and future work is to explore the use of SSM in creating an information strategy in an organization. This avoids the problems of having to restrain an open-ended process of inquiry which is user-dependent in a prescriptive straitjacket, but is not without its own difficulties, not the least of which is that so many people—managers and computers professionals—cannot yet distinguish between an information strategy and an IT strategy! In addition, this strand of work also faces the problems of making links between SSM's models and the detailed considerations of data and technology which enable an IT strategy to be created within a wider IS strategy.

That work in these areas is still urgently needed is suggested when we examine an SSM study carried out in 1978 in the Information and Library Services Department (ILSD) of what was then ICI Organics (Checkland and Scholes, 1990, Ch. 3). The work was regarded as successful in its main aim of helping ILSD rethink its role. At the presentation of the results of the study to a management audience, the three members of ILSD who had worked on the team described the main outcomes; I was asked to look ahead and present a more radical view. This part of the presentation is given in the Appendix to Chapter 3 of *Soft Systems Methodology in Action* (Checkland and Scholes, 1990). It argues for the view that organizations now have to think seriously about managing information as a prime resource. Given the combination of the technical revolution (cheap distributed computing) and the revolution in social attitudes embodied in the rejection of hierarchies and the demand for 'participation', it suggests (p. 85) the following picture of an organization that gives prime importance to information:

—organizations are likely to move towards a mode of operation in which autonomous groups, where possible small enough to be self-organising, are linked in an information network; out of the question will be the management style, obsolescent for some years now, in which the manager's power is based on the withholding of information;

—the need for the high-level management of information (in defining protocols, etc.) will lead to an information function having the kind of status now accorded to other support functions focused on knowledge, money or people;

—the information function of the future will fill an enabling role, defining the rationality of the information net and the rules governing access to it, and beyond that making sure that resources are available which will allow the net to adapt to changing circumstances.

On the occasion of this presentation in 1978 the audience listened politely but there was no evidence of the message being heard. Fifteen years later such things as: the increasing interest in computer-aided co-operative work; the greater readiness of organizations to take seriously the idea of formulating a coherent information strategy; and the existence of some Directors of Information (though this is often narrowly conceived as an IT role), suggests that at least *some* progress has been made. But the main impression is that the progress has been both halting and modest in scope. This is a pity, given that the image outlined is of a more humane form of organization than that which most people experience. There is clearly much to do in this field as work on information systems in the true sense of the phrase slowly establishes itself as complementary to the technological (IT) thinking that has been dominant so far. SSM has a role to play in these developments.

REFERENCES

Blum, F. H. (1955) 'Action research—a scientific approach?', *Philosophy of Science*, **22** (1) 1–7.

Bulow, I. von (1989) 'The bounding of a problem situation and the concept of a boundary in soft systems methodology', *Journal of Applied Systems Analysis*, **16**, 35–41.

CCTA (1989) ' "*Compact*" *Manual, Version 1.1*', No. 1, Central Computer and Telecommunications Agency, Norwich.

CCTA (1991) *SSADM Version 4 Reference Manual: Feasibility—Soft Systems Methodology*, Central Computer and Telecommunication Agency, Norwich.

Checkland, P. B. (1981) *Systems Thinking Systems Practice*, Wiley, Chichester.

Checkland, P. B. (1983) 'OR and the systems movement: mappings and conflicts', *Journal of the Operational Research Society*, **34** (8), 661–675.

Checkland, P. B. (1988a) 'The case for "holon" ', *Systems Practice*, **1** (3), 235–238.

Checkland, P. B. (1988b) 'Information systems and systems thinking: time to unite?', *International Journal of Information Management*, **8**, 239–248.

Checkland, P. B. (1991) 'From framework through experience to learning: the essential nature of action research', in *Information Systems Research: Contemporary Approaches and Emergent Traditions* (H. E. Nissen, H. K. Klein and R. Hirschheim, eds), North-Holland, Amsterdam.

Checkland, P. B. (1992) 'SSM in information systems design: history and some current issues', *Systemist*, **14** (3), UK Systems Society, 90–92.

Checkland, P. B. (1993) Review of Patching (1990) see *Systems Practice*, **6** (4), 435–438.

Checkland, P. B. and Casar, A. (1986) 'Vickers' concept of an appreciative system: a systemic account', *Journal of Applied Systems Analysis*, **13**, 3–17.

Checkland, P. B. and Griffin, R. (1970) 'Management information systems: a systems view', *Journal of Systems Engineering*, **1** (2), 29–42.

Checkland, P. B. and Holwell, S. E. (1990) 'SSM in information systems studies: some rethinking'. Internal Discussion Paper 2/90, Department of Systems and Information Management, Lancaster University.

Checkland, P. B. and Holwell, S.E. (1993) 'Information management and organisational processes: an approach through soft systems methodology', *Journal of Information Systems*, **3** (1), 3–16.

Checkland, P. B. and Scholes, J. (1990) *Soft Systems Methodology in Action*, Wiley, Chichester.

Clark, P. A. (1972) *Action Research and Organisational Change*, Harper and Row, London.

Foster, M. (1972) 'An introduction to the theory and practice of action research in work organisations', *Human Relations*, **25** (6), 529–556.

Gilmore, T., Krantz, J. and Ramirez, R. (1985) 'Action based modes of inquiry and the host–researcher relationship', *Consultation*, **5** (3), 160–176.

Holwell, S. E. (1990) Msc dissertation. 'Department of Systems and Information Management, Lancaster University.

Hult, M. and Lennung, S. (1980) 'Towards a definition of action research: a note and a bibliography', *Journal of Management Studies*, **17** (2), 242–250.

Lewis, P. J. (1991) 'The decision making basis for information systems: the contribution of Vickers' concept of appreciation to a soft systems perspective', *European Journal of Information Systems*, **1** (1), 33–43.

Lewis, P. J. (1992) 'Rich picture building in the soft systems methodology', *European Journal of Information Systems*, **1** (5), 351–360.

Lewis, P. J. (1993) 'Linking soft systems methodology with data-focused information systems development', *Journal of Information Systems*, **3**, 169–186.

Miles, R. K. (1988) 'Combining "soft" and "hard" systems practice: grafting or embedding?', *Journal of Applied Systems Analysis*, **15**, 55–60.

Nissen, H.-E., Klein, H. K. and Hirschheim, R. (eds) (1991) *Information Systems Research: Contemporary Approaches and Emergent Traditions*, North-Holland, Amsterdam.

Patching, D. (1990) *Practical Soft Systems Analysis*, Pitman, London.

Susman, G. and Evered, R. D. (1978) 'An assessment of the scientific merits of action research', *Administrative Science Quarterly*, **23** (December), 582–603.

Systemist (1992) 'Special edition on information systems', *Systemist*, **14** (3), UK Systems Society.

Vickers, G. (1965) *The Art of Judgement*, Chapman and Hall, London; reprinted 1983, Harper and Row, London.

Wilson, B. (1990) *Systems: Concepts, Methodologies and Applications* (2nd edn), Wiley, Chichester.

2

USING SOFT SYSTEMS METHODOLOGY IN THE DESIGN OF INFORMATION SYSTEMS

John Mingers
Warwick Business School, University of Warwick

INTRODUCTION

The aim of this chapter is to provide an overview of the influence that soft systems methodology (SSM) has had on IS development and to introduce the wide variety of methods that have been advocated. We then look at the reasons for using SSM in IS design and provide a commentary on various approaches. The final section gives a critical appraisal of the problems and possibilities afforded by them.

THE NEED FOR A SOFT APPROACH TO INFORMATION SYSTEMS DESIGN

This section explores the motivation for trying to link SSM to IS design from both philosophical and practical viewpoints. One of the most compelling reasons for thinking a soft approach to information systems is worth while is simply the extensive and well-documented failures of systems designed by conventional methods. As this chapter is being written, the London Ambulance Service has just scrapped a brand new £10m computer system for controlling ambulances. When it was first put into operation it performed so disastrously that it was never used again. The head of the Ambulance Service resigned. Similar total failures have recently occurred with the London Stock Exchange's Taurus system (£75m) and a UK government system for the unemployed (£48m). Unfortunately, these are by no means isolated instances. Jayaratna (1990) points out figures from the US General Accounting Office (Blum, 1987) concerning US federal software projects which had failed or were failing. Less than 2 per cent of software products were used as delivered, a further 3 per cent being used after change; 19 per cent were abandoned or reworked, and a staggering 29 per cent were paid for but never delivered. Most interestingly, though, the remaining 47 per cent were delivered but never used. Presumably, they were never used because they were found not to meet the users' real needs. As far back as 1975, the failure of information systems to 'deliver the goods' had been noted (Lucas, 1975). By the late 1980s there was extensive literature on the topic. Lyytinen and Hirschheim (1987) and Lyytinen (1988) conducted a comprehensive survey of the empirical literature concerning information systems failures and concluded (Lyytinen, 1988, p. 61) that:

> Studies ranging from personal biographies, and case studies up to statistical surveys all show that information systems problems are so widely spread and pervasive that one may speak of IS failures. ... Many reports show that somewhere between one-third to half of all systems fail, and some researchers have reported even higher failure rates.

The nature and causes of these failures were extremely varied, but Lyytinen and Hirschheim argue that they can all be seen ultimately as failures of expectation—that is, the final IS system did not meet in some way the legitimate expectations of the stakeholders. They developed a framework for classifying failures in terms of types of failure and reasons for the failure, and suggested that SSM may well be valuable in addressing these problems.

It has been argued that many of these IS failures ultimately occur as a result of limitations in conventional (or 'hard') IS design methodologies such as SSADM, structured systems analysis or Jackson systems development (JSD). It has been further argued that soft methodologies, such as SSM, can alleviate a significant number of these problems. In the next section we shall identify and discuss these weaknesses in detail.

Firstly, conventional methods are geared primarily towards the technological aspects of design. Both they, and the CASE tools that they have spawned, focus on modelling data, data flows and systems functions. This causes a concentration on technical solutions to what may be complex social, organizational and communicational problems. Secondly, they are usually either oriented towards computerizing existing processes, and thus assuming that these processes are effective, or they assume that the users know what they want and that eliciting user requirements is straightforward (Galliers, 1987). Thirdly, and following from the first, conventional methods pay little attention to the wider business and organizational settings within which the information system must operate. Fourthly, they implicitly assume a particular positivist (or objectivist) philosophy towards both information and the organizational context which many argue is inappropriate.

Looking at requirements analysis, Hirschheim and Shafer (1988) have argued that this view—that information requirements somehow 'emerge' through the process of systems analysis—simply ignores the multiplicity of issues (and assumptions) associated with the individual's 'needs' (Hirschheim and Shafer, 1988). They identify and criticize three beliefs about information requirements that come out of the literature on IS methodologies.

Firstly, the belief that specifying requirements is a first, informal step towards producing detailed specifications. There are several problems with this assumption; the main one is the belief that users can explicitly specify their requirements, but most practical evidence points to the contrary. Users can describe what they currently do, but they find it difficult to visualize how they might use a computer system or how the whole task might be re-engineered. They have to learn about information systems in the same way as analysts have to learn about their work. Indeed, Ackoff (1992), in the context of total quality management, argued that users only come to discover what they want through their participation in the process of design. Other problems with this belief are (1) information systems are part of social systems and their use cannot be specified wholly in technical terms; and (2) the technical orientation of analysts often leads to a gap between 'what the user wants' and 'what the analyst thinks the user wants'. The second belief is that requirements focus on the technical characteristics of the system. This may be how the analyst sees the situation but is not how it is seen by the user. Users are concerned with business tasks and objectives and formulate requirements in these terms. They are concerned not with the system itself, but with what it can achieve. This is a problem that the analyst must overcome by trying to see the world as the user does, but conventional methodologies have little to offer in this respect. The third belief is that the initial requirements can form a complete and objective specification of the system which can then be taken off and designed by the analysts. The reality is quite different as many decisions have to be taken down the line as the design progresses and, indeed, there are decisions which do not need to be taken until later. It is important that the users are continually involved in these later processes and not simply forgotten after the statement of requirements.

Moving on to the philosophical question, it is clear that, both ontologically and epistemologically, traditional methodologies are underpinned by a positivist or objectivist viewpoint (Hirschheim and Klein, 1989). Many writers (for example, Boland, 1985; Miles, 1985; Lyytinen and Klein, 1985; Winograd and Flores, 1987; Checkland and Scholes, 1990; Stowell, 1991; Lewis, 1993), have argued that this is inappropriate for designing information systems which are but a part of the whole process of human communication. This is not the place to cover this complex debate, but one of the alternatives to positivism, namely interpretivism, has had strong arguments made for it.

Interpretivism (Hirschheim, 1992; Galliers, 1992a) is a rather vague term, but essentially it argues that human interaction inevitably involves understanding and meaning. That is, our actions and conversations are not open to simple objective recording by an outside observer. Rather, an observer must come to understand, to interpret, the meaning that social acts have for participants. Moreover, this is not the case only for outside observers but is the fundamental process of social interaction itself. According to this view, the analyst's task is not simply the objective description of particular information flows and data structures but the interpretation and elicitation of the socially constructed patterns of meaning which generate observed behaviour. As Checkland has stated (Checkland and Scholes, 1990, p. 303), 'information equals data plus meaning.' Data by itself does nothing; it is only when a particular person interprets it in the light of his or her own context and meaning system that it becomes usable information.

SSM, at first sight, provides answers to many of the above problems. Philosophically, SSM is explicitly in the interpretive camp, being concerned with the exploration of different people's systems of meaning, not with describing some 'objective' reality. The initial aim is to generate a rich understanding of the relevant situation before exploring potential improvements. This involves considering notional activities which may, or may not, already exist, and may well lead to 'business process re-engineering' (Hammer, 1990; Galliers, 1993b) before the information system design is considered. SSM philosophy is highly participative and would encourage users to be fully involved at all stages. The overall process is seen as a learning system geared towards fostering greater understanding and involvement among all concerned.

USING SSM IN THE DESIGN OF INFORMATION SYSTEMS

Much has already been written describing soft systems methodology, not least Checkland (1981) and Checkland and Scholes (1990), and a chapter is devoted to the subject in this book. So, I shall assume a familiarity with basic SSM and concentrate on the particular adaptions and modifications related to designing information systems. At times, this may make the approaches appear excessively mechanical and almost incompatible with the philosophy of soft systems. This, in fact, is probably not the case but is simply a result of focusing on one, fairly technical, part of a wider inquiring process.

STANDARD LANCASTER METHOD

The use of soft systems in helping to design information systems goes back to the beginning of the development of SSM at Lancaster. One of the earliest published papers on SSM was entitled 'Management information systems: a systemic view' (Checkland and Griffin, 1970). But the first systematic account of a method for generating information system requirements from an SSM study was developed and published by Wilson

(1984). Other early applications are Galliers (1984) and Le Fevre and Pattison (1986). The overall philosophy of the approach is that, firstly, a general SSM study is performed in order to identify a set of activities that must be carried out by the organization (or department). These activities will be independent of any particular organizational structure and will not, in general, be simply a description of what actually happens. Rather, they will be based on a conceptualization of what the organization does resulting from a thorough analysis of the stakeholders involved and the issues current at the time. Given these activities, it is then possible to specify the information necessary for their occurrence and the informational links between them. After this conceptual analysis the actual organizational structure can be mapped in terms of particular managers/departments with particular roles covering various activities. Finally, the information needs of the activities can be mapped to the roles and a comparison made of the desired information needs with the actual information provision. Figure 2.1 shows the overall process in more detail.

Stage 1 (covering activities 1 to 4 in Figure 2.1) involves the development of a primary task conceptual model depicting necessary organizational activities. This involves iterations around the main stages of SSM. Firstly, an issue-based analysis is conducted to identify and explore the main stakeholders, their views and expectations about the information system, and any particular problematic issues. This is done by constructing and debating a number of root definitions (RDs) and conceptual models (CMs) relevant to the primary tasks of the organization or part thereof. This should eventually lead to a consensus (or at least an accommodation) among the actors about the fundamental activities that the information system is to support. The final primary task model will consist of all the necessary relations and their logical interrelations. It may well be very detailed with a number of resolution levels and up to one or two hundred activities.

It is important to emphasize that the conceptual model is a concept. It is a logical expansion of a particular idea, not a description or mapping of what actually exists. The real world will certainly contain activities not included in the CM.

Stage 2 (activities 5 and 6) takes the primary task model and develops the information necessary to carry out these activities. For each activity three things are specified: (a) the information inputs that the activity requires; (b) the information outputs relevant to other activities that the activity produces; and (c) the monitoring and control information necessary to allow the measures of performance defined for the activity to be checked. This stage produces a very large number of different items of information and some form of grouping procedure is necessary. Wilson suggests that similar items should be grouped into information categories—that is, 'family names' for particular

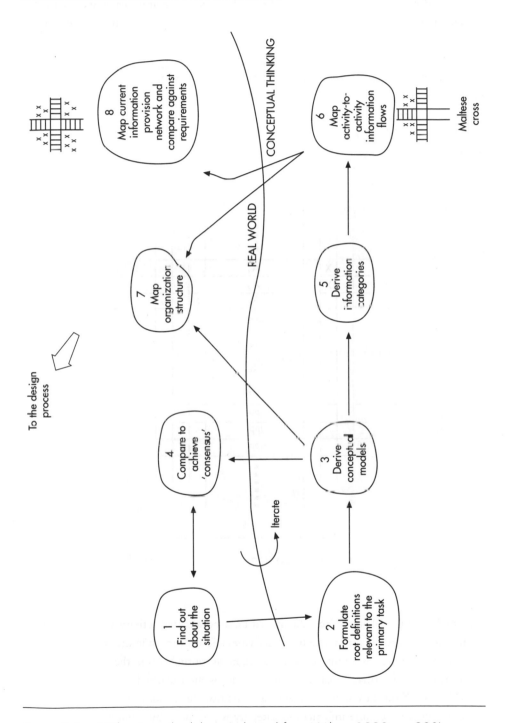

Figure 2.1   Wilson's methodology (adapted from Wilson, 1990, p. 233)

sets of related data (Wilson, 1990, p. 220). Within an information category the different data items can be described by a data model which shows how they relate to each other.

The information required and produced by the different activities can be displayed in different ways: on the actual conceptual model; in a simple matrix showing the activities against the categories (Wilson, 1990, p. 222); or in a special form called a Maltese Cross which facilitates comparison of the information needs with the current information-processing systems (see Figure 2.2).

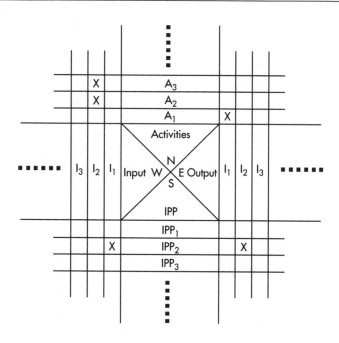

Figure 2.2   Maltese Cross (adapted from Wilson, 1990, p. 235)

The top half of the Maltese Cross shows that these conceptual activity-to-activity information flows. In the centre is the list of activities and on each side the information categories: on the left as input to and the right as output from the activities. Each combination of information category and activity is then marked. Apart from providing a record of the flows, this also focuses attention on possible inconsistencies—for example, where the same information category is produced by a number of activities, or where the same information is used by a number of activities.

Stage 3 (activities 7 and 8) moves away from the conceptual, 'below-the-line', tasks to describing the real situation. Firstly, actual departmental boundaries and managerial roles are mapped onto the conceptual model. This shows which sets of activities particular managers undertake, and thus which information categories they need, and which they are responsible for producing. From this the flows of information from activity to activity can be converted into role-to-role. In the case of a green-field situation, this organizational mapping can be used to create appropriate roles and boundaries in the first instance.

Secondly, the existing information-processing procedures (IPPs) are analysed. Typically, these will be both manual and computerized. The main IPPs are determined and treated like the activities in terms of their information inputs and outputs. This information can be entered into the bottom half of the Maltese Cross if this is being used. This allows a formal and detailed comparison of the information needs, as shown in the north-west corner, with the information currently produced by existing systems, in the south-east corner. The deficiencies (or indeed redundancies) identified by this comparison provide a basic source of information requirements that need to be met, and the best way to effect this can then be considered, given the existing set of IPPs. The outputs from stage 3—namely the new information requirements and the information needs and responsibilities of the managerial roles—then form the basis of the detailed design and implementation work.

A number of weaknesses particular to this approach can be identified (see also Galliers, 1991; Holwell, 1992). Firstly, the exclusive use of a single primary task model inevitably leads to a very narrow IS definition. Only those activities that can be agreed as uncontroversial can be included, and much of the richness of analysis in terms of issues and stakeholders will be lost. The SSM view of organizations as socially constructed and pluralistic is reduced to the traditional task-oriented functionalist view. Secondly, the espoused distinction between data and information (information is data plus meaning) seems in danger of being lost. Information categories and data models appear unproblemmatically with no apparent recognition that information is meaning-dependent or that any particular set of information categories inevitably reflects a particular Weltanschauung. Thirdly, the actual derivation of information, information categories and data models from the activities is rather *ad hoc*. There is no systematic way of determining the information needed and produced by an activity, nor of developing data models. Finally, there is no connection to standard IS design methodologies or case tools to facilitate the detailed design work after the requirements have been identified. Wilson (1990, p. 252) does suggest that a 'Gane and Sarson' diagram could be used but does not detail how.

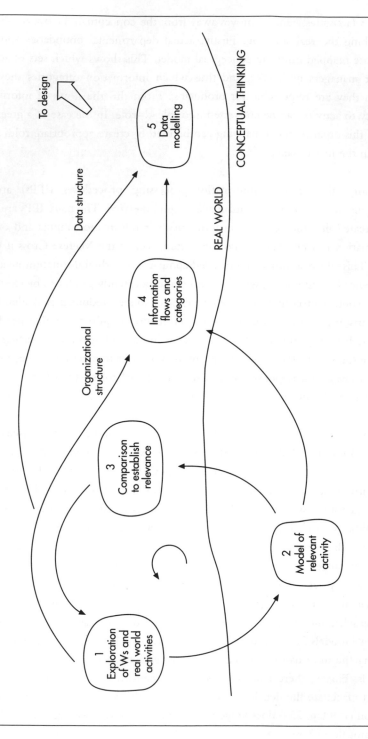

Figure 2.3   Checkland's approach

Checkland has also considered SSM for IS work in a way that is a modified version of Wilson's (Checkland and Scholes, 1990, pp. 53ff). The first stage (see Figure 2.3) uses SSM to explore the meanings and Weltanschauungen that actors in the situation hold in order to develop a model of purposeful activity (CM) that is agreed to be 'truly relevant' to the situation. This could be a straightforward primary task model or could be the result of a long period of reappraisal and debate. At the second stage, given this activity model, the information requirements for each activity are established, as are the people who are sources of and recipients of this information. The activity model is then converted to a model of the information flows and the information categories existing in the information are specified. In the final stage, the information categories are expressed in suitable data structures and these then form the basis of information system design.

Checkland expresses some reservations about this approach. He recognizes that the data structures are not simply derivable from the information categories but must be reconciled with data structures that already exist within the situation. (It would seem that bringing real-world actors into the specification of the information flows means that this activity too is not simply conceptual.) Checkland concludes that the detailed linking of SSM to detailed design of computerized data manipulation systems has not yet been accomplished (Checkland and Scholes, 1990, p. 57). This must be seen as work still in progress and in a more recent work (Checkland and Holwell, 1993) the idea of adding specific 'information-related activities' to the activity model is illustrated.

While Wilson and Checkland have not made formal attempts to link SSM to existing structured systems design (SSD) methodologies, others have and it is to these that we now turn.

LINKING SSM TO EXISTING STRUCTURED DESIGN METHODS

The idea of linking SSM to existing structured design methods was first surfaced by Stowell (1985) who suggested that an agreed conceptual model could be expanded into a detailed data specification using a data flow diagram (DFD). There are indeed quite strong resemblances between a conceptual model and a DFD: the conceptual model shows activities and the logical links between them while the DFD shows data flows and the activities that transform one into another. A detailed comparison of CMs and de Marco-type DFDs (de Marco, 1980) was carried out by Mingers (1988). The conclusions were that there were superficial similarities but that there were also major differences in the underlying philosophies of the two methodologies—one being objectivist and the other being subjectivist. Nevertheless, it was suggested that a well-constructed and detailed conceptual model might usefully and easily be converted into a DFD (Mingers, 1988, p. 378). In fact, it turns out that the conversion is not straight-

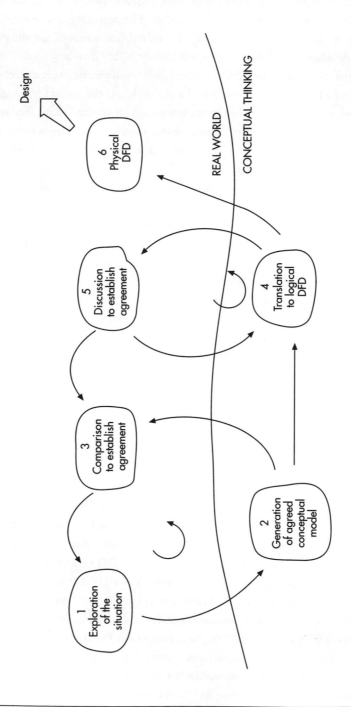

Figure 2.4   Prior's approach using logical DFDs

forward, either technically or philosophically, as we shall see. Nevertheless, DFDs have been the main link although Jackson system development (JSD) has also been used.

One difference of approach highlighted by Miles (1988) is between 'grafting' SSM to SSD methods and 'embedding' SSD methods within SSM. In the former approach SSM is used as a front-end to an SSD method—the output from SSM in the form of an activity model is linked to, say, a DFD and then the traditional systems design method takes over. In the latter approach, the whole study from start to finish is controlled through SSM but hard design elements from traditional SSDs are incorporated within SSM as appropriate. Miles is critical of the grafting approach, arguing that most of the benefits of the SSM study will be lost in the technical design of the system although he accepts that the grafting approach has the virtue of simplicity. Criticisms have been made of the idea of linking these different types of methodologies, particularly because of the epistemological differences, and these will be discussed later.

PRIOR'S APPROACH

Prior (1990) suggests a way of directly converting an agreed CM (a 'finalized' conceptual model) into a DFD. He emphasizes that this is not simply a mechanical process but is iterative and interpretive. He outlines two stages: firstly, producing a conceptual DFD which is very close to the activity model and then converting this into a working DFD for the system (see Figure 2.4).

Stage 1 (activities 1 to 5): produce a conceptual DFD that is very close in its scope and level to the CM. However, there is no simple one-to-one conversion of CM activities into DFD activities or logical connections into data flows. It is necessary to concentrate on the data flows that are necessary for the activities in the CM. Often these will come directly from the activity which will then appear as a data flow in the DFD. For example, an activity such as 'Receive information about potential customers' will become a data flow of customer information. On the other hand, some activities will themselves be transforming information and so will appear as a transform in the DFD. For example, 'Select which customers to visit' would be a transform converting the 'potential customers' data flow into the 'customers to visit' data flow.

Stage 2 (activity 6): convert this conceptual DFD into a working DFD for the actual system. In later papers (Prior, 1991, 1992), partly in response to criticisms (Doyle and Wood, 1991a, 1991b), Prior has clarified some of the more general aspects of his approach. Firstly, he emphasizes that the DFDs derived from conceptual models are not to be seen as objective accounts of real-world systems. In traditional SSD methods DFDs are generally taken to be real-world descriptions not least because there is no clear recognition of the distinction between conceptual and real-world descriptions

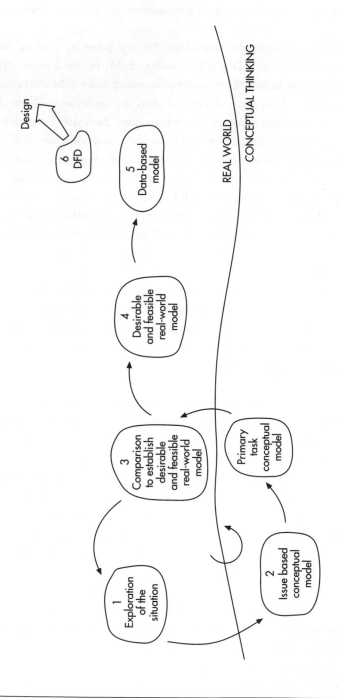

Figure 2.5   Sawyer's approach

(although De Marco does distinguish between logical and physical DFDs). Prior is clear that his DFDs remain conceptual, being a particular view taken of a possible system based on the Weltanschauung inherent in the conceptual model. They remain 'below the line' in SSM terms. Secondly, he reiterates that the translation is not at all mechanical, but a continuing interpretation and development of the ideas expressed in the CM. As such, it should be undertaken by the SSM analyst, not left to a technical systems designer, and should involve the clients as much as in the earlier SSM work. Thirdly, he agrees with Miles that embedding is the best approach—using SSM to structure the whole design process with DFDs simply being a specific data mapping technique within SSM.

SAWYER'S APPROACH

Sawyer (1991) sees the process of translation from CM to DFD as involving two distinct types of transformation: from a conceptual model to a real-world model and from an activity model to a data model. He refers to these as two epistemological shifts—firstly, the transformation of an issue-based activity model into a desirable and feasible real-world activity model and, secondly, the conversion of this real-world activity model to a real-world data-based model which can then easily be translated into a DFD (see Figure 2.5).

Stage 1 (activities 1 to 4): firstly, SSM is used in a traditional way in order to explore the problem situation and develop issue-based activity models. After a debate, one of these issue-based models is chosen for development. The aim is to create a real-world model of desirable and feasible activities. It is suggested that the best way to approach this is by converting the issue-based model into a primary-task model. This is done by expanding the issue-based model, which will tend to have a well-defined Weltanschauung (W) but a rather general transformation (T), to a level of detail where the transformations are very clear and detailed. Then, through a process of comparison and debate, a real-world version can be developed. This will be a mixture of activities that already exist and potential activities that are agreed to be both desirable and feasible.

Stage 2 (activities 5 and 6) involves translating the activity model into a data-based model. This may mean various potential changes to both the activities and the flows. Each activity is examined to discover its input and output information requirements. The activity may then be changed—e.g. to make it reflect the actual data transformation; the flows may be augmented and named in terms of the data; and some activities may become sources or sinks for data. The result is a model showing the flows of data and the transforming activities which can easily be developed into a logical, desirable DFD. Sawyer then sees that a structured approach such a SSADM may be used, the

SSM being very much a front-end. Sawyer (Sawyer and Trahern, 1991; Sawyer, 1992) has also developed a wider methodology called OPIUM in which the linking of SSM and DFDs forms but a part.

In contrast to Prior, Sawyer, makes the transition from the conceptual world to the real world at the activity model stage. His data models are thus already descriptions of the real world, while Prior's remain conceptual and part of the ongoing SSM process.

GREGORY'S AND MERALI'S APPROACH

Gregory (1992) draws on philosophical logic and the philosophy of meaning to address the problem of SSM and information system design. The result is, he claims, a practical method that is grounded on well-recognized theory. Unlike other writers on SSM, Gregory uses formal calculi such as propositional, predicate and modal logics to develop his case. His strategy is to increase the logical content of stakeholder-constructed conceptual models to the point where an information system design can be derived by formal methods.

Gregory distinguishes between two information theories: that of Shannon and Weaver (1949) who take information to be physical, and that of Bar-Hillel and Carnap (1952) who take information to be logical. The physical theory of information suggests an empirical and inductive approach to information system design. The logical theory suggests an analytic and deductive approach. According to Gregory (1992, 1993b), SSM is firmly in the logical camp. He sees the building of a conceptual model as being a Wittgensteinian language game in which the stakeholders create a language to describe a desirable system.

There are two problems in moving from an SSM conceptual model to an information system design that can deal with events in the physical world. One is that the models do not have the power to represent causal sequences. The other is that the models are notional and not even intended to represent a physical state of affairs.

The first problem is dealt with by the inclusion of two new logical connectives in the conceptual model. The arrows in standard conceptual models are intended to represent logical contingency (Checkland and Scholes, 1990)—in causal terms they correspond to necessary conditions. An adequate account of causation requires a connective corresponding to a necessary and sufficient condition and a connective corresponding to a sufficient but unnecessary condition. Gregory (1993a) introduces a double-headed arrow and a broken arrow to represent these connectives. The result is called a logico-linguistic model and can be expressed in the propositional calculus.

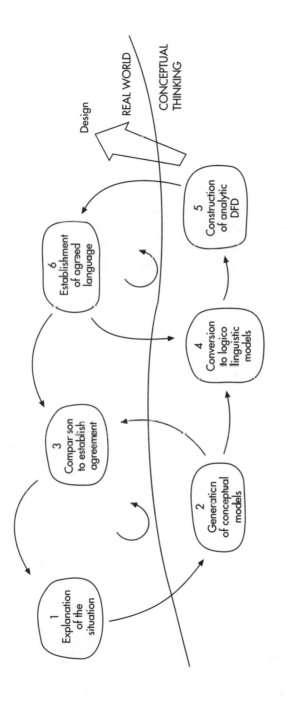

Figure 2.6   Gregory and Merali's approach

Merali (1992) takes the logico-linguistic model as the starting point for the construction of an analytic data flow diagram (see Figure 2.6). For Merali, DFDs can be used as tools for thinking and need not be confined to physical representations, i.e. they can be seen as conceptual. Merali's diagrams have three types of element: the first identify objects that exist independently of the system and are similar to conventional sources and sinks; the second are elements that require further resolution and may require real-world action; the third are conventional processing transforms that will constitute the operational processing core of the system. The analytic DFD is not intended as just a process-modelling tool, but the first and third type of element can be used for the development of de Marco style DFDs.

The second problem identified by Gregory is more complex and requires a more complicated solution. He develops the models by expressing them in predicate logic. Two types of universal are then distinguished, these being definitions and inductive hypotheses (Gregory, 1993b). He argues that traditional SSM models are definitional (Gregory, 1993c) but that inductive hypotheses are required to solve the problem of real-world mapping that occurs when we try to use notional models to describe physical events (Gregory, 1993d). He introduces modal operators into the models to distinguish definitions from inductive hypotheses and particulars.

The process of adding the inductive hypotheses can be described as knowledge elicitation and the resulting models described as a form of knowledge representation. In this way SSM has application in the design of knowledge-based systems.

The final part of the theory (Gregory and Merali, 1993) expresses the models in Prolog, the artificial intelligence language. The system contains two types of 'rule'. Logically necessary rules and rules derived from them are taken as expressions of the definitions from the stakeholder-driven language game. Contingent rules and rules derived from them are inductive hypotheses taken from the stakeholders' knowledge about the situation. 'Facts' cannot be entered into the system if they conflict with a logical rule. However, if a fact conflicts with a contingent rule it can be entered and its entry will indicate that the rule has been falsified. Given this, the system learns in a way that conforms to a Popperian account of scientific method.

MILES: EMBEDDING IS METHODS WITHIN SSM

Miles (1988) argued that front-ending (or grafting) SSM onto hard methods was the wrong approach. Rather, SSM should guide the whole project and, when appropriate, should have hard design elements embedded within it. This approach is elaborated in a later paper (Miles, 1992). Rather than converting CMs into DFDs, new constructs—a conceptual flow model and a conceptual data model—are added into SSM at the con-

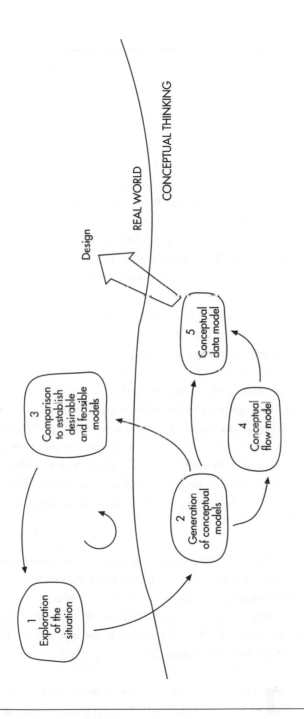

Figure 2.7   Miles' embedded method

ceptual modelling stage. The description of these new constructs is brief. The flow model depicts flows of information between activities, but is not intended as a conceptual DFD. It has no data stores and has the same activities as the activity model itself. The data model consists of data entities and their relations and is derived from the flow model. It is therefore presumably very similar to a standard entity–relationship diagram. Miles does not explain in any detail how these are produced.

Once produced, however, they fit neatly into the standard SSM format—they are concepts to be compared with the real-world in order to agree desirable changes. Flows or entities missing in the real-world might indicate possible systems development, while flows or entities not in the model(s) might indicate redundancy or a changing situation. In either event, changes will already be in a form suitable for hard requirements definition (see Figure 2.7).

SAVAGE AND MINGERS: LINKING SSM TO JSD

While most work explicitly linking SSM to SSD methods has concentrated on the use of DFDs and, to some extent, entity diagrams, it is also possible to consider links to other types of methodologies. In particular, linking to the Jackson system development (JSD) methodology (Cameron, 1989) was suggested by Wood and Doyle (1989) and has been investigated by Savage and Mingers (1993).

JSD differs significantly from structured methodologies of the de Marco/Yourdon type. Firstly, it is object-oriented, concentrating attention not on data and data flows but on the entities existing in the situation and the actions they perform or suffer; secondly, it makes the time dimension more explicit by being structured around the life cycles of the entities; and, thirdly, its emphasis is on building a model of the real situation rather than logical data models. As these characteristics are also antithetical to SSM, it might appear to be an unlikely partner; nevertheless it can provide a useful complement to SSM.

There are three phases to JSD: a modelling phase in which model processes, entities and actions are selected and defined; a network phase in which the detailed specification including input/output functions and communication processes are designed; and an implementation phase in which the processes and data are fitted onto the existing technology. The developed SSM/JSD framework concentrates on fitting the modelling phase into SSM, as shown in Figure 2.8.

After several iterations of SSM, one or more activity models seen as relevant will be selected for development. For each, a JSD entity structure diagram is derived but this remains a purely conceptual diagram rather than a real-world description as in conven-

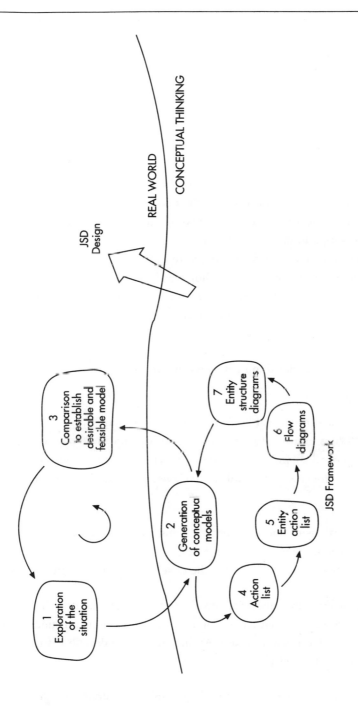

Figure 2.8   Savage and Minger's link to JSD

tional JSD. This conceptual entity structure diagram is then considered alongside the activity model in a debate about desirable and feasible changes. Depending on the outcome, particular JSD diagrams could form the basis of the network and implementation stages within an overall SSM framework.

In this case, the derivation of the JSD diagram from the activity model is quite complicated because of the different orientations of the models: activities against entities. The main steps are:

(1) Drawing up an action list. This uses the activities of the conceptual model to identify entities in the situation and their actions.
(2) Convert the action list to an entity-action list by assigning the actions to the entities that perform or suffer them.
(3) Draw flow diagrams for entities with more than one action to identify which are concurrent or may involve a choice between alternatives.
(4) Construct conceptual JSD entity structure diagrams for each entity.
(5) Produce a function and entity attribute list, identifying the information necessary to carry out the activities.

This process is intended to be iterative and to involve the clients.

MULTIVIEW

This approach, developed by Avison and Wood-Harper (1990, 1992), Wood-Harper *et al.* (1985) is in many ways the most formalized methodology combining SSM (or at least parts of SSM) with other IS development tools. As it is well known and has been extensively documented, it will be reviewed only briefly. Multiview consists of five stages:

Stage 1 (analysis of human activity systems) involves an initial analysis of the human activity systems within which the information system is embedded. Essentially it involves SSM up to and including the development of conceptual models.

Stage 2 (information modelling) involves more traditional IS techniques. A functional model is developed from one of the root definitions—the functions being analysed in as much detail as is felt necessary. At the same time a data flow diagram is produced as well as an entity model.

Stage 3 (analysis of socio-technical systems): the purpose of this stage is to bring into consideration important social objectives and values—to generate different possible systems designs so that the participants and users will be able to control the final result.

Stage 4 (design of the human–computer interface) is concerned with the detailed design of the user interface. It is the last input into the final design of the system.

Stage 5 (designing technical subsystems) is the most technical stage where the detailed specification is carried out. It is informed by both the information analysis of stage 2 and the social and user-oriented objectives of stages 3 and 4.

Overall, this methodology has much to recommend it—especially the incorporation of stages 3 and 4 which are seldom given the attention they deserve. However, the point of interest is the move from stage 1 to stage 2 and here Multiview is singularly weak. The soft analysis carried out in stage 1 culminates in a conceptual model, but this is really left in the air. The next stage begins almost anew with an analysis of the functions of the new system. Quite how this new system was decided upon and how the functions and entities relate to the conceptual model is not clear. Multiview has potential, but in comparison with other methods it needs much more work on this link to make it useful.

OTHER METHODOLOGIES

There are a number of other methodologies incorporating some SSMs which are beyond the scope of this chapter. In particular:

(1) Functional Analysis of Office Requirements (FAOR) (Shafer, 1988) which, as its name suggests, is tailored towards developing office systems.
(2) COMPACT (CCTA, 1989), which is a method, developed by the Government's Central Computer and Telecommunications Agency, to link SSM to the standard design method SSADM. It is understood that future versions of SSADM may well have some elements of SSM specified within them, although the idea of embedding soft within hard seems entirely the wrong way round.

SSM AND INFORMATION MANAGEMENT

So far in this chapter the emphasis has been on the development of a single information system in response to a particular problem. However, SSM has also been used at the more general level of information management, and particularly for strategic information systems planning.

Galliers (1992b, 1993a) argues for the importance of information systems being conceived strategically rather than in isolation. Organizations need to have a planned information systems (and technology) strategy to guide their activities over a number of years and, crucially, this information systems strategy must be linked to the overall business strategy (assuming there is one). This integration is a difficult activity to undertake

successfully since it involves the differing perspectives of business, information requirements, and information technology.

The approach advocated by Galliers is based on SSM and aims not at the development
of particular information systems but the construction of a flexible information architecture for the business as a whole which is robust enough to respond to changing
future requirements. The method is a development of Wilson's approach (see Figure
2.9), but the primary task modelling and Maltese Cross are both rejected.

Stage 1 (activities 1 to 4) concerns the analysis of the organization and its situation. Here
extra emphasis is paid to 'scanning the environment' in order to understand future
trends. Attention is paid not only to the strengths and weaknesses of the organization
but also to the threats and opportunities arising from its environment in terms of the
current situation and the possible future. Debate and participation are encouraged and
a range of possible scenarios are developed.

Stage 2 (activities 5 to 7) involves the development of root definitions, activity models
and information requirements in a similar manner to Wilson but with one major difference. A number of scenarios are maintained in the analysis and activity models are
developed for each. It is accepted that there will be divergence of opinion about future
developments and even about the nature and purpose of the business itself. No attempt
is made to generate or force a consensus, rather the richness is welcomed as it will help
to avoid blind spots and may well aid implementation through a feeling of participation and ownership.

The different scenarios will generate different information requirements but there will
be differing degrees of overlap between them. Some requirements will be common to
all the scenarios, while others will be shared to a greater or lesser degree. Decisions need
to be made at this stage about what information is to be maintained. The balance is
between the cost of collection and maintenance of all the possible requirements and the
benefits of creating a flexible information architecture able to detect and adapt to the
changing future.

Stage 3 (activities 8 to 11) takes the activity models and the information requirements
back 'above the line' to initiate a debate about both the effectiveness of the current
organization and the relationship between the desired information requirements and
the current information provision. The aim is the generation of recommendations
across the whole IS/IT spectrum, including inter organizational IS, in line with the current and future business strategy.

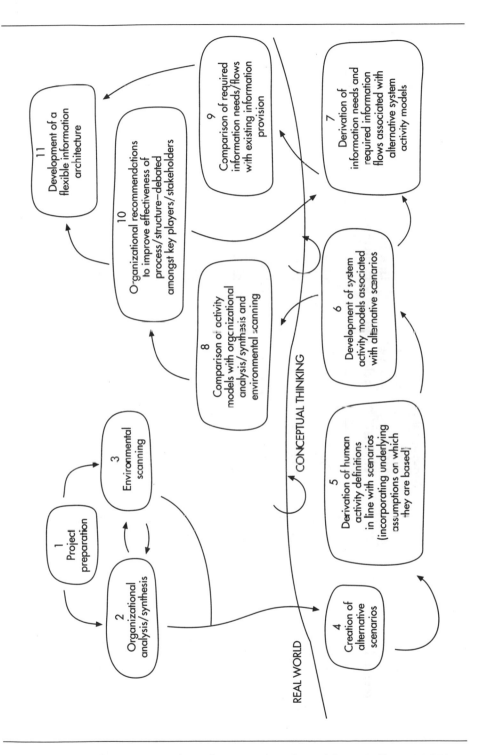

Figure 2.9 Galliers' scenario-based approach (adapted from Galliers, 1993)

| Method | Conceptual model | | | Link to IS method | Additional SSM constructs |
	Type of CM	Number of CMs	Data model above/below line		
Wilson	Primary	One	Below	None	Maltese Cross
Checkland	'Relevant'	One	Above	None	
Prior	'Agreed'	One	Below	DFD	
Sawyer	Issue to primary	One	Above	DFD	
Gregory and Merali	'Agreed'	One	Below	DFD	Logico-linguistic model
Miles	'Agreed'	One	Below	None	Conceptual flow model Conceptual data model
Savage and Mingers	'Relevant'	One or more	Below	JSD	JSD framework
Galliers	'Relevant'	Multiple	Below	None	Scenarios

Table 2.1   Comparison of methods for linking SSM to IS

SUMMARY OF THE METHODS

A comparison of the methods in summary form is shown in Table 2.1.

The main dimensions of difference concern the conceptual model: whether it is a primary task or an issue-based one; whether it is seen as conceptual (below the line) or descriptive of the real world (above the line) ; and whether one or several CMs are used. The other differences shown in the table are whether there is an explicit link to an established IS method, and whether new constructs have been added to SSM.

CRITICAL DISCUSSION OF LINKING SSM AND IS

So far this chapter has surveyed, fairly uncritically, a range of different approaches to linking SSM and IS. A strong argument was made in the first section for considering SSM in IS development, but this is very much a developing area and there are a number of difficulties and questions that must be addressed.

GENERAL ISSUES

Do we accept that attempting to link SSM and SSD in a fairly mechanistic way is worth while, or will it end up being the worst of both worlds? Objections to the thrust of much of this work have been raised by Doyle and Wood (1991a, 1991b). In their first article the main point was that SSM and IS embodied different and conflicting epistemologies and that there was no simple way to link them. Doyle and Wood agreed that it was necessary to have both soft analysis and hard analysis yet saw the two as essentially incompatible—it was just not possible to graft or embed the two easily. Any links will be the result of hard work moving between the two approaches. In a later paper, responding to critics, they reiterate that shifting from one paradigm to another is a difficult matter, but agree that you can complement a CM by, for example, a DFD. In this case they argue, rather like Miles, that the DFD/CM should remain conceptual and under-the-line. The main problem that they see is maintaining debate about what is to be created. For them, the derivation of a DFD from an agreed set of activities is trivial, as it is just a discussion about real-world implementation rather than a conceptual debate about different subjective viewpoints. A way must be found of combining SSM and SSD without compromising either.

A second concern is that in linking SSM to traditional IS methodologies much of the richness of the SSM analysis will be lost. At a practical level, the SSM approach tends to generate an enormous amount of varied information, particularly concerning different viewpoints and possible activities. Most of this must be lost in the need to fix on a single agreed activity model and then convert this into a particular narrow representation such as a DFD.

At the philosophical level, it appears that this particular way of using SSM contradicts its own premises. The whole philosophical thrust of SSM and interpretivism is to recognize the different meanings and interpretations that may be given validly to the world and to information within it. Indeed, SSM starts with the proposition that information only comes into being when data is interpreted in the light of particular meanings. Yet this recognition is suppressed in the interests of developing a single hegemonic information system. A similar point is made by Galliers (1991) in terms of defining strategic information requirements, and by Keys and Roberts (1991) and Wood (1992). Is it not possible to retain this diversity of view in the developed system?

TECHNICAL ISSUES

Accepting for the moment that there are significant benefits to be gained by some formal linking, then there are a number of questions which need further research. First, is it satisfactory to graft an output from SSM onto some SSD or should we embed, making SSM the overall guiding methodology? Is the latter case realistic given the preponderance of hard methods already in use? Related to this, there is a problem about the people who would actually do it. Currently, most analysts have a technology bias/background and tend to be much more comfortable with technical issues. On the other hand, the (relatively few) SSM practitioners rarely have the necessary detailed technical skills and knowledge to create practicable systems. This would seem to imply the need for significant retraining of IS analysts, but is this feasible? And even if it were done, the process and management skills that SSM requires may be difficult for the technically-oriented analysts to acquire. Secondly, at what point, if at all, should the involvement of managers/users and the debate stop? Should it all be within a standard cycle of SSM, resulting in an agreed CM which is then taken as a blueprint, or does debate carry on throughout the development of (several) DFDs or entity models? Indeed, might it not carry on throughout the entire project? Thirdly, what is the best way of linking SSM into some form of SSD method, or indeed is there any systematic way of doing this? Relatedly, what is the best SSD method to aim for? Concentration has been on DFDs and data analysis–type methods with some attention to JSD, which is more activity based. Should other approaches, such as Ethics, be considered, or should SSM (or parts of it) be embedded in some specific methodology such as Multiview or FAOR? It seems to me that there is much scope for a research programme, using action research, to begin to answer these questions.

CONCLUSION

In conclusion, I would like to put forward my own answers to some of these questions and to make some suggestions for significant future research.

Firstly, the philosophical incompatibility identified by Doyle and Wood does not seem to be a very significant problem. All design starts as concepts and ideas which are debated and developed, but there must be a path towards greater concreteness. For example, architects develop many conceptual models and eventually one or more is embodied in a design drawing which is then physically modelled and is finally used to create the building. This does not mean that the drawing is definitive—it changes and develops as building progresses. Somewhere, however, concepts have to be embodied; they have to enter the real world in order to generate real-world artifacts.

Secondly, I am certainly in favour of the idea of embedding rather than grafting. SSM has important advantages over hard methodologies for controlling the entire project process. For example, it explicitly encourages user involvement from the beginning; it is a methodology that focuses on learning, which is appropriate because the entire development cycle is based on learning, both by analysts about the organizational context and by users about the developing system; and it encourages iteration—information requirements are often changed and developed even late in the project as circumstances alter and users become more aware of the developments

Thirdly, I have no particular favourite among the linking methods—that, hopefully, will be an interesting outcome of further research—but I do think a fairly systematic, almost mechanical, result would be beneficial as it would allow changes to be easily embodied in actual systems in a prototyping type mode. CASE tools might help here in two different ways. A CASE-type tool could be created for SSM itself, and work has already been done on this (Keys and Roberts, 1991; Avison et al., 1992; Stowell et al., 1991), although the idea of automating SSM in some way is controversial. Alternatively, it might be possible to create a CASE tool that generated actual code from a detailed specification in, say, JSD. Prototype systems could then be generated quickly and easily within an SSM-controlled participative framework.

Finally, the incompatibility between SSM's interpretivism and the single resulting information system is important, and I make two suggestions:

(1) It should be possible to keep a number of different conceptual models/Ws going throughout the process and to try to develop systems that are compatible with them all. This may well involve maintaining different definitions of apparently the same concept. For example, as we all have experienced in our own institutions, costs can be calculated in many different ways and in practice we actually use different figures for different purposes, and there may well be debate about this. So why not build this in and make it explicit? Get the machine to do the work and let people have the debates.

(2) The work of Winograd and Flores (1987), based in part on Maturana's theory of autopoiesis and structural coupling (Maturana and Varela, 1980), is of great interest. This can be read as providing a detailed underpinning for interpretivism. It suggests that systems should be developed that allow the users to create their own language and conversations rather than defining everything for people. This would mean that the same system might appear quite differently to different users and would contain different concepts and sets of information, each reflecting different shared views of reality. Some work already exists in this area—see, for example, Winograd (1987), Harnden and Mullery (1991), Stephens and Wood (1991), Kensing and Winograd (1991)—and Mingers (1993a, b) has developed an analysis of the nature of information and meaning from this intersubjective position.

In conclusion, research into the use of SSM in IS development is vital as it holds out the promise of rich rewards, both practically and intellectually.

REFERENCES

Ackoff, R. (1992) *Beyond Total Quality Management*, Centre for Systems Studies Publication, University of Hull, Hull, UK.

Avison, D. and Wood-Harper, A. T. (1990) *Multiview: An Exploration in Information Systems Development*, Blackwell, Oxford.

Avison, D. and Wood-Harper, A. T. (1992) 'Reflections from the experience of using Multiview: through the lens of soft systems methodology', *Systemist*, **14** (3), 136–45.

Avison, D., Golder, P. and Shah, H. (1992) 'Towards an SSM toolkit', *European Journal of Information Systems*, **1** (6), 397–407.

Bar-Hillel, Y. and Carnap, R. (1952) 'An outline of a theory of semantic information', Technical Report 247, Research Laboratory of Electronics, MIT.

Blum, B. (1987) JAD Report FGMSD–80–4 revisited ACM S16 soft *Software Engineering Notes*, **12** (1), 49–50.

Boland, R. (1985) 'Phenomenology: a preferred approach to research on IS', in *Research Methods in Information Systems* (E. Mumford, R. Hirschheim, G. Fitzgerald and T. Wood-Harper, eds), Elsevier, Amsterdam, 363–79.

Cameron, J. (1989) *JSP and JSD: the Jackson approach to Software Development*, IEEE Computer Society Press, New York.

CCTA (1989) *Compact Manual version 1.1*, CCTA, Norwich.

Checkland, P. B. (1981) *Systems Thinking, Systems Practice*, Wiley, Chichester.

Checkland, P. B. and Griffin, R. (1970) 'Management information systems: a systemic view', *Journal of Systems Engineering*, **1** (2), 29–42.

Checkland, P. B. and Holwell, S. (1993) 'Information management and organizational processes: an approach through soft systems methodology', *Journal of Information Systems*, **3**, 3–16.

Checkland, P. B. and Scholes, J. (1990) *Soft Systems Methodology in Action*, Wiley, Chichester.

De Marco, T. (1980) *Structured Analysis and Systems Specification*, Yourdon, New York.

Doyle, K. and Wood, R. (1991a) 'Systems thinking, systems practice: dangerous liaisons', *Systemist*, **13** (1), 28–30.

Doyle, K. and Wood, R. (1991b) 'The paradigm shift and the protozoon', *Systemist*, **13** (3), 131–4.

Galliers, R. (1984) 'An approach to information needs analysis', in *Human-Computer Interaction—INTERACT '84* (B Shackel, ed.), Elsevier, North-Holland, Amsterdam, 619–28.

Galliers, R. (1987) *Information Analysis: Selected Readings*, Addison-Wesley, Sydney.

Galliers, R. (1991) 'A scenario-based approach to strategic information systems planning', in *Systems Thinking in Europe* (M. Jackson, G. Mansell, R. Flood, R. Blackham and S. Probert, eds), Plenum, London.

Galliers, R. (1992a) 'Choosing information systems research approaches', in *Information Systems Research: Issues, Methods and Practical Guidelines* (R. Galliers, ed.) Blackwell, Oxford, 144 62.

Galliers, R. (1992b) 'Soft systems, scenarios, and the planning and development of information systems', *Systemist*, **14** (3), 146–59.

Galliers, R. (1993a) 'Towards a flexible information architecture: integrating business strategies, information systems strategies and business process redesign', *Journal of Information Systems*, **3** (3), 199–213.

Galliers, R. (1993b) 'Information systems and business reengineering', in *IFORS Conference, Lisbon*, 11–16 July.

Gregory, F. (1992) 'SSM to information systems: a logical account', *Systemist*, **14** (3), 180–9.

Gregory, F. (1993a) 'Cause, effect, efficiency and soft systems models', *Journal of the Operational Research Society*, **44** (4).

Gregory, F. (1993b) 'Logic and meaning in conceptual models: implications for information system design', *Systemist*, **15** (1), 28–43.

Gregory, F. (1993c) 'SSM to information systems: a Wittgensteinian approach', *Journal of Information Systems*, **3**, (3), 149–68.

Gregory, F. (1993d) 'Mapping conceptual models on to the real world', in *Proceedings of the United Kingdom Systems Society 3rd International Conference*, Plenum, New York.

Gregory, F. and Merali, Y. (1993) 'Inductions, modality and conceptual modelling'. Warwick Business School Research Bureau Research Paper 79, Warwick University.

Hammer, M. (1990) 'Reengineering work: don't automate, obliterate', *Harvard Business Review*, **68** (4), 104–12.

Harnden, R. and Mullery, G. (1991) 'Enabling network systems (ENS)', *Systems Practice*, **4** (6), 579–98.

Hirschheim, R. (1992) 'Information systems epistemology: an historical perspective', in *Information Systems Research: Issues, Methods and Practical Guidelines* (R. Galliers, ed.), Blackwell, Oxford, 28–60.

Hirschheim, R. and Klein, H. (1989) 'Four paradigms of information systems development', *Communications of the ACM*, **32** (10), 1199–215.

Hirschheim, R. and Shafer, G. (1988) 'Requirements analysis: a new look at an old topic', *Journal of Applied Systems Analysis*, **15**, 101–18.

Holwell, S. (1992) 'SSM information approach: a critique', *Systemist*, **14** (3), 93–8.

Kensing, F. and Winograd, T. (1991) 'The language/action approach to the design of computer support for cooperative work: a preliminary study in work mapping', in *Collaborative Work, Social Communications and Information Systems* (R. Stamper, P. Kerola, R. Lee and K. Lyytinen, eds), Elsevier North-Holland, Amsterdam, 311–32.

Keys, P. and Roberts, M. (1991) 'Information systems development and soft systems thinking: towards an improved methodology', in *Systems Thinking in Europe* (M. Jackson, G. Mansell, R. Flood, R. Blackham and S. Probert, eds), Plenum, London.

Jayaratna, N. (1990) 'Systems analysis: the need for a better understanding', *International Journal of Information Management*, **10**, 228–34.

Le Fevre, A. and Pattison, E. (1986) 'Planning for hospital IS using the Lancaster SSM', *Australian Computer Journal*, **18** (4), 180–5.

Lewis, P. (1993) 'Linking soft systems methodology with data-focussed information systems development', *Journal of Information Systems*, **3** (3), 169–86.

Lucas, H. (1975) *Why Information Systems Fail*, Columbia University Press, New York.

Lyytinen, K. (1988) 'Stakeholders, information system failures and soft systems methodology: an assessment', *Journal of Applied Systems Analysis*, **15**, 61–81.

Lyytinen, K. and Hirschheim, R. (1987) 'Information systems failures: a survey and classification of empirical literature', *Oxford Surveys in Information Technology*, **4**.

Lyytinen, K. and Klein, H. (1985) 'The critical theory of Jurgen Habermas as a basis for a theory of information systems, in *Research Methods in Information Systems* (E. Mumford, R. Hirschheim, G. Fitzgerald and T. Wood-Harper, eds), Elsevier, Amsterdam, 219–31.

Maturana, H. and Varela, F. (1980) *Autopoiesis and Cognition*, Reidel, Dordrecht.

Merali, Y. (1992) 'Analytic data flow diagrams: an alternative to physicalism', *Systemist*, **14** (3) 190–8.

Miles, R. (1985) 'Computer systems analysis: the constraints of the hard systems approach', *Journal of Applied Systems Analysis*, **12**, 55–65.

Miles, R. (1988) 'Combining "hard" and "soft" systems practice: grafting or embedding', *Journal of Applied Systems Analysis*, **15**, 55–60.

Miles, R. (1992) 'Combining "hard" and "soft" systems practice: grafting and embedding revisited', *Systemist*, **14** (2), 62–6.

Mingers, J. (1988) 'Comparing conceptual models and data flow diagrams', *The Computer Journal*, **31** (4), 376–9.

Mingers, J. (1993a) 'Information and meaning: foundations for an intersubjective account'. Warwick Business School Research Bureau Research Paper 74, University of Warwick, Coventry, UK.

Mingers, J. (1993b) 'Information and meaning: towards intersubjective meaning systems'. Warwick Business School Research Bureau Research Paper 75, University of Warwick, Coventry, UK.

Prior, R. (1990) 'Deriving data flow diagrams from a "soft systems" conceptual model', *Systemist*, **12** (2), 65–75.

Prior, R. (1991) 'Dangerous liaisons: a reply to Doyle and Wood', *Systemist*, **13** (2), 81–5.

Prior, R. (1992) 'Linking SSM and IS development', *Systemist*, **14** (3), 128–32.

Savage, A. and Mingers, J. (1993) 'A framework for linking soft systems methodology and Jackson systems development'. Warwick Business School Research Bureau Research Paper 80, Warwick University, Coventry, UK.

Sawyer, K. (1991) 'Linking SSM to DFDs: the two epistemological differences', *Systemist*, **13** (2), 76–80.

Sawyer, K. (1992) 'A contribution towards the debate on linking SSM to IS', *Systemist*, **14** (3), 199–201.

Sawyer, K. and Trahern, P. (1991) 'Integrating hard and soft thinking: the use of the "current activities description" in OPIUM', in *Systems Thinking in Europe* (M. Jackson, G. Mansell, R. Flood, R. Blackham and S. Probert, eds), Plenum, New York, 571–6.

Shafer, G. (1988) *Functional Analysis of Office Requirements: A Multiperspective Approach*, Wiley, Chichester.

Shannon, C. and Weaver, W. (1949) *The Mathematical Theory of Communication*, University of Illinois Press, Ill.

Stevens, R. and Wood, R. (1991) 'Information systems as linguistic systems: a constructivist perspective', in *Systems Thinking in Europe* (M. Jackson, G. Mansell, R. Flood, R. Blackham and S. Probert, eds), Plenum, New York.

Stowell, F. (1985) 'Experience with soft systems methodology and data analysis', *Information Technology Training*, May, 48–50.

Stowell, F. (1991) 'Towards client-led development of information systems', *Journal of Information Systems*, **1**, 173–89.

Stowell, F., West, D. and Stansfield, M. (1991) 'The application of an expert system shell to an unstructured domain of expertise: using expert systems technology to teach SSM', *European Journal of Information Systems*, **1** (4), 281–90.

Wilson, B. (1984) *Systems: Concepts, Methodologies, and Applications*, Wiley, Chichester [2nd edition 1990].

Winograd, T. (1987) 'A language/action perspective on the design of cooperative work', *Human-Computer Interaction*, **3**, 3–30.

Winograd, T. and Flores, F. (1987) *Understanding Computers and Cognition*, Ablex, New York.

Wood R. (1992) 'Linking soft systems methodology and information systems', *Systemist*, **14** (3), 133–5.

Wood R. and Doyle, K. (1989) 'Doing the right thing right: an exploration between soft systems methodology and Jackson system development', ISGSR Conference, Edinburgh.

Wood-Harper, A., Antill, L. and Avison, D. (1985) *Information Systems Definition: The Multiview Approach*, Blackwell, Oxford.

3

RE-ORIENTING INFORMATION SYSTEMS STRATEGY: INTEGRATING INFORMATION SYSTEMS INTO THE BUSINESS

Bob Galliers
Warwick Business School, University of Warwick

INTRODUCTION

It is becoming generally accepted that a key to successful information systems strategy formation lies in the *integration* of the information systems strategy with that of the business strategy on the one hand, and information systems development and the management of organizational change on the other. While there is general agreement that there *should* be this integration, it is still the case that in many organizations the linkage is tenuous, at best.

Integration is improved if, *inter alia*:

- key stakeholders, at all levels within the organization (and sometimes in other closely related organizations) are involved in, and are committed to, the formation and implementation of the plan;
- the process of strategy formation, implementation and review is integrated into on-going management activities;
- there is a senior management 'champion' and/or 'sponsor', who is prepared to take responsibility to ensure that this process is taken seriously;
- there is a partnership based on mutual respect and trust between information systems staff and their business colleagues;
- the information systems function is organized and staffed in such a way that it 'fits' with that of the organization as a whole;
- the richness associated with business systems strategy formulation is transferred to information systems development, and

- the information systems development process incorporates business process redesign ... and the information systems strategy itself takes account of required business and organizational change, brought about by changed business imperatives and the opportunities afforded by information technology.

There is nothing very new in the above list of factors that might improve the integration of information systems strategies with business strategies. However, it is still the case that organizations find difficulty in achieving success in their information systems strategy formation and implementation efforts. This is partly the result of a lack of awareness by managers and their information systems colleagues: the former are often happy in the mistaken belief that information technology can be left to the technologists, and many of the latter are happier to have an information systems strategy and an information systems development that are more concerned with technological issues than with business imperatives—with as little as possible involvement from business executives. It is also partly due to the very nature of the two processes, as currently practised: the one creative and synthetical; the other mechanistic and analytical. Having said that, there have been attempts to combine the two philosophies, as a result of growing awareness that we have not been as successful as we would have liked in developing information systems that have a real impact on business performance.

It should be noted, however, that our view of information systems strategy has developed over the years. Figures 3.1 and 3.2 illustrate the changing perceptions of the outcomes of, and process of formulating, an information systems strategy. From a mere list of potential information systems developments as the outcome from the process, one can discern a transition in thinking that has gone on to include a portfolio of information systems applications across the business, and the issues associated with organizational impacts introduced above. Similarly, the process itself was seen in the early days of business data processing, primarily as an isolated task associated with improved computer efficiency. Multiple (Earl, 1989) or eclectic (Sullivan, 1985) methods are now seen to be required, incorporating business-driven and creative approaches which include the search for strategic opportunities and associated organizational change brought about by information systems as well as dealing with matters of information systems efficiency and effectiveness.

INFORMATION TECHNOLOGY, STRATEGIC OPPORTUNITIES AND ORGANIZATIONAL CHANGE: THE RECEIVED WISDOM

Much has been claimed regarding the impact that information technology (IT) can have on organizational competitiveness (e.g. Porter, 1980, 1985; McFarlan, 1984), on

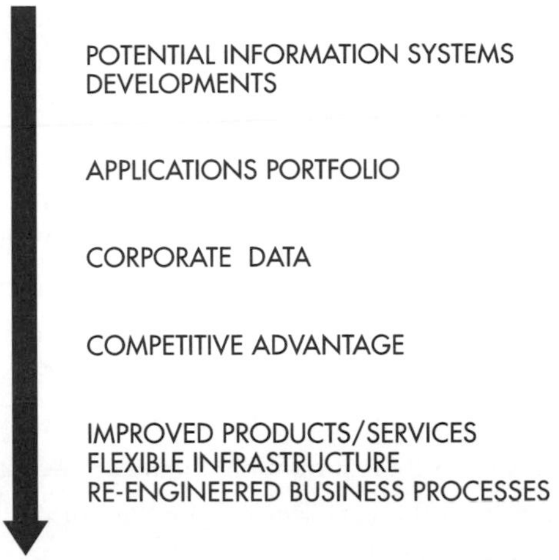

POTENTIAL INFORMATION SYSTEMS
DEVELOPMENTS

APPLICATIONS PORTFOLIO

CORPORATE DATA

COMPETITIVE ADVANTAGE

IMPROVED PRODUCTS/SERVICES
FLEXIBLE INFRASTRUCTURE
RE-ENGINEERED BUSINESS PROCESSES

Figure 3.1   Trends in strategic IS planning: the changing nature of desired
outcomes

redrawing organizational boundaries (Cash and Konsynski, 1985; Keen, 1991), in
informing decision making (e.g. Zuboff, 1988), in enabling the redesigning of business
processes (Hammer, 1990) and a redefinition of the very purpose of the business itself
(Scott Morton, 1991). While some of the earlier claims have been called into ques-

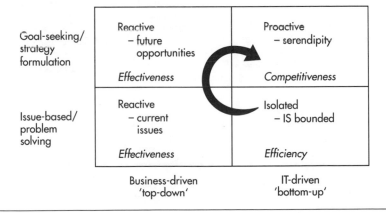

Figure 3.2   The shifting focus of IS strategy formulation: from technological
efficiency to business competitiveness (amended from Galliers,
1987c, p. 226)

tion—e.g. with respect to the inability of businesses to *sustain* any competitive advantage brought about by IT (Clemons, 1986)—it is generally accepted that IT should be treated as a strategic rather than a tactical issue, and as a concern of business executives rather than a peripheral issue to be dealt with by technicians alone.

The transitions that organizations might pass through with respect to the impact of IT is illustrated by the work of Venkatraman as part of MIT's 'Management in the 1990s' research programme (Scott Morton, 1991). Figure 3.3 summarizes the argument which identifies two earlier, evolutionary, stages concerned with localized exploitation of IT followed by cross-functional integration. These may be followed by more radical changes to the way business is undertaken: the redesign of key business processes, the integration of processes across organizational boundaries—inter-organizational systems—and the redefinition of the very scope and nature of the business, all as a direct result of harnessing the power of IT.

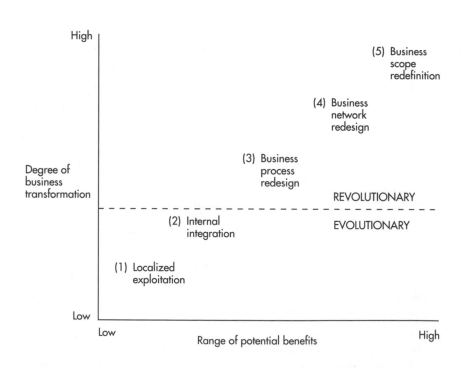

Figure 3.3   Stages of IT-induced business transformation (amended from Venkatraman, 1991, p. 127)

INFORMATION TECHNOLOGY AND BUSINESS RE-ENGINEERING

There tend to be two quite opposing viewpoints as to the strategic impact of IT: one, suggesting that the changes IT can bring about are profound and overwhelmingly beneficial; the other, pointing out the disappointing results even following quite massive investments in IT (Galliers, 1992a). A contributing factor to the more negative perspective on IT would seem to be the fact that, in many instances, existing processes are left intact and IT is used simply to make these more efficient (Hammer, 1990, p. 104). We should, perhaps, have learned from the lessons of old that the mere automation of existing processes that are themselves ineffective, will at best lead to more efficient—but no more effective—processes. Leavitt's (1965) analysis and, more recently, the approach to information systems development following organizational change advocated by Lundeberg *et al.* (1981, p. 125; *italics* added) should surely have warned us not simply to attempt to automate existing ways of doing business:

> Information systems have value only if they contribute to improve the situation for people in the organization They have no value of their own. It is therefore not enough that we study the contents of the information systems so that we can form am opinion about their values. We *must instead study* the activities that *people perform* in the organization and that somehow should be improved.

However, the short and not altogether glorious history of IT is reapplied with examples of failures that should have prepared us to take on board this fairly simple message. Indeed, we have but to go back to March 1993 for the spectacular failure of the London Stock Exchange's Taurus share settlement system. Costing, according to the Stock Exchange, £75m (and possibly as much as £250m) in development costs and lasting 12 years, this project failed to take into account the possibilities for new processes to take the place of the existing procedures, and the differing interests and viewpoints of key stakeholders. As a result, it was practically doomed to fail from its inception (Green-Armytage, 1993).

It is because of this limited view and the sometimes disastrous results that ensue, that advocates of business process redesign (Hammer, 1990) and business reconfiguration (Venkatraman, 1991) argue for a more radical approach (see Figure 3.3). Hammer (1990, p. 107), for example, suggests that:

> At the heart of re-engineering is the notion of discontinuous thinking—of recognizing and breaking away from the outdated rules and fundamental assumptions that underlie operations. Unless we change

these rules, we are merely rearranging deck chairs on the *Titanic*. We cannot achieve breakthroughs in performance by cutting fat or automating existing processes. Rather, we must challenge old assumptions and shed the old rules that made the business underperform in the first place.

But how do we go about *discontinuous thinking*? Hammer suggests a number of principles that might aid us in this creative process. These include (see Hammer, 1990, pp. 108–12):

- organize around outcomes, rather than tasks
- arrange for those who use the output of a process actually to perform that process
- subsume information processing work into the 'real' work that produces the information
- treat geographically dispersed resources as if they were centralized
- link or integrate parallel activities rather than merge the information that arises from them
- make decisions where the work is performed, and build control into the process itself
- capture information just once, and at source.

These principles, while useful, are not of themselves particularly helpful. Linked, as they often are, with an assumed IT solution, they may actually be dangerous! For example, it may be, having read such articles, that executives aim to put their messages into action: to introduce radically new methods of working, and/or to pursue new market opportunities, utilizing the latest IT. Were they to have good quality information systems (IS) resources, in terms not just of technology but also of information systems applications and of the requisite skills—among users and providers alike—this may well be an appropriate strategy. Conversely, were such resources to be inadequate, it is likely that competitive *disadvantage* would ensue. Figure 3.4 illustrates the point. Based on the work of McLaughlan *et al.* (1983), Figure 3.4 suggests that organizations with sound IS resources and having identified good business opportunities from the application of IS/IT should consider an aggressive strategy with respect to harnessing the potential that IS/IT has to offer. In organizations where there is both low potential and relatively poor resources, there is likely to be little to be gained from such a strategy, and little likelihood of attack from the competition.

Conversely, organizations with good quality resources but apparently little potential should quietly explore opportunities, in case some are identified over time. Should there be high potential added value, but low competence, such companies should beware on two fronts: (1) they are vulnerable to attack by better placed competitors; (2) should they try to exploit IS/IT, they are more likely to fail in view of their relative lack of competence—in other words, they are in a 'Catch 22' position.

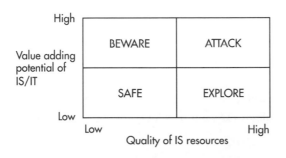

Figure 3.4   Choosing an appropriate strategic approach to the utilization of IS/IT (amended from McLaughlin *et al.*, 1983)

PUTTING IT IN ITS PLACE

One of the problems with the literature on business re-engineering is that it often takes too much of a proactive stance when discussing the question of IT and its strategic impact on organizations. While a proactive stance, of itself, is no bad thing, there is a danger in IT being viewed as the solution to problems of organizational inefficiency and ineffectiveness:

> Nobody could deny the importance of IT. No organization, to my knowledge, that has invested heavily in IT would now return to its pre-computer methods even if they were permitted to claw back their investments in IT. But IT does not have the centrality in transformation which often appears to be tacitly claimed by some ... authors. ... For example, a successful organization has first to manage its primary function competently. The most successful banks are those that successfully manage their substantive roles as bankers. There is little evidence that IT helps them improve their competence as bankers. ... IT plays an important part in achieving success if the primary function is carried out excellently. Organizations which have transformed successfully have done so by performing this transformation over a wide range of activities and processes. IT may act as an enabler or catalyst but it can only be one element in the process of building success.   (Land, 1992a, pp. 111–12)

In addition, note the terminology that is often applied in this context. Business process redesign (Hammer, 1990), business design (Keen, 1991) and business reconfiguration (Venkatraman, 1991) are three commonly used terms in the IS literature. In practice, we also hear of such terms as workflow restructuring and process innovation (Aryanpur, 1993). Each suggests a partial view only of the range of change that may be necessary when implementing one's strategy. It may not only be a matter of simplifying the business processes in line with defined business objectives and automating some of these processes; it may not simply be a question of redesigning organizational entities, or even reconsidering the very nature of the business itself in line with the opportunities provided by IT. It is just as likely that the nature of the necessary change will include *each* of these aspects, *together with* changing attitudes, skills and even personnel. Certainly, IS/IT may have a key role to play, but it will be only one aspect of the whole change process.

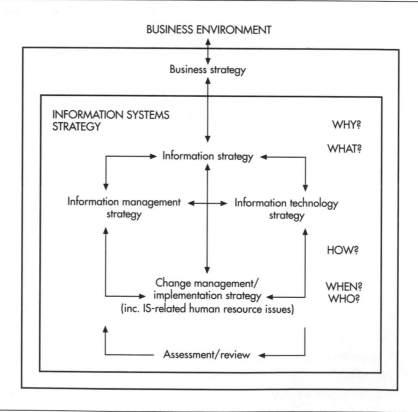

Figure 3.5   Information systems strategy as but one aspect of business strategy (amended from Galliers, 1991, p. 60; 1992c, p. 161; and 1993b, p. 201)

A framework for information systems strategy that attempts to incorporate the above lessons is provided as Figure 3.5. The framework emphasizes the central role that information strategy plays in linking the business and information systems strategy processes. The linkage is two-way: the business strategy may be analysed to identify key management and operational information requirements, while information may also be provided to question whether the business strategy needs to be amended in the light of changed circumstances or new information. For example, information arising from the assumptions upon which the business strategy is based may be questioned with a view to changing business directions. Similarly, information arising from the process of assessing and reviewing past information systems strategies or the implementation of the current strategy might lead to new thinking on the business strategy.

INFORMATION: A FORGOTTEN ELEMENT OF INFORMATION SYSTEMS STRATEGIES?

In all the debate and evolution of thinking and practice, however, a key question is often overlooked. This relates to the difficulty that managers and information systems professionals have in determining key information requirements to meet individual needs, and—just as importantly, if not more so—key information requirements and flows throughout the organization. While this is certainly seen as being a major issue by American IT directors, who cite developing an 'information architecture' as the single most critical issue they face at present (Niedermann *et al.*, 1991), there is a danger in assuming that the informatory quality of IT (Zuboff, 1988) is an automatic outcome of the introduction of IT, as argued by Ackoff (1967) in the early days of management information systems.

The difficulty arises not only in deciding current requirements, but also in anticipating what is likely to be required in the future—a problem exacerbated by business environments that are characterized by constant change; the global nature of much of today's business activity and competition; and a growing focus on information requirements and flows outside organizational boundaries (with a view to improving supplier/customer relationships and the establishment of electronic communications between collaborating organizations, for example).

ON INFORMATION REQUIREMENTS AND FLOWS

Let us now consider a means by which managers can identify the changing nature of their organization's information requirements, while at the same time improving mutual understanding about the confusing and very different worlds of business, information and IT and the integration of IS/IT developments and business process redesign. The approach described is based on an extension of soft systems methodology

(Checkland, 1972, 1981), first articulated by Wilson (1980). The approach has been refined in many applications throughout the 1980s and into the 1990s. It has been found useful, not only in clarifying current and future information requirements and flows, but also in forging a closer relationship between business and information systems strategic thinking, and in integrating IS development with business process redesign. As a result, a closer relationship (and a much improved understanding between corporate, business unit management and information systems management) has ensued. The approach aims at the development of a flexible information architecture to meet changing information needs and to revise business processes in line with changing business imperatives, rather than the development of specific IS applications.

Before turning to the approach itself, it is perhaps advisable first to consider the subject of information if we are to appreciate what an effective information architecture might be. This is because of the desire to develop a flexible *information* systems environment (i.e. one that *informs*) rather than simply developing *data-processing* systems (i.e. systems that automate an operational task). The latter may be accomplished by replicating observable actions (Yadav, 1983), while the former requires considerable awareness of the context in which information may be required and the manner in which it is likely to be interpreted to enable a required activity or decision to be made, namely:

> ... information is that collection of data, which, when presented in a particular manner and at an appropriate time, improves the knowledge of the person receiving it in such a way that he/she is better able to undertake a [required] activity or make a [required] decision.
>
> (Galliers, 1987a, p. 4)

In other words, information may be understood as being both *enabling* and *contextual*, while data is context-free and simply the raw material from which information (meaning) may be *attributed* (Galliers, 1987a, p. 4; Checkland and Scholes, 1990, pp. 54–6).

> From these considerations ... two consequences flow. Firstly, the boundary of an [information system] ... will always have to include the attribution of meaning ... [and] will consist of both data manipulation, which machines do, and the transformation of data into information, [which humans do] ... Secondly, designing an [information system] will require explicit attention to the purposeful action which [it] serves. ...   (Checkland and Scholes, 1990, p. 55)

This argument is illustrated in Figure 3.6, which takes pains to show the central location of the information users and their use of data obtained directly from the 'real world' and via informal mechanisms, as well as formal, designed information systems. It illustrates the fact that individuals will choose different data to capture, from different sources, depending on their way of perceiving the world and, further, will interpret that data differently, again dependent on their individual perspectives. They will also wish to utilize formal systems to a lesser or greater degree.

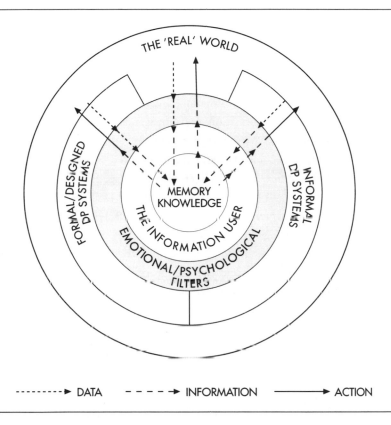

------▶ DATA   – – – ▶ INFORMATION   ──────▶ ACTION

Figure 3.6   An individual's information system (Galliers, 1993a, p. 93; 1993b, p. 203: amended from Land, 1992b, p. 8)

It follows that a reasonable approach to the development of a flexible information architecture must taken into account the context in which necessary actions and decisions are to take place, and the manner in which information is to be inferred from the data provided. Soft systems methodology would appear to be a good candidate for this, given its emphasis on obtaining a shared understanding of complex situations about which there may be considerable debate, and its ability to clarify the activities that are required to meet objectives which may be only dimly perceived. It also follows that the development of IS cannot be considered in isolation from the activities they are to support. IS development methodologies should therefore incorporate the means of identifying required changes in activities/business processes in line with desired objectives or new directions—but few do.

However, as argued above, we should not be lulled into a false sense of security regarding the ease by which information requirements can be determined. We could easily form the mistaken belief that this process is simply a matter of rational analysis, based on an understanding of required activity. Indeed, there is something of this flavour in the writings of, for example, Zuboff (1988) and Scott Morton (1991), when they talk of the *informating* characteristic of IT as if this were an *automatic* outcome from the use of computer-based information systems (see Galliers, 1992a). There is, as argued above, an element of subjectivity about information, given, for example, the power that can come with it; the use of information for propaganda purposes (see, for example, Argyris, 1980; Feldman and March, 1981; Hedberg and Jonsson, 1978; Land and Kennedy-McGregor, 1981), and the difficulties associated with communicating needs between the analyst and the potential user of the IS (see, for example, Oliver and Langford, 1984; Valusek and Fryback, 1985; Mittermeir *et al.*, 1982). Add to this the changing nature of information requirements (Land, 1982)—owing to changes in the business environment, changes in job content/role, and changes in what is actually informative (brought about by the development in individual users' capabilities/knowledge)—and it soon becomes evident that the process requires a complex mixture of rational analysis and subjective inquiry, synthesized into conclusions that are acceptable and recognizable by the key stakeholders involved.

A SOFT SYSTEMS APPROACH TO INFORMATION REQUIREMENTS ANALYSIS

Much has been written on the basic approach to, and application of, soft systems methodology and the way in which it has developed over the years (e.g. Checkland, 1972, 1981; Checkland and Scholes, 1990). The basic approach will therefore not be described here in any detail. It may be useful, however, to describe in outline an extension of the approach that has been developed by Wilson (1980, 1984, 1990) with a view to identifying information to support required organizational activities, and the manner in which this information should flow between these activities.

Wilson's approach is summarized in Figure 3.7. Noteworthy features include the following (see Wilson, 1990, pp. 231–2):

- the identification of information requirements and flows is based on modelling a 'primary task' (as opposed to 'issue based') root definition of the organization (see Checkland and Wilson, 1980);

- taking the existing organizational structure, 'activity-to-activity' information flows are converted to 'role-to-role' information flows in order to identify individual managers' information requirements, based upon an analysis of the activities for which each is responsible;
- required information systems are then determined, based on an analysis of the performance needs of each of the activities identified.

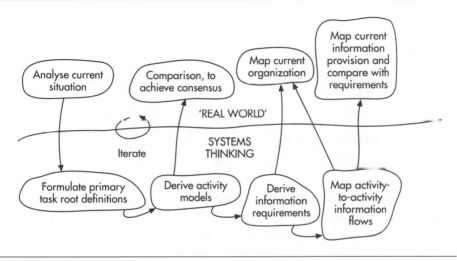

Figure 3.7   Information requirements analysis based on soft systems methodology (amended from Wilson, 1990, p. 233)

Using Ormerod's (1993) framework—which distinguishes between those information systems strategy approaches that focus their analysis on either decisions or on data and are either participative or conventional in their mode of enquiry—the basic approach outlined in Figure 3.7 has tended to be (though not necessarily so) conventional and decision-oriented. The extended approach described below is invariably a participative, decision-oriented approach, as shown in Figure 3.8. Other approaches in common usage, such as information engineering (e.g. Martin, 1982) and IBM's PQM (Ward, 1990) can be classified in the same way, as shown.

A SCENARIO-BASED APPROACH

In work undertaken over the past decade in the area of information systems strategy formation and implementation, the basic approach described above has been further developed to take account of the particular issues associated with linking business and IS strategies and change management issues. Examples of the manner in which these

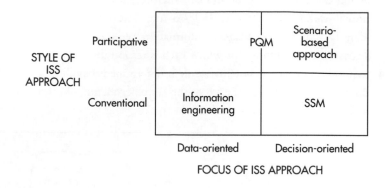

Figure 3.8   Classifying IS strategy approaches (based on Ormerod, 1993)

ideas have developed can be found in Galliers (1984, 1985, 1987b); Le Fevre and Pattison (1986) and Watson and Smith (1988).

The variation on the approach being advocated here attempts to take account of the following situations which executives often face when attempting to develop appropriate business (information) strategies (see Chapter 4).

- Published mission statements (where these exist) may not reflect actual management activities and decisions, and may not be sufficiently detailed to assist in identifying key performance indicators let alone information requirements.
- Key executives may have deeply held assumptions about the nature (both current and future) of the business and its environment which cloud their own perceptions, are not debated with their colleagues, and may not be shared by them in line with the above.
- Perfectly plausible (but sometimes quite radically different) views of the future may be held by different executives, which could lead to quite different requirements in terms of organizational arrangements and activities.
- Information organizational boundaries and managerial roles often arise almost as accidents of history, and may be inappropriate for current and future circumstances, and a change in management strategy has therefore to be incorporated into the strategy approach.

(Cf. arguments for 'change analysis' in Lundeberg et al., 1981, and the socio–technical framework for information systems strategy advocated by Galliers, 1991, p. 60.) The 'scenario-based' approach is illustrated in outline in Figure 3.9. Firstly, however, some of its key features are highlighted.

Some key features of the scenario-based approach

Rather than describe in detail the various aspects and techniques of the scenario-based approach, a summary of some of its key features will be provided, pointing out in particular where the approach departs from those advocated by Checkland (1981); see also Checkland and Scholes (1990) and Wilson (1980, 1984, 1990).

The first distinguishing feature is that particular attention is paid to preparation as a critical first step. As has been noted in other studies (e.g. Ward, 1990), a key to a successful information systems strategy includes a briefing with the project sponsor regarding the aims, objectives and methods of the study, study team membership and the various roles that will need to be filled. Sometimes it is necessary to establish a project steering committee. Secondly, the 'analyse current situation' step described by Wilson (see Figure 3.7) has been divided into two: one concerned with scanning the environment and the other concerned with organizational analysis/synthesis. The reasons for this include the need for greater attention to be paid to environmental factors in strategy studies than may be the case in those studies which focus on organizational problem solving (which was the focus of much early soft systems methodology work). Methods that are of particular utility here include Porter's (1980, 1985) analysis of competitive forces and of the extended value chain (i.e. to include suppliers and customers), a review of industry trends in the use of IT, and the opportunities and threats that emerge from the organization's wider environment. The organizational analysis/synthesis aspect is assisted by using such methods as (a) Rockart's (1979) critical success factors approach (supplemented by a consideration of critical *failure* factors, critical decisions and critical assumptions), (b) Lincoln's (1980) constraints analysis, and (c) the various stages of growth models which assist in locating the development of the organization in the management and planning of their IT utilization and data resources (see, e.g. Nolan, 1979; Earl, 1989; Galliers, 1991; Galliers and Sutherland, 1991). The aim here is to synthesize a range of views on the strengths and weaknesses of the organization and its aims and objectives, in the context of the environmental impositions and trends and its historical setting, all in the context of its management of the information resource. As a result, a number of alternative scenarios for the future may be identified.

These scenarios will enable the identification of appropriate alternative strategies for the organization to follow, and on which appropriate 'root definitions' can be based. The scenarios are themselves developed by considering those aspects that may be held fairly constant over the planning period selected, and by identifying the major trends that may reasonably be considered to continue and those over which there is (or could be)

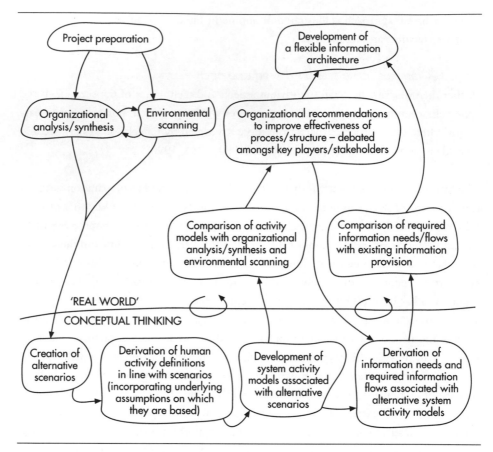

Figure 3.9   A scenario-based approach to information systems strategy
(amended from Wilson, 1984, p. 208; 1990, p. 233; Galliers,
1985, p. 5; 1987b, p. 10; 1992c, p. 152; 1993b, p. 206;
and Galliers *et al.*, 1988, p. 92)

debate. In this way perhaps three or four scenarios (and attendant strategies) can be devised, one of which can usefully be counter-intuitive, given the unpredictability of the future business and political environment in which we work. Alternative perspectives and assumptions are identified and incorporated into the scenarios. A shared understanding and vision, rather than consensus, is the objective here—all with a view to countering the possibility of 'group think' (Galliers *et al.*, 1991, 1993).

Scenarios can be built up by reviewing

- those key elements that are expected to remain *constant* during the planning period (e.g. the major focus of the University of Warwick will remain the provision of high-quality education and research: it will not diversify into manufacturing widgets!);

- those trends that appear likely to continue (e.g. the university might expect that government funding for institutions of higher education in the UK will continue to be tightly controlled); and

- those *issues* over which there is some debate (e.g. the extent to which the business school involves itself in executive education, while maintaining its research focus).

A counter-intuitive scenario might also be included, so that key stakeholders would consider their strategic options in a situation that is unexpected (e.g. what might the university do should government funding increase significantly in the planning period, or what might the business school do if demand for its postgraduate courses were to tail off from the current high levels being experienced?). Clearly, the earlier analysis of competitive forces, competitor activity, and political, economic, social and technological (PEST) trends will be helpful in formulating alternative scenarios.

This emphasis on the use of scenarios relates to the concern that most IS strategy formation that takes place in practice, and the approaches advocated in theory, rely on a single, taken-for-granted view of the future. Clearly, in the turbulent world in which we live, this philosophy is inappropriate and likely to lead to rigid information architectures that are unable to cope with change. The remainder of the approach is more or less similar to that advocated by Wilson (see Figure 3.7) except that the creation of so-called 'Maltese Crosses' is omitted, and greater attention is paid to the development of a flexible information architecture, as described in more detail below, and of the management of change issues discussed above.

Perhaps the most significant distinguishing feature of the approach, in comparison with that advocated by Wilson, is its acceptance of the likelihood that key stakeholders *will* express a range of views regarding an organization's primary purpose, goals and environment. One could go further: as a result of an application of the scenario-based approach, open disagreement regarding these issues can often result. Certainly, it is most likely that a range of opinion will be expressed about the business environment that is expected, and the most appropriate responses to changing business imperatives in the light of these changed circumstances. Critical assumptions upon which business views are expressed, and upon which business decisions would be taken, are brought to the surface as a result of the debate that takes place in the organizational analysis/synthesis phase. While this requires careful handling (cf. the role of the facilitator, as described in Galliers *et al.*, 1991, 1993), it is essential that 'taken-for-granted' views of key players in relation to both the current and future business environment are brought to the surface so that a shared understanding and shared vision of alternative futures can be obtained. Without this, the *implementation* of the resultant strategy may well be problematic, but also, key information requirements of a strategic nature may well not be identified.

As indicated above, different 'futures' (scenarios) for the organization can be established by identifying those environmental and organizational factors that appear likely to be fairly constant over the planning period; those that appear to be subject to perceptible trends; and those over which there may be (considerable) debate. Once these different 'futures' have been debated and an appropriate organizational response to each agreed, systems activity models can be built in the usual manner. Similarly, required information and information flows associated with each 'future' can be identified. It is very probable that the information requirement associated with a particular 'future' will overlap to a lesser or greater degree with the required information associated with other 'futures'. For the sake of argument, let us assume that we have identified three 'futures' for our business and that associated information requirements are represented by the areas F_1, F_2 and F_3 as shown in Figure 3.10. It is then a matter of judgement as to the extent to which all the required information is collected.

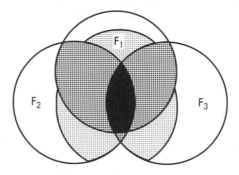

Figure 3.10 Required information associated with alternative 'futures' (Galliers, 1987d, p. 361; 1992c, p. 156; 1993b, p. 209)

It is most likely that provision should be made to collect the information represented by the area shaded black, since this appears to be required no matter what 'future' emerges. In addition, we may decide to make provision for the collection of information represented by the hashed areas, since this appears to be required in two cases out of three. Further, there may be some absolutely critical information associated with a single 'future' (represented by the dotted areas) which we also decide to collect. In this way, while not being absolutely certain that we have prepared ourselves for every even-tuality, we have at least placed ourselves in a position whereby we can develop reas-onably flexible information systems, capable of being adapted in line with changed business imperatives. In addition, given that we constantly monitor the environment in order to reassess the underlying assumptions upon which our business strategy is built, we can equip ourselves with strategic information systems which provide early warn-ing of changed circumstances requiring control action.

CONCLUSION

It is hoped that this chapter has served to illustrate the range of information required to support differing strategies that might be adopted in line with different scenarios. It has also suggested a means by which underlying assumptions can be tested. As a result of this process, business strategies can be evaluated on an on-going basis and informed decisions can be made as to the extent of information provision likely to be needed, given the alternative scenarios that are identified and studied. As key information is obtained, the scenarios themselves can be tested and altered, so that a flexible informa-tion architecture is maintained in the light of changing circumstances. In addition, nec-essary changes to the organization structure and processes are also identified *as an integral part of the approach*.

Some key points, which are almost by-products of the approach, are that senior exec-utive involvement and on-going commitment are maintained and the strategy forma-tion process becomes an integral part of on-going management activities and concerns. Other stakeholders should also be involved in what is very much a participative approach in which a range of views is expected to be aired and key assumptions are questioned.

In addition, given that the process is seen to be highly relevant from a senior executive perspective (as it helps to formulate appropriate business strategies and to provide useful IS for senior executives), it tends to be championed by either chief executive officers or highly influential board members, thus increasing the chances of successful implementation of the IS strategy. Further, and for the same reasons, it tends to raise the profile of the information systems function, and helps to forge partnerships based on mutual respect and understanding between information systems and business unit executives. All in all, however, it is likely that the shared understanding and vision (although not necessarily consensus) that emerge among key stakeholders is the major contribution that the process offers. Also, the approach attempts to deal with issues of organizational change, including business process redesign and business recon-figuration. But, as has been emphasized, this is not its exclusive focus. While the approach

- takes account of the potential of IS/IT;
- takes account of the guiding principles of business process redesign enunciated by Hammer (1990) above;
- focuses on key business processes associated with appropriate business strategies, which themselves take account of the changing business, economic and technological environment; and
- also considers other change issues such as organizational boundary changes, changes in attitude, skills and personnel

it does not place IT centre stage. The principal message is that IS strategy formation and implementation is but one aspect of business strategy and the management of change. There are likely to be many outcomes from the approach advocated here, and not all will concern IS/IT *per se*. The changes that have to be managed can (and often do) relate not just to innovative uses of IT but to changes in direction, objectives, management style, attitudes, procedures and organization structure. New skills and personnel may well be identified as being required in order that this range of change can be implemented more readily.

Notes

This chapter utilizes aspects of the following of the author's papers: A scenario-based approach to strategic information systems planning, in M. C. Jackson *et al.* (eds), *Systems Thinking in Europe*, Plenum, New York, 1991, pp. 73–87; Soft systems, scenarios and the planning and development of information systems, *Systemist*, **14** (3), August 1992, 146–59 and *Journal of Information Systems*, **3** (3), July 1993, 199–213, and Information systems and business re-engineering. Warwick Business School Research Papers, No. 89, May 1993.

REFERENCES

Ackoff, R. L. (1967) 'Management misinformation systems', *Management Science*, **14** (4), December B147–56.

Argyris, C. (1980) 'Some inner contradictions in management information systems', in *The Information Systems Environment* (H. C. Lucas *et al.*, eds), North-Holland, Amsterdam; reproduced in R. D. Galliers (ed.), 1987a, 99–111.

Aryanpur S. (1993) 'On the mend', *Computer Weekly*, 25 March, p. 39.

Cash, J. I. Jr and Konsynski, B. R. (1985) 'IS redraws competitive boundaries', *Harvard Business Review*, **63** (2), March–April, 134–42.

Checkland, P. B. (1972) 'Towards a systems-based methodology for real-world problem-solving', *Journal of Systems Engineering*, **3** (2).

Checkland, P. B. (1981) *Systems Thinking, Systems Practice*, Wiley, Chichester.

Checkland, P. B. and Scholes, J. (1990) *Soft Systems Methodology in Action*, Wiley, Chichester.

Checkland, P. B. and Wilson, B. (1980) 'Primary task and issue-based root definitions in systems studies', *Journal of Applied Systems Analysis*, **7**, 51–4.

Clemons, E. K. (1986) 'Information systems for sustainable competitive advantage', *Information & Management*, **11**, 131–6.

Earl, M. J. (1989) *Management Strategies for Information Technology*, Prentice-Hall, New York.

Feldman, M. S. and March, J. G. (1981) 'Information in organizations as signal and symbol', *Administrative Science Quarterly*, **26** (2), June, 171–86; reproduced in R. D. Galliers, (ed.), 1987a, 45–61.

Galliers, R. D. (1984) 'An approach to information analysis', in *Proceedings of the First IFIP International Conference on Human-Computer Interaction*, London, 4–7 September; reproduced in *Human-Computer Interaction – INTERACT '84* (B. Shackel, ed.), North-Holland, Amsterdam, pp. 619–28; also in R. D. Galliers (ed.), 1987a, 291–304.

Galliers, R. D. (1985) 'Providing a coherent information planning environment to meet changing organizational and individual information needs', *WAIT Computing and Quantitative Studies Working Paper*, Perth, Western Australia, January

Galliers, R. D. (ed.) (1987a) *Information Analysis: Selected Readings*, Addison-Wesley, Wokingham.

Galliers, R. D. (1987b) 'Applied research in information systems planning', in *Information Management and Planning* (P. Feldman, L. Bhabuta and S. Holloway, eds), Gower Technical, Aldershot, 45–58.

Galliers, R. D. (1987c) 'Information systems planning in the United Kingdom and Australia—a comparison of current practice', *Oxford Surveys in Information Technology*, **4**, 223–55.

Galliers, R. D. (1987d) 'Information systems planning in Britain and Australia in the mid-1980s: key success factors', Unpublished PhD Thesis, London School of Economics, June.

Galliers, R. D. (1991) 'Strategic information systems planning: myths, reality and guidelines for successful implementation', *European Journal of Information Systems*, **1** (1), January, 55–64.

Galliers, R. D. (1992a) 'Information technology: management's boon or bane?', *Journal of Strategic Information Systems*, **1** (2), March, 50–6.

Galliers, R. D. (ed.) (1992b) *Information Systems Research: Issues, Methods and Practical Guidelines*, Blackwell, Oxford.

Galliers, R. D. (1992c) 'Integrating information systems into business: research at Warwick Business School', *International Journal of Information Management*, **12** (2), 160–3.

Galliers, R. D. (1993a) 'Research issues in information systems', *Journal of Information Technology*, **8** (2), June, 92–8.

Galliers, R. D. (1993b) 'Towards a flexible information architecture: integrating business strategies, information systems strategies and business process redesign', *Journal of
Information Systems*, **3** (3), July, 199–213.

Galliers, R. D. and Sutherland, A. R. (1991) 'Information systems management and
strategy formulation: the "stages of growth" model revisited', *Journal of Information
Systems*, **1** (2), April, 89–114.

Galliers, R. D., Marshall, P. H., Pervan, G. P. and Klass, D. J., (1988) 'DSS development within an information systems planning framework', in *DSS-88 Transactions.
Eighth International Conference on Decision Support Systems, Boston, MA*, 6–9 June,
85–94; also in *Decision Support and Execution Information Systems* (P. Gray, ed.),
Prentice-Hall, Englewood Cliffs, NJ, 1994, 66–77.

Galliers, R. D., Klass, D. J., Levy, M. and Pattison, E. M. (1991) 'Effective strategy
formulation using decision conferencing and soft systems methodology', in *Collaborative Work, Social Communications and Information Systems. Proceedings of the IFIP
TC8 Conference, Helsinki, Finland*, 27–29 August (R. Stamper, P. Kerola, R. Lee, and
K. Lyytinen, eds), Elsevier, Amsterdam, 157–79.

Galliers, R. D., Pattison, E. M. and Reponen, T. (1993) 'Strategic information systems
workshops: lessons from three cases. Paper presented at the SISnet European
Conference on Information Systems, Tilburg University, The Netherlands, 7–9
June also in *International Journal of Information Management*, **14** (1), February 1994,
51–66.

Green-Armytage, J. (1993) 'Why Taurus was always ill-starred', *Computer Weekly*, 18
March, 10.

Hammer, M. (1990) 'Re-engineering work: don't automate, obliterate', *Harvard
Business Review*, **68** (4), July–August, 104–12.

Hedberg, B. and Jonsson, S. (1978) 'Designing semi-confusing information systems for
organizations in changing environments', *Accounting, Organizations and Society*, **3** (1),
47–64; reproduced in R. D. Galliers (ed.) 1987a, 179–202.

Keen, P. G. W. (1991) *Shaping the Future: Business Design through Information Technology*,
Harvard Business School Press, Boston, Mass.

Land, F. F. (1982) 'Adapting to changing user requirements', *Information and
Management*, **5**, 59–75; reproduced in R. D. Galliers (ed.) 1987a, 203–29.

Land, F. F. (1992a) 'Book Review of M. S. Scott Morton (ed.) 1991; *Journal of Strategic
Information Systems*, **1** (2), 111–12.

Land, F. F. (1992b) 'The information systems domain', in R. D. Galliers (ed.), 1992b,
6–13.

Land, F. F. and Kennedy-McGregor, M. (1981) 'Effective use of internal information',
Proceedings of the First European Workshop on Information Systems Teaching (FEWIST),
Aix-en-Provence, April; reproduced under the title 'Information and information sys-
tems: concepts and perspectives', in R. D. Galliers (ed.), 1987a, 63–91.

Leavitt, H. L. (1965) 'Applied organizational change in industry: structural, technological and humanistic approaches', in J. G. March (ed.), (1965), 1144–1170.

Le Fevre, A. M. and Pattison, E. M. (1986) 'Planning for hospital information systems using the Lancaster soft systems methodology', *Australian Computer Journal*, **18** (4), November, 180–5.

Lincoln, T. J. (1980) 'Information systems constraints—a strategic review', in *Information Processing 80* (S. H. Lavington, ed.), North-Holland, Amsterdam.

Lincoln, T. (ed.) (1990) *Managing Information Systems for Profit*, Wiley, Chichester.

Lundeberg, M., Goldkuhl, C. and Nilsson, A. (1981) *Information Systems Development: A Systematic Approach*, Prentice-Hall, Englewood Cliffs, N.J.

McFarlan, F. W. (1984) 'Information technology changes the way you compete', *Harvard Business Review*, **62** (3), May–June, 98–102.

McLaughlin, M., Howe, R. and Cash, J. I. Jr (1983) 'Changing competitive ground rules: The impact of computers and communications in the 1980s'. Unpublished Working Paper, Graduate School of Business Administration, Harvard University, Boston, Mass.

March, J. G. (ed.) (1965) *Handbook of Organizations*, R and McNally, Chicago

Martin. J. (1982) *Strategic Data Planning Methodologies*, Prentice-Hall, Englewood Cliffs, N.J.

Mittermeir, R. T., Hsia, P. and Yeh, R. T. (1982) 'Alternatives to overcome the communication problem of formal requirements analysis', in *Requirements Engineering Environments* (Y. Ohno, ed.), North-Holland, Amsterdam; reproduced in R. D. Galliers (ed.), 1987a, pp. 153–65.

Niedermann, F., Brancheau, J. C. and Wetherbe, J. C. (1991) 'Information Systems Management issues in the 1990s', *MIS Quarterly*, **16** (4), pp. 474–500.

Nolan, R. L. (1979) 'Managing the crises in data processing', *Harvard Business Review*, **57** (2), March–April, 115–26.

Oliver, I. and Langford, H. (1984) 'Myths of demons and users', *Proceedings of the Australian Computer Conference*, Australian Computer Society Inc., Sydney, Australia, November; reproduced in R. D. Galliers (ed.), 1987a, 113–23.

Ormerod, R. J. (1993) 'On the nature of information systems strategy development', *Proceedings: First European Conference on Information Systems*, Henley, 29–30 March, 455–63.

Porter, M. E. (1980) *Competitive Strategy*, The Free Press, New York.

Porter, M. E. (1985) *Competitive Advantage*, The Free Press, New York.

Rockart, J. F. (1979) 'Chief executives define their own data needs', *Harvard Business Review*, **57** (2), March–April; reproduced in R. D. Galliers (ed.), (1987a), 267–89.

Scott Morton, M. S. (ed.) (1991) *The Corporation of the 1990s: Information Technology and Organizational Transformation*, Oxford University Press, Oxford.

Sullivan, C. H. Jr, (1985) 'Systems planning in the information age', *Sloan Management Review*, **27** (4), 3–12.

Valusek, J. R. and Fryback, D. G., (1985) 'Information requirements determination: obstacles within, among and between participants', *Proceedings of the End-User Computing Conference*, Association of Computing Machinery Inc., Minnesota; reproduced in R. D. Galliers (ed.), 1987a, 139–51.

Venkatraman, N. (1991) 'IT-induced business reconfiguration', in M. S. Scott Morton (ed.), 1991, 122–58.

Ward, B. (1990) 'Planning for profit', in T. Lincoln (ed.) 1990, 103–46.

Watson, R. H. and Smith, R. (1988) 'Applications of the Lancaster soft systems methodology in Australia', *Journal of Applied Systems Analysis*, **15**, 3–26.

Wilson, B. (1980) 'The Maltese Cross: A tool for information systems analysis and design', *Journal of Applied Systems Analysis*, **7**, 55–65.

Wilson, B. (1984) *Systems: Concepts, Methodologies and Applications*, Wiley, Chichester.

Wilson, B. (1990) *Systems: Concepts, Methodologies and Applications*, (2nd edn), Wiley, Chichester.

Yadav, S. B. (1983) 'Determining an organization's information requirements', *Data Base*, **14** (3), Spring.

Zuboff, S. (1988) *In the Age of the Smart Machine: The Future of Work and Power*, Heinemann, Oxford.

4

THE ROLE OF METHODOLOGIES IN SYSTEMS STRATEGY DEVELOPMENT: REFLECTIONS ON EXPERIENCE

Richard Ormerod

Warwick Business School, University of Warwick

INTRODUCTION

The approach adopted in this chapter will be to relate a number of cases involving the development of a systems strategy and to comment on the role of methodologies in general and SSM in particular. The cases are taken from the experience of the author and are presented chronologically over the period 1984 to 1991. The sample has a personal bias representing the major strategy exercises with which the author has been associated. By no means all the cases use SSM, but each provides the opportunity to reflect on the role SSM could have played.

In practice, the first step in any systems strategy exercise is a negotiation between interested parties to define what is required from the exercise in the particular context at that particular time. This, of course, means defining the nature of the end result. The answers to this initial question can vary immensely and the methodological questions raised are correspondingly rich. The chapter is about practice: the practice contained in eight cases, and any theory will be contained in the reflections. The status of the cases and the reflections is thus different. The cases are a description written by one of the actors involved. The accounts are greatly abbreviated and therefore selective, but they are written with the intention of being a factual account of what happened and why. The reflections are much more speculative in nature. At every stage in each case choices were made. The results in terms of problems arising, targets being met and satisfaction of those involved can be ascertained. What would have happened if different choices had been made is a matter for conjecture, arrived at with the benefit of hindsight and with no responsibility for the consequences. At the beginning of any major strategy exercise, the designer of the process (perhaps called the project manager) is faced with the responsibility of deciding who will be involved at each stage, what tasks will be done, which models or frameworks will be used and what results will be delivered. The choices will be discussed and negotiated with the sponsor of the exercise. Guidance may be sought from some framework such as Earl (1989), Galliers (1991), Scott Morton (1991) or Ormerod (1993a) but the approach will more probably be based on experience of previous strategy exercises and understanding of the particular context, the business needs, and the expectations of powerful actors.

Some of the cases have already been described in Ormerod (1992 and 1993b). This chapter draws on that material and adds to it. The first case describes a strategy exercise carried out in 1984/5. Although Checkland's *Systems Thinking, Systems Practice* was published, SSM was not widely known or used, and certainly played no part in the case described. But could it have done? Would the result have been a better process of intervention?

CASE A: BRITISH COAL—A NEW ORGANIZATION FOR IT

In 1986 British Coal created a new department to bring together their disparate IT resources under one management. Up to that time separate groups of IT resources had developed, one with expertise in data processing and data communication, another with expertise in process control and underground communication, and a third with expertise in office systems and voice communication. Overlap was starting to occur between the groups; users were showing signs of frustration; and senior managers were concerned about control.

The new IT organization was the result of a major strategy exercise that reviewed the totality of IT resources throughout the organization and engaged the management in a widespread process of consultation. At the time of the exercise (1984/5), British Coal included a deep-mined operation with a production capacity of 100 million tonnes of coal from 170 mines employing 180 000 miners, an opencast operation with a capacity of 15 million tonnes and a coal-processing division that converted coal to coke and other fuels and chemicals.

At a time when industrial relations problems were at their height and the chairman, Ian MacGregor, was changing the management style of the business, organizational issues were high on the agenda including:

- separation of policy and service functions at the centre

- devolvement of decision making to the Areas (regional groupings of between 10 and 20 pits)
- development of profit centres
- cutting of overhead costs.

During the strategy exercise a large number of interviews were conducted across the organization. The results of the interviews were captured in entity–relationship models and fed back to those interviewed. In addition, groups of managers with differing expertise and interests were involved in structured group sessions where each participant made a presentation on a defined issued, followed by a discussion and summary by the facilitator. One particular group involved the managers in charge of each IT resource area, referred to as the 'stakeholder' group. This participative approach was liked by the users but the IT professionals wanted more direct control over the process that would determine their future.

The key issue at the centre of the debate was the relative role of pits, the Areas and the centre in the light of the new managerial style. The technology favoured central servicing of pits directly without passing through Areas. The new managerial style called for a reduction in central services and emphasized the role of Areas as decision-making and profit centres. The IT strategy exercise was one forum where new relationships between the parties were being decided.

Groups were again used to evaluate the organizational options, developing the criteria, weighting them against each other and scoring the organizational options against the criteria to obtain multi-criteria preferences.

REFLECTIONS ON CASE A

This is an early example of a process that tried to involve managers in the development of an information strategy. Methodology played a part in four areas. Firstly, in the fact-gathering stage the results of interviews were captured in notes of meetings supported by diagrams based on the entity–relationship model. Secondly, organizational options were developed by considering different ways of grouping the necessary IT functions. Thirdly, the group sessions were structured to allow a wide number of people to provide an input into the thinking. Fourthly, a method was used to evaluate the options.

A typical example of a high level entity–relationship diagram is given in Figure 4.1. These diagrams were supported by data flow diagrams, hierarchical functional decompositions and what were referred to as 'communications' diagrams (these simply showed the major information flows with other parts of the organization and external bodies). This method of recording was thought to be desirable because it would result in an

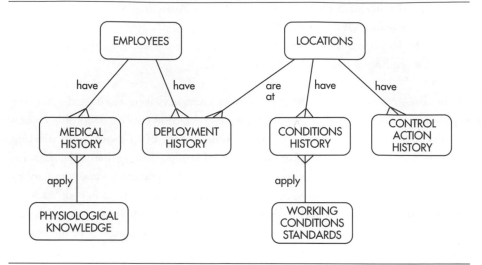

Figure 4.1   Medical department high level data model

'enterprise model' that would prove of enduring value. This seems to be a case of the consultants involved refighting their last battle. The approach had apparently been successful on a previous occasion where an overall systems architecture had been required. The requirement at British Coal was quite different, the emphasis being on organization. The use of this approach as the central methodology was misguided and little use was made of the results in the substantive debate which followed. The use of the diagrams did, however, have some value. The diagrams were unfamiliar and generated interest. They gave a vehicle for discussion and a feeling that something tangible had resulted from the interviews. The process of deriving the diagrams did lead to greater understanding. Together with the interview notes, in effect a rich picture was built up. In practice therefore the role of the data-oriented methods was, in this particular instance, simply to express the situation. If SSM had been used, emphasis would have been placed on rich pictures but undoubtedly records of meetings and some structured diagrams would also have resulted from the 'understanding' phase. SSM would have focused on the actors involved and their viewpoints. In practice, without SSM, the exercise was dominated by the views of stakeholders and other powerful actors, a fact that was anticipated from the start. The formation of a Steering Committee of Board Members was in response to the known and anticipated divergence of views, as was the adoption of an unprecedented degree of consultation.

At each group session a topic or topics was given to participants prior to the meeting. On the day each participant is allowed a fixed period of time to make his or her case (10 minutes). A period is then set aside for discussion (45 minutes). The chairman then summarizes (20 minutes). Notes are taken and the session recorded. The format of the sessions created a sense of occasion which did result in active participation. Issues were tabled and there was a sense of fairness. The participants lacked common frameworks for organizational debate and none was offered. It seems possible that if the sessions had been built round the task of defining a root definition, a shared understanding of the issues may have been possible. To be effective this would have needed the involvement of people from a higher level of recursion. In this case that meant the board members who were on the steering committee. At the time, the board members were having to deal with a major strike (the 1984–85 miners' strike) and its consequences. No methodology is likely to overcome such difficulties.

The third potential area for methodology was in the design of organizational options for evaluation. The approach taken was to draw up a list of the functions required to be undertaken and then to group them into alternative organizational structures. For instance, one option pulled the various resource groups together in a new central organization; another envisaged strengthening the role of Areas. Organizations were designed on the basis of the tasks that needed to be done and the interfaces with the various user groups. Other industries were used to provide working examples. This process is not dissimilar to the development of a conceptual model in SSM terms to debate how the activities should be grouped within an organizational structure. SSM could well have been used for this process but was not known to the participants at the time. Other ways of viewing organizations could have been helpful, such as metaphors (Morgan, 1986). The metaphor of autopoiesis (Mingers, 1989) would have been particularly apposite as the motivation for the strategy exercise was a belief that some of the IT resource groups had become overly self-referential and were not responding to the requirements of the greater whole in an effective manner—a thought that was also very much in the minds of senior managers in the next case.

Finally, multi-criteria decision making was used to evaluate the options. The analysis went well beyond the initial check of cultural feasibility and systemic desirability, envisaged by SSM. This seemed necessary to try to bring some semblance of rationality to highly emotional and politicized questions. It was not clear that the sophisticated analysis used did guide decisions. The process was accepted as sensible but the weight that should be attached to any particular actor was uncertain. If a powerful player felt the outcome was unacceptable (as several did), the political process continued.

The striking thing about the approach described above is not the differences when contrasted to SSM but the similarities. Most, if not all, of the activities described above would have sat quite comfortably within a framework of SSM. SSM would have enhanced the intervention, not so much because very different things would have been done but because it would have provided a philosophical underpinning which the approach lacked. It would have undoubtedly provided a common language for the intervention and the debate that it orchestrated.

The tentative conclusion from the first case is that SSM would seem to articulate an approach to intervention which chimes well with practice in the information systems strategy development field. The initial stage of gaining an unstructured understanding is a natural precursor to strategy exercises. The emphasis on people and viewpoints is inherent in practical strategy formulation. Identifying changes which are acceptable (cultural feasibility) is as important as establishing that they improve the situation (systemic desirability). Perhaps SSM's continuously iterative debate is more realistic than formal attempts to close the decision.

CASE B: GAINING CONTROL OF IT AT VOLKSKAS—STAGES OF GROWTH

Volkskas is a medium-sized (ranked 300 in world terms) retail bank in South Africa with some 200 branches offering a full range of retail and corporate services. In 1987 a major expansion in IS activity was underway in terms of money and the numbers of staff, and the senior managers were concerned about the control of IS expenditure and the impact on the bank's bottom line. A team of consultants was engaged to investigate the position. As a framework they used a four-stages-of-growth model based on Gibson and Nolan (1974). Viewing the Management Services Division (MSD) as a business they measured in various ways the stage that the MSD product (applications portfolio), customers (users), resources (funding, people and technology), and structure (organization, process, controls) had reached on the maturity model. Their mode of operation was investigatory, employing interviews, fact gathering and questionnaires. The results were presented to senior management and refined.

The conclusions noted a lack of balance. Some aspects, such as the technology used and the organization adopted, were reaching into the maturity stage, whereas the application portfolio and the users' IS knowledge and awareness were only in the second (contagion) stage. Control in particular was felt to be underdeveloped.

As a result of this investigation a steering committee was formed with the expressed task of formulating the strategy and controlling its implementation. The issue here was not one of identifying new opportunities, but of determining how to shape the many opportunities already identified into a controlled plan that would deliver the maximum business benefits. At the centre of the approach a priority setting method was developed against which each proposed project could be evaluated. The framework is shown in Figure 4.2. At the end of the day the senior managers had to make difficult choices: should they continue down the automation routes or should they concentrate on electronic delivery? As a medium-sized bank they could not afford to do everything at once.

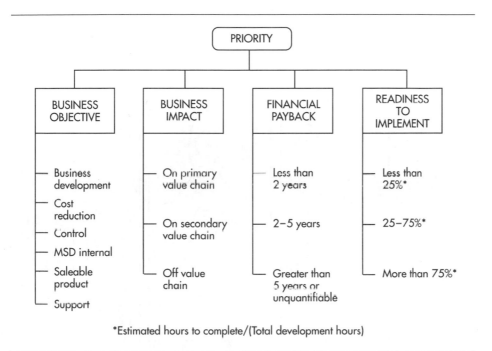

Figure 4.2   Priority framework

REFLECTIONS ON CASE B

The Gibson and Nolan model, extended by Nolan (1979) and Galliers and Sutherland (1991), has proved an enduring and popular framework. The model has been criticized (see, for instance, King and Kramer, 1987 and Doukidis and Mylonopoulos, 1993) but the basic idea has a certain plausibility even if its calibration is problematic. As a stimulant for discussion it is undoubtedly useful. There is no equivalent model in SSM. However, SSM may have been helpful in designing the framework for quantification against the stages. The list of headings used, based on viewing MSD as a business, lacked a cohesive explanation which SSM could have provided.

The need to look for opportunities and issues by examining the functions of the bank along the lines of Checkland and Scholes (1990) and Wilson (1990) was absent in this case. A considerable amount of analysis had already been conducted using entity–relationship models and functional models (the relative merits of these and SSM

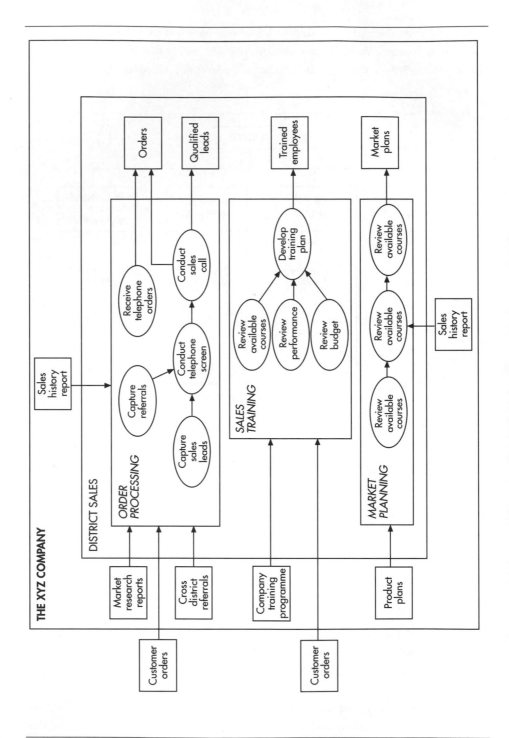

Figure 4.3   Process analysis

conceptual models are considered below) within a structured methodology. The use of the priority framework illustrated in Figure 4.2 goes beyond the SSM consideration of systemic desirability and cultural feasibility. However, these two headings may have been a useful starting point in designing the priority framework.

Perhaps the most interesting comparison with the use of SSM arises out of some analysis carried out as part of the project to better define roles within MSD. A recursive 'process model' was drawn for each group at each organizational level. An example of the type of model used is shown in Figure 4.3. Note that each work group has a series of activities joined together as a flow. These activities are connected to other work groups (e.g. marketing) or external groups (e.g. customers) by document flows (e.g. market research reports, customer orders). These diagrams share many features with SSM's conceptual models. The method of analysis is, however, distinctly different. In SSM this part of the analysis starts with a root definition containing a transformation. From the root definition the activities are derived forming the basis of the conceptual model. The process analysis starts with products and services, derives the activities required to deliver those products and services and then works back to the resource inputs required. This procedure is very similar to the analytical approaches currently used in business process re-engineering. SSM is an obvious contender for this type of analysis.

In reflecting on this case, the direct applicability of SSM has been less apparent than in Case A. However the process of comparison using SSM as the point of reference has been helpful in understanding the role of disparate techniques. There may be more specific ways of approaching a particular analytical task than SSM. There may be a need for detail. There may be a specific need for closure which the continuing debate of SSM does not support. However, whatever is required, SSM would seem to help when thinking about what is needed even if it is not used directly. At this point the usefulness of SSM as a point of reference or meta-language is noted. This theme will be developed further after Case D.

CASE C: A STRATEGY FOR MERGER AT NICHOLAS LABORATORIES—FEASIBLE OPTIONS

Nicholas Laboratories in the UK, a subsidiary of Sara Lee of Chicago, was determined to extract the benefits of merging with Ashe Consumer Products, another UK Sara Lee subsidiary. Both companies produced a wide range of toiletries and health care products, selling them through wholesale and retail outlets. The aim was to obtain the benefits of merger as rapidly as possible The need for a systems strategy to support the changes in the business was recognized early. An exercise to develop the systems strategy was initiated at the beginning of 1988 (see Galliers, 1991, Ch. 3).

Early in the project it was decided to eliminate the Ashe head office, amalgamate the salesforces of the two companies, but retain both companies' manufacturing sites. Beyond that no decisions had been made. Although a merger task force was in place, the decisions about marketing and salesforce structure, distribution, manufacturing and product-stocking policy were subject to continuous speculation. At this point it was also not clear how or if Ashe senior managers would be absorbed into the Nicholas management structure. Despite this business uncertainty, the systems issues needed to be addressed.

In essence each company had four major systems:

- sales order processing
- manufacturing
- finance
- sales statistics.

Although broadly similar in function, the systems of the two companies were very different in detail. Furthermore, they operated on different, mixed and incompatible platforms. For each of the major systems there was the option of sticking with two different

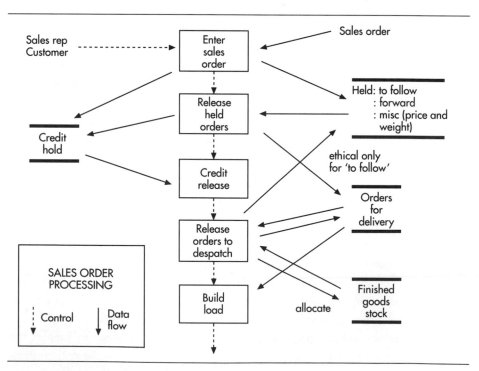

Figure 4.4   Example data flow diagram

systems, converting one company to the other company's system (in effect two options: conversion to Ashe or conversion to Nicholas) or replacing both by a new system. This gave four options for each of the four major systems. The large number of combined options was narrowed down by examining current performance of the systems, the logical relationship between systems, and the need for integration to support identified or potential business change. Once the options had been narrowed to five or so, a detailed examination was made of the amount of investment in new hardware that would be required, the fit with company policy, the amount of redevelopment of the software, the availability and suitability of new packaged software and many other issues. The only analytical technique used was data flow diagrams to understand the interfaces that would be required between each system in each option. An example of the data flow diagrams used is shown in Figure 4.4.

Once all the relevant analyses had been completed the options were evaluated against a series of criteria reflecting short- and long-term business objectives. Key requirements were that the business should not be disrupted and that systems should not put any merger timetable at risk. A multi-criteria analysis was used with senior managers providing the weights for the different criteria. The result was a systems strategy to support the merger.

REFLECTIONS ON CASE C

The approach taken in this case has most in common with the strategic choice approach (Friend and Hickling, 1987). Most of the effort went into identifying the decision areas and the options, working out the logical relationships and designing decision schemes. The evaluation process was also not unlike that in strategic choice. Even the nature of the final decision was similar to the 'commitment package' suggested in strategic choice; there was an immediate decision on a systems strategy to support the merger, with a deferred decision on a move to new systems to be determined after further exploratory work. This raises the question of SSM's relative merits compared to strategic choice and other 'soft' approaches. Should we stick to one approach as the protagonists of each tends to do in practice?, or should the approach adopted be contingent on the particular context and issue at hand?, or should the methods be mixed?

Before moving on from this case it should be noted that despite the final success in implementing the strategy, the path was not without difficulty. In retrospect a greater degree of participation of departmental managers may have achieved more commitment. However, as a result of the merger and the resulting uncertainties, the atmosphere was very fraught and managers were very busy. Perhaps a more structured approach to resolving the overall business issues would have had the greatest beneficial impact on the systems project. Again, whether SSM or strategic choice would have provided most support for the process of deciding the overall merger strategy, is a moot point. Perhaps the need for a decision suggests that strategic choice would be preferred. The question of choice between approaches is discussed again after Case E.

CASE D: IS STRATEGY AT NATIONAL GRID—A DATA-ORIENTED APPROACH

Until it was privatized the Central Electricity Generating Board (CEGB) was responsible for the generation and transmission of electricity in England and Wales. In 1988 it had been decided that the CEGB would be split into three companies: two were to be engaged in electricity generation and the third, National Grid, was to be responsible for transmission. National Grid would be owned by the 12 Regional Electricity Companies, who would also be privatized. Late in 1988 the CEGB set up three teams to develop systems strategies for the three proposed new privatized electricity companies resulting from the break up of the CEGB. The National Grid team consisted of three analysts from the CEGB's IT department and an external consultant. At that stage a White Paper had been published, the future directors had been identified but not appointed and no staff had been allocated to the company. For existing functions the team could look at the grid management and operational functions within the CEGB. The team followed a traditional route (interviews, analysis, report, discussions led by the analyst) despite the far from clear shape, form and style of the new enterprise.

The analysis fell into three broad phases: business analysis, design of systems architecture and bases of data, and planning. In the design phase two models were developed. The first, the functional decomposition model—sometimes called a hierarchical business or enterprise model—was derived through discussion and agreement with senior executives (see Figure 4.5 for an example of part of a model). It provided a comprehensive description of all the anticipated activities of the new company. It was subjective in nature but was treated as objective by the participants and emphasis was placed on its independence of any particular organizational form. The second model was an entity–relationship model which was partly derived from an existing CEGB-wide model and partly by considering what data would be required by the decisions embedded in the functional model. The main analytical tool was an entity–usage matrix showing the input and use of data by system. The matrix was sorted to derive an information systems architecture showing data flows, subject databases and systems and a dependency diagram to guide implementation planning.

An important aspect of the study was the first cut definition of the new company's mission and a debate about the desired management style. The mission was subsequently reworked and published as part of an internal document, *The National Grid Company:*

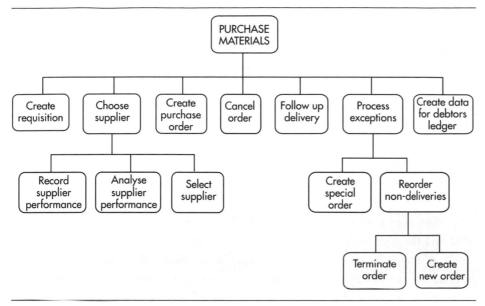

Figure 4.5   Functional decomposition

'A Blueprint for the Future' (NGC, 1989). The debate about management style formed an appendix to the systems strategy. The envisaged loosening of central control implied that the strategy needed to embrace the possibility that operational units carrying out similar functions may choose to adopt a diversity of controls, procedures and data. Thus flexibility, allowing multiple viewpoints, was built into the approach from the beginning. The softer issues of culture and control were central to the development of the IS strategy.

REFLECTIONS ON CASE D

The development of a data architecture is a common centrepiece of a systems strategy. Most large organizations have gone down this path at some point. It has the advantage of completeness, giving a view of the whole systems domain. It is also a structured approach with some useful deliverables, such as build sequence and first cut database design. Much of the work can be carried out by analysts and computers can be used to support the process. The disadvantages include (a) the implicit assumption that everything is going to be supported by an integrated set of computer systems, (b) an internal rather than external focus and (c) lack of perspective about the relative importance of different areas of the business.

One consequence of the approach adopted for this type of strategy exercise is that it is difficult to run in a participative mode or, perhaps more to the point, it is easy to run in a non-participative mode. As a result there is often a lack of ownership and commitment by the managers who will be responsible for implementing the resulting strategy. It is possible to use SSM to get to approximately the same result following, for instance, Wilson (1990). The similarity between the functional model and the conceptual model has already been noted. Wilson's Maltese Cross performs the same function as the entity–usage matrix favoured in this case. Whether Wilson's Maltese Cross is any more amenable to a participative approach is a question worth exploring. Experience with using SSM in a participative mode leads to the alternative thought that functional diagrams could be the basis of a much more participative approach within data–oriented systems strategies.

One SSM issue that has received considerable attention is the relationship between SSM and the systems development process that follows (Miles, 1988, 1992; Mingers, 1992). Although in this case a traditional approach, which derived functions and high-level entities to describe the proposed new systems, had been adopted, the project teams found this input of minimal help as they set off on their demanding task of defining and developing a practical working system. This was in spite of the fact that the development approach adopted was data centred and entirely consistent with the strategy approach described above.

SSM either has embedded in it the technical tools required (root definitions and conceptual models) or it can be simply extended (e.g. using Wilson's Maltese Cross) to carry out this type of data-oriented approach. SSM has the potential, but should it be preferred? The advantages of SSM lie in its philosophy, not the mechanics—its emphasis on human activity systems, differing points of view and cultural feasibility. The mechanics of the more conventional data-oriented approach are quite good, being supported by computer software. If the added value is indeed in its philosophical stance then perhaps the ideal approach is to use conventional tools within SSM as the overarching methodology. Again we return to the possibility of SSM as a meta-language, a language to design the process and choose the tools and ensure that the whole orchestrates the right conversations about viewpoints within a human activity system.] ?

CASE E: IS STRATEGY AT SAINSBURY'S—USE OF 'SOFT' APPROACHES

Sainsbury's is the leading grocery and food chain in the UK. Towards the end of the 1980s they employed some 70 000 staff in 300 stores and were placed in the top 20 of UK companies by market value on the London Stock Exchange. In 1989 Sainsbury's decided to develop a new systems strategy to take them through the 1990s and maintain their systems lead in the food supermarket sector. The process adopted was quite different in nature from those discussed above, having at its centre a task force of hand-picked senior line managers (16 in number) who were to conduct the investigation themselves. The role of the task force was to analyse the business, identify systems opportunities and make the business case for the systems. Architectures and database design were not at issue. Cognitive mapping (Eden *et al.*, 1983) helped the task force explore the current business strategy and its implications, providing a bridge between the thinking of board members and the senior management in the task force. The output was a series of cognitive maps which identified key relationships in the business and points of leverage with the competition, and a better shared understanding of the nature of the food supermarket business.

SSM was used as a simple stepped framework and guide for the task force members as they conducted their inquiry into chosen areas of the business to identify systems opportunities. They were encouraged to identify actors, viewpoints and interactions and then follow the SSM steps (Checkland, 1981; Checkland and Scholes, 1990). The outputs of this part of the analysis were conceptual models of the business and candidate systems (very loosely defined) for further consideration. An example of the conceptual models is shown in Figure 4.6.

The individuals in the task force were to provide the bridge between the understanding generated in the strategy exercise and the subsequent project teams (formed jointly

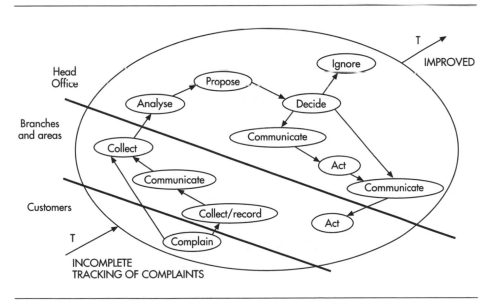

Figure 4.6   Example conceptual diagram

of systems specialists and line management) set up to develop the new systems. No formal, mechanistic links were sought.

REFLECTIONS ON CASE E

In this case three approaches were used on the same project. Each was used in a different part of the study but they were each consistent with a pluralistic, participative approach (Ormerod, 1993c). The question as to which approach will best suit a particular exercise can be addressed by considering, firstly, the nature of the transformation to be achieved by the strategy exercise and, secondly, the nature of the approach to be adopted; the second, in part, being dependent on the first.

A strategic exercise will normally be organized in a number of sequential steps or phases. The sequential nature is a simplification but is necessary if the exercise is to progress towards a conclusion. In practice, debates initiated in one phase will continue through later phases, and the process is iterative. The phases adopted for the Sainsbury's exercise were:

- Phase 0 *Involvement*
- Phase 1 (Business) *Imperatives*
- Phase 2 *Insight*
- Phase 3 (Strategic) *Intent*
- Phase 4 *Initiatives*.

Together these are referred to as the 'Five I' approach. The potential use during each phase of a selection of methods is shown in Table 4.1.

Table 4.1   Potential methods/models

	Phase 0	Phase 1	Phase 2	Phase 3	Phase 4
Cognitive mapping	√	√	√	•	•
SSM	√	•	√	•	√
VSM	•	•	√	•	•
Decision conference	√	√	•	√	•
Strategic choice	√	√	•	√	√
BIAIT 7 questions	•	•	√	•	•
CSF	√	√	•	√	
Entity diagrams	•	•	√	•	√
Functional models	•	√	√	•	√
Porter	•	√	√	•	•

√ indicates potential for use

For different strategy exercises the emphasis will be on different phases. For instance, at Nicholas the key thing was to reach a decision: the emphasis is therefore on the *Intent* phase. For the National Grid the business imperatives needed to be understood and translated into a systems architecture and build sequence: the emphasis is on *Imperatives* and *Initiatives*. These requirements may indicate a preferred method but, before choosing, two decisions need to be taken about the nature of the strategy development exercise: (1) is the mode of inquiry to be conventional (analysts, interviews and reports) or participative (facilitators, workshops and ownership)? and (2) is the focus of analysis to be data-oriented or decision-oriented? (Ormerod, 1993a). Ormerod suggests that the contextual factors that should determine choice include management culture, information intensity and IS planning maturity. The Sainsbury's exercise was participative and decision-oriented. Figure 4.7 positions the cases considered so far in this chapter on the grid based on the two decisions: conventional or participative, data- or decision-oriented.

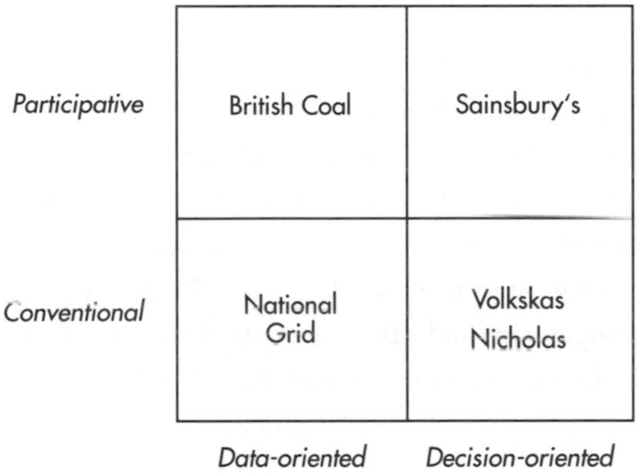

Participative	British Coal	Sainsbury's
Conventional	National Grid	Volkskas Nicholas
	Data-oriented	Decision-oriented

Figure 4.7   Classification of strategy approaches

The choice of a participative, decision-oriented approach at Sainsbury's resulted in the choice of methods shown in Table 4.2. The overall approach was designed to be within the spirit of Ackoff's interactive planning. The use of SSM by the task force provided guidance while being sufficiently flexibile to allow the issues to be debated. The rich pictures, root definitions and conceptual models provided focal points for discussion and a parsimonious method of recording the thinking. Different viewpoints were vigorously represented because of the non-hierarchical, cross-functional nature of the teams.

Table 4.2   Actual methods/models used

	Phase 0	Phase 1	Phase 2	Phase 3	Phase 4
Cognitive mapping	•	•••			
SSM			•••		•
VSM				•	
Decision conference					
Strategic choice		•		••	
BIAIT 7 questions		•	•		
CSF					
Entity diagrams	•				•
Functional models			•	•	
Porter	•	•			

••• indicates major use   • indicates minor use

The conceptual models were recursive and can be depicted, if so desired, as a hierarchical functional (activity) model as illustrated in Figure 4.5. To do so would incur two losses: hierarchical models lose the arrows between the concepts (functions) at the level of focus and the icon value of a jointly derived picture is also lost (most people find it easier to relate to pictures than text). In fact, in the Sainsbury's case a functional model was developed in the background to cross-check that the less-structured approach of the task force was covering the ground. (Both the conceptual models and the functional hierarchy were later fed into the team of business analysts whose task it was to support the use of IEW/IEF methodologies by the development teams.)

SSM provides no special assistance in moving from function to data. As in the more traditional approach adopted for National Grid, the data required is derived from the functional requirements through a process of examining the functions that are carried out and the decisions taken. In the case of Sainsbury's, the transition to data was left to the subsequent project teams who made use of structured development methods. It is a moot point whether the carryover from SSM to structured development is sufficient. The main connection was the continuity of people involved, with task force members being given roles in the development project teams.

The cases so far have suggested a number of ways that SSM could be deployed in an IS strategy development exercise: as the overall methodology to be used (British Coal), as a meta-language for design of the process (Volkskas) and as a functional analysis tool (National Grid). In other cases (Nicholas), other approaches have seemed potentially more powerful (strategic choice). In the Sainsbury's case SSM's value as a practical tool for loosely structured enquiry has been encountered. The rich pictures, root definitions and conceptual models provided stepping stones to the identification of systems opportunities. In each case the purpose of the strategy development was different and the context unique. In the next case IS strategy is interpreted in a new way, providing a different challenge for SSM.

CASE F: AN IS STRATEGY FOR BP OIL—ENABLING CULTURAL CHANGE

In 1990 two decisions dominated the thoughts of the IS community in BP. Firstly, Robert Horton, the new chairman and CEO, determined to change the culture of BP through a change programme called 'Project 1990'. Secondly, as part of the drive to reduce the role of the corporate centre it was announced that headquarters would be reduced by over 1000 staff. By far the largest reductions were in the Information Systems Service (ISS) group which provided computing services and developed IS strategy.

In a series of 'Dear Colleague' letters to all members of staff, Horton set out the BP Vision, Values and Themes and explained Project 1990. The project's aims were to:

- reduce complexity throughout the corporation
- redesign the central organization
- reposition the corporation in approach and style for the 1990s.

The reduction in IS resources at the corporate centre was achieved by outsourcing computing services, transferring some resources out of the corporate centre. The central IS activities were reduced to small groups engaged in Group IT strategy, telecommunication services and support for head office functions. The initiative for developing IS capability and providing IS support was delegated to the four businesses: Exploration, Oil, Chemicals and Nutrition.

In BP Oil, which was responsible for the distribution, refining and marketing of crude and oil products, the process of decentralizing IS did not stop there. Responsibility for developing and operating systems was the responsibility of the regions, Europe, North America, Australasia, South East Asia, South Africa, etc. A small IS strategy unit, called Oil Systems World (OSW) and located at the centre of BP Oil, was asked by BP Oil's CEO to develop a new IS strategy in the light of the changes in the company's direction and character.

OSW had a problem. What would a strategy for BP Oil look like? What should it contain? How could IS respond to the new open, non-hierarchical, action-oriented management culture being implemented by BP Oil's CEO under the phrase 'The way we do things round here'? The guidance that the CEO gave was that he wanted not so much a strategy, but more a philosophy, and certainly nothing like the technical document resulting from the previous IS strategy exercise. He suggested that 'orders of magnitude change' should be identified and further indicated that he would be prepared to reserve some powers to the centre should the case be made.

OSW's response was to involve the regional line managers and their IS staff in a series of workshops to debate the issues. Armed with some conclusions and some questions they sought a wide range of views outside the company about the direction of the technology and possible organizational responses. They were, for instance, able to take advantage of the ideas emerging from the major research exercise 'Management in the 1990s', conducted by MIT and reported in Scott Morton (1991).

The result was a series of focal areas within which actions were identified that would use IS to facilitate the new management style. The senior management of BP Oil found the results both refreshingly accessible and fully consistent with their business direction. On one point, however, OSW were firm. Seeking 'orders of magnitude change' could only be achieved by the regions responsible for the business processes. The centre should only facilitate the take up of new ideas and technology, set minimal standards, encourage best practice and ensure interregional communications.

REFLECTIONS ON CASE F

In the BP Oil case, the 'Five I' method was used as a loose framework. At this point in time the author was familiar with SSM and it would have been a natural choice. The new management style suggested that a participative approach would be appropriate and would help to reinforce the change itself. Thus SSM could have a role because of its participative characteristics. From the beginning it was recognized that a data-oriented approach was inappropriate at the BP Oil level of focus. More conventional IS strategies would be the provenance of the regions or even lower in the organization if the regions so chose. Thus the use of conceptual diagrams as a stepping stone to identifying systems opportunities or data flows was not appropriate.

In the event no overall methodology was adopted. A participative approach was designed involving senior managers in workshops in each of the major regions of the world. The workshops focused on the appropriate role of the centre in the light of the new management style. Recognizing different viewpoints was inherent in the process. However, a second SSM concept was immensely powerful: the concept of transformation. The key to building the bridge between the management strategy and the IS strategy was to identify the transformation required by each element of the management strategy and to identify the role of the centre (if any) in using IT to enable those transformations.

The project itself was complex, involving managers all over the world and a series of subprojects. Its organization could have been thought of in systems terms, as advocated by Checkland (1993). It is not clear that anything would have been gained (or anything lost) because it is quite natural when designing a strategy project to think in terms of overall aims (transformation), linked tasks (conceptual model), who should be involved (viewpoints and actors) and the political and cultural context. Mode 2 SSM (Checkland and Scholes, 1990) is a useful framework for thinking about the process of intervention if an awareness of the softer issues is lacking. Certainly such thinking is a necessary antidote to conventional project management textbooks and it has the advantage of being well articulated. An alternative articulation of the process of inquiry from the systems perspective can be obtained in Miser and Quade (1985, 1988; including a contribution from Checkland).

In an exercise that is concerned with issues of management style and the relative roles of different parts of the business, SSM needs to be enriched with other ideas. Organizational thinking such as the metaphors of Morgan (1986) needs to be utilized. An understanding of the issues involved in managing global companies in general (Bartlett and Ghoshal, 1989) and IS in global companies in particular (Ormerod, 1993d) need to be incorporated into the thinking. Ironically when the soft issues are the focus of attention in a managerially sophisticated arena, SSM may not bring enough insight to the situation.

CASE G: IS STRATEGY AT PALABORA—FOCUS ON PRIMARY TASKS

In 1991, the Palabora Mine (a large copper mine operated and partly owned by RTZ) embarked on a strategy development exercise that had to be dovetailed into three one-week visits. The purpose was to develop a method that could be applied at mines throughout the world, to be known as PIMS (participative information management strategy). The approach evolved out of that used at Sainsbury's, becoming more direct and less overtly SSM in nature in the process. Nevertheless, the underlying 'Five I' framework was the same and many features of SSM are still recognizable.

As in Sainsbury's the investigation was conducted by a task force of line managers divided into cross-functional teams. Initially the teams investigated different parts of the business in an unstructured way. They were encouraged to use rich pictures but in practice preferred more structured diagrams. The team then engaged in a structured analytical process to establish rapidly an agreed model of the main functions to be analysed. There are strong similarities with the primary task approach of Wilson (1990). Figure 4.8 shows how the objectives of different parts of the business were defined using a modified CATWOE root definition.

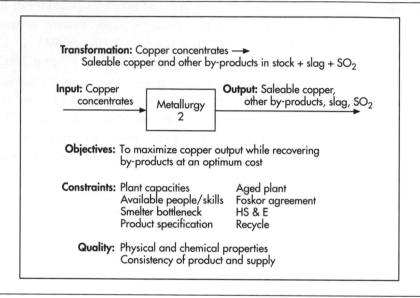

Figure 4.8   Objectives definition

From the root definition, process (conceptual) diagrams were drawn. In the Palabora analysis the focus was on the management of the primary tasks, identifying planning, monitoring, scheduling and control opportunities. For important processes a 'critical analysis' was carried out [critical in the sense used by Rockart (1979)] to identify the critical success factors (CSFs) for that process, the critical decisions and hence the critical information requirements. As in the Sainsbury's case, identification of the data requirements was left to the systems design process.

By the time groups of line managers are examining a large number of processes, the subtleties of the method invoke a simple desire to find ways of improving the situation (meaning more control, higher throughput, lower costs, better quality, less pollution). The candidate systems that resulted were evaluated using a Palabora specific framework, similar to that shown in Figure 4.2. The highest priority systems were then scheduled according to the availability of the resource groups to form the basis of the strategy.

REFLECTIONS ON CASE G

The Palabora strategy exercise can be understood as a developed form of SSM, its main features being an unstructured investigation, an analysis using root definitions, conceptual models and 'critical' analysis, and a multi-criteria evaluation scheme. The emphasis was on the primary processes and the business administrative systems to support them. Despite this close fit with SSM, and the participative spirit in which it was conducted, the approach lacked some of the subtlety that might be expected with SSM. This resulted from two factors. Firstly, there was a need to provide a tight structure in order both to restrict the strategy exercise into a very limited time frame, and to test out a framework that could be used again at other mines. In other words, there was a need to package the approach to a greater degree than would be required when using SSM with a free hand. Secondly, at a mine located at a remote site there is a strong shared sense of reality. To have tried to engineer a debate about the nature of the mine from different viewpoints would have seemed very artificial. Different viewpoints were encountered about the purpose, value and fitness-for-purpose of specific systems, as would be expected, but the definition of processes was not controversial. Controversial issues that certainly would have provoked a variety of conflicting opinions were not addressed.

Although this was not the best example of applied SSM in terms of putting all the philosophy into practice, Palabora does demonstrate that SSM can be used to derive an approach that is robust in a difficult environment. The concept of PIMS has since been confirmed by its use elsewhere.

CASE H: SYSTEMS SPECIFICATION AT HAMERSLEY IRON—FROM VIEWPOINTS TO FUNCTION AND SCOPE

More of the subtlety of the SSM approach was retained when an *individual* systems development was addressed rather than a whole strategy at Hamersley Iron, one of the world's largest iron ore producers and part of the CRA group which is 49 per cent owned by RTZ. The objective was 'to identify beneficial change to operational practice which could be supported by the introduction of new technology'. The idea was to apply the same participative approach to project definition as had been used for the IS strategy at Palabora. The issue identified was operations scheduling and the development method was to be an expert systems approach (an approach which is itself highly sensitive to context, actors and the way that these actors within context perceive the decisions they are taking). The key tasks were to identify the opportunities to control operations, to determine the control strategy to be adopted and to define the scope of the project. The project would draw on the experience gained in developing an expert scheduling system, SCHEDEX, for the smelter operation at Palabora (see Pauley, 1992).

At Hamersley Iron some of the mechanics of SSM have melted into the background but the underlying philosophy still underpins the whole approach. Rich pictures, transformations and conceptual models are in evidence, complemented by techniques to draw out the benefits of potential functions of the system. The nature of the system envisaged meant that data analysis and structure were not considered to be critical. The real issues were business objectives and management style, organizational structure and operational control, reward systems, operational feasibility, costs and the delivery of benefits. The availability and cost of data were important considerations, of course, but relatively simple compared to the management issues.

REFLECTIONS ON CASE H

The conclusion from the Hamersley Iron experience is that, in an environment that does not use formal systems methods, if a 'soft' approach centred on people and their decisions is embraced throughout, the interface with SSM is not problematic. SSM can form a continuous framework for each stage of the development process. In particular, at each stage of analysis questions will be raised: what should the interface look like?; what should be inside and what outside the system?; and what is the value of a particular feature of the proposed system? SSM can help with the process of gaining insight and clarity, can encourage the right debate to take place and can ensure that different voices are heard.

The integrated role of SSM in the development process is labelled *embedded* by Miles (1992). This is contrasted with a *grafted* use of SSM in which the SSM approach stops with the handover of the conceptual model of the object system or referent system to the systems development process. Hamersley is an example of *embedding* whereas the Sainsbury's and Palabora approaches are examples of *grafting*. There is a difference in the way Miles envisages *embedding* to work. Miles sees the distinction between the two approaches hinging on the treatment of data as part of (*embedded*) or distinct from (*grafted*) the conceptual model. At Hamersley the issue is primarily to draw the systems boundary and define the human–machine interface, testing at every step the value of the functionality provided against the business benefit. This is a continuous process taking place within the detailed design phase as well as during the earlier scoping. Thus the concept of viewpoints continues to be relevant within the design process, an idea that has appealed to Galliers (see Chapter 3) and Mingers (1992).

With the focus of attention in many organizations moving from transactional processing towards managerial and strategic systems, the nature of systems development methodologies will evolve. Less emphasis will be placed on delivering against an accurate specification. More emphasis will be placed on continuous interaction with users. If so *grafting* is likely to give way to *embedding*, not necessarily by including data in the

SSM conceptual model but also by conceptual modelling becoming embedded in the design process. It can be concluded that the future direction of systems development is likely to offer greater opportunities for the use of SSM.

CONCLUSION

At the end of this chapter of cases and reflection on the use and potential use of SSM, how does SSM emerge? It would seem that SSM can be usefully employed in several modes (extending Checkland and Scholes, 1990): as a methodology for a complete problem-solving intervention (Mode 1); as a methodology for a problem-solving phase within a wider project (Mode 1*); as a method for building conceptual models for information systems strategy and design purposes (Mode 1**); as a basis for organizing a systemic process of inquiry (Mode 2); as a meta-language for designing and evaluating interventions (Mode 3). SSM, therefore, is a formidable tool and should be part of the repertoires of all aspiring problem solvers or strategy developers. It should, however, come with a reminder that it may need to be complemented by other approaches, and may not always be the preferred approach. It lacks the requisite variety to do everything. The variety must be provided by other approaches and models and the skill and ingenuity of the problem solvers (intervention designers, facilitators and participants) in adapting and using methods in particular contexts. This leaves open the intriguing possibility that SSM in Mode 3 can be used to oversee the choice of approach—a process that might result in the rejection of SSM in Mode 2. Can SSM reject SSM?

REFERENCES

Bartlett, C. A. and Ghoshal, S. (1989) '*Managing Across Borders: The Transnational Solution*', Harvard Business School Press, Boston.

Checkland, P. B. (1981) *Systems Thinking, Systems Practice*, Wiley, Chichester.

Checkland, P. B. (1993) 'Systems science', in *Systems Science: Addressing Global Issues* (F. A. Stowell, D. West and J. G. Howell, eds), Plenum, New York, 415–20.

Checkland, P. B. and Scholes, J. (1990) *Soft Systems Methodology in Action*, Wiley, Chichester.

Doukidis, G. I. and Mylonopoulos, N. A. (1993) 'Strategic information systems planning within medium environments: a critique of IS growth models'. Paper presented at IFORS, Lisbon.

Earl, M. J. (1989) *Management Strategies for Information Technology*, Prentice-Hall, Hemel Hempstead.

Eden, C., Jones, S. and Sims, D. (1983) *Messing About in Problems*, Pergamon, Oxford.

Friend, J. K. and Hickling, A. (1987) *Planning under Pressure: The Strategic Choice Approach*, Pergamon, Oxford.

Galliers, R. D. (1991) 'Strategic information systems planning: myths, reality and guidelines for successful implementation', *European Journal of Information Systems*, **1** (1), 55–6.

Galliers, R. D. and Sutherland, A. R. (1991) 'Information systems management and strategy formulation: the "stages of growth" model revisited', *Journal of Information Systems*, **1** (2), 89–114.

Gibson, C. F. and Nolan, R. L. (1974) 'Managing the four stages of EDP growth', *Harvard Business Review*, January–February, 76–88.

King, J. L. and Kramer, K. L. (1987) 'Evolution and organisational information systems: an assessment of Nolan's stage model', *Communications of the ACM*, **27** (5), May.

Miles, R. (1988) 'Combining "hard" and "soft" systems practice: grafting or embedding', *Journal of Applied Systems Analysis*, **15**, 55–60.

Miles, R. (1992) 'Combining "hard" and "soft" systems practice: grafting or embedding revisited', *Systemist*, **14** (2), 62–6.

Mingers, J. (1989) 'An introduction to autopoiesis—implications and applications', *Systems Practice*, **2** (2), 158–80.

Mingers, J. (1992) 'SSM and information systems: an overview', *Systemist*, **14** (3), 82–9.

Miser, H. J. and Quade, E. S. (eds) (1985) *Handbook of Systems Analysis: Overview of Uses, Procedures, Applications and Practice*, North-Holland, New York.

Miser, H. J. and Quade, E. S. (eds) (1988) *Handbook of Systems Analysis: Craft Issues and Procedural Choices*, North-Holland, New York.

Morgan, G. (1986) *Images of Organisation*, Sage, Beverly Hills, CA.

NGC (1989) *The National Grid Company: 'A Blueprint for the Future'*, Internal National Grid document. The National Grid Company plc, Kirby Corner Road, Coventry.

Nolan, R. L. (1979) 'Managing the crisis in data processing', *Harvard Business Review*, March–April, 115–26.

Ormerod, R. J. (1992) 'Combining hard and soft systems practice', *Systemist*, **14** (3), 160–5.

Ormerod, R. J. (1993a) 'On the nature of information systems strategy development', in *Proceedings of the First European Conference on Information Systems* (E. A. Whitley, ed.), 455–63.

Ormerod, R. J. (1993b) 'Information and management style in IT strategy development', *Systemist*, **15** (1), 44–52.

Ormerod, R. J. (1993c) 'Putting soft OR methods to work—a case study'. Warwick Working Paper, No. 90, University of Warwick.

Ormerod, R. J. (1993d) 'Managing IS in global companies', in *Systems Science: Addressing Global Issues* (F. A. Stowell, D. West and J. G. Howell, eds), Plenum, New York, 415–20.

Pauley, G. S. (1992) 'Successful implementation of a knowledge-based, smelter operations scheduling system at the Palabora Mine in South Africa', *IDASCO 92*, Oxford.

Rockart, J. F. (1979) 'Chief executives define their own information needs', *Harvard Business Review*, March–April, 81–93.

Scott Morton, M. S. (1991) *The Corporation of the 1990's: Information Technology and Organisational Transformation*, Oxford University Press, Oxford.

Wilson, B. (1990) *Systems: Concepts, Methodologies and Applications* (2nd edn), Wiley, Chichester.

5

EXPERIENCE OF USING MULTIVIEW: SOME REFLECTIONS

David Avison
*Department of Accounting
and Management Science,
University of Southampton*

Trevor Wood-Harper
*Information Systems
Research Centre,
University of Salford*

INTRODUCTION

The Multiview framework is an attempt to combine soft and hard approaches to information systems development. Particularly strong influences have been the work of Checkland and Mumford. The analysis of human activity through the use of modified soft systems methodology (SSM) (Checkland, 1984; Checkland and Scholes, 1990), along with socio-technical systems (Mumford, 1981; Land and Hirschheim, 1983) has been wedded to more conventional work on data analysis (Rock-Evans, 1981) and structured analysis (Gane and Sarson, 1979; De Marco, 1979). However, these earlier works have been interpreted in a particular way (indeed, the original authors may not agree with the interpretation) and since the publication of the original text on Multiview (Wood-Harper, *et al.*, 1985) other work has been assimilated into the Multiview framework (Avison and Wood-Harper, 1986, 1990). It has continued to develop so that, for example, its latest version incorporates an object-oriented approach.

This combination of approaches has created a theoretical framework which attempts (1) to account for the different viewpoints of all those involved in using a computer system and (2) to reconcile issue-based with task-related aspects. An issue-related question is, 'What do we hope to achieve for the company as a result of installing a computer?'; a task-related question is, 'What jobs is the computer going to have to do?' Conventional methodologies stress task-related aspects.

We use the term 'framework' in the context of Multiview advisedly; it acts as a guide for those developing an information systems application. This contrasts with the view of a methodology as a constraining force. Such a 'prescription' cannot be appropriate for all applications for the following reasons:

- The 'fuzziness' of some applications require an attack on several fronts. This 'exploration' may lead to an understanding of the problem area and hence to a reasonable solution.
- As an information system project develops, it takes on very different perspectives or 'views' and any approach adopted should incorporate these views, which may be organizational, technical, economic, and so on.
- The tools and techniques appropriate for one set of circumstances may not be appropriate for others.

Nevertheless, the term 'methodology' is often used to describe prescriptive approaches to information systems development, such as SSADM, STRADIS, IE and MERISE (see Avison and Fitzgerald, 1988), and we shall follow that terminology in this paper, using the term 'framework' or 'approach' to information systems development when referring to Multiview.

Many authors and practitioners have argued that a more flexible approach to information systems development is likely to be more useful than a 'one best way' model which can lead to 'elaborate and bureaucratic methodologies' (Benyon and Skidmore, 1987). A methodology, in the Multiview context, is that unique set of methods, tools and techniques that have been adopted by a particular group of users and analysts as appropriate for a particular problem situation.

We have had various experiences of using the approach in action research projects, some of which are discussed in Avison and Wood-Harper (1990) and in more detail in Wood-Harper (1989) and Avison (1990). Multiview is a contingency approach and these varied experiences and others have shaped and developed the framework, the techniques, and the tools used. This chapter discusses some reflections based on this experience.

As we have seen, the chase for the perfect methodology is somewhat illusory because different methodologies represent different views of the world. Information systems design could be seen as a logical, technical or people problem. Different analysts have adopted different methods because they have taken different views of the situation. There are also differences in the systems analysis and design approaches used that are caused by differences in the situation in which the analyst is working. Approaches that may be successful in a large bureaucratic organization may well be different from those that work in a small fast-moving company.

In systems analysis and design practice there is a three-way relationship between the analyst/user group, the Multiview approach and the situation, shown in Figure 5.1, but parts of the relationship are missing in many expositions of information systems development methodologies. For example, many methodologies implicitly assume that each situation is essentially the same and that analysts are similar in background and experience (Davies and Wood-Harper, 1989).

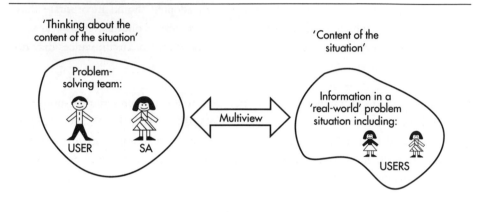

Figure 5.1   A framework for reflection on information systems development in practice

In the following section we briefly outline the Multiview approach. We then turn to the main purpose of this chapter, which is to discuss our reflections as we learned from our experiences of using Multiview in practice (the action research learning cycle seen in Figure 5.2) and attempt to recast this experience through the lens of SSM.

AN OVERVIEW OF MULTIVIEW

This section describes an approach to information systems development that combines important aspects of some of the major methodologies and themes—discussed in Avison and Fitzgerald (1988), for example—into a coherent and yet flexible approach. The approach covers five different stages of systems analysis and design, each with its own appropriate view of the problem, and each with methods for tackling that aspect of the problem.

The stages of the Multiview framework and their interrelationships are shown in Figure 5.3 and in more detail in Figure 5.4. The five questions to which Figure 5.3 refers show the wide area that Multiview addresses.

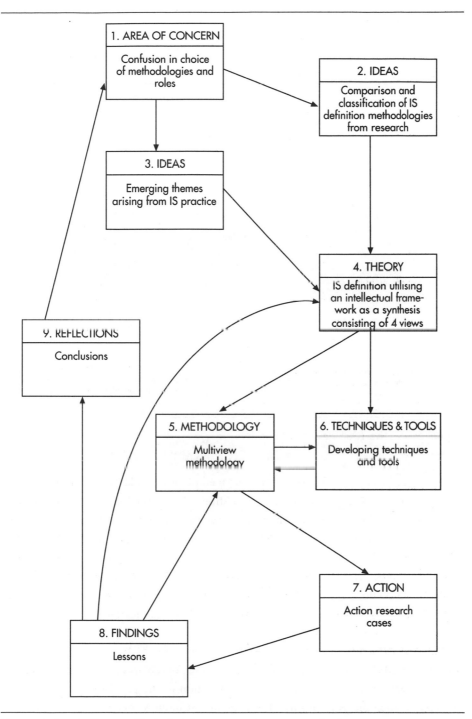

Figure 5.2   Reflections from the theories and practice of information systems
development (adapted from Avison and Wood-Harper, 1991)

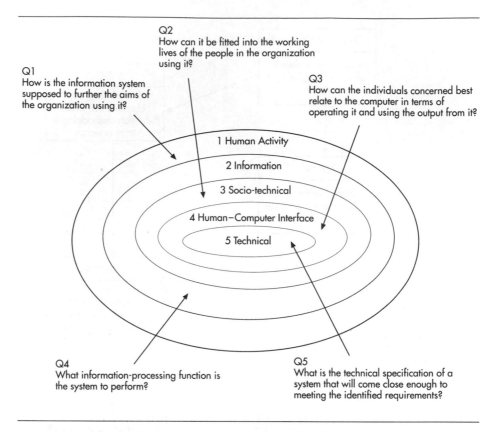

Q2
How can it be fitted into the working
lives of the people in the organization
using it?

Q1
How is the information system
supposed to further the aims of
the organization using it?

Q3
How can the individuals concerned best
relate to the computer in terms of
operating it and using the output from it?

1 Human Activity

2 Information

3 Socio-technical

4 Human–Computer Interface

5 Technical

Q4
What information-processing function is
the system to perform?

Q5
What is the technical specification of a
system that will come close enough to
meeting the identified requirements?

Figure 5.3   The Multiview framework

Whereas conventional information systems methodologies address questions 4 and 5 (and perhaps 3), Multiview addresses question 1 (addressed also by Soft Systems Methodology, which is not an information systems development methodology) and question 2 (which few approaches address, one exception being ETHICS). The boxes in Figure 5.4 refer to the analysis stages and the circles to the design stages. The arrows between them describe the interrelationships. Some of the outputs of one stage are used in a following stage. The dotted arrows show other major outputs. The five stages, described fully in Avison and Wood-Harper (1990), are summarized below:

1. Analysis of human activity

This stage in Multiview concerns the search for views of the organization. The rich picture represents a subjective and objective perception of the problem situation in diagrammatic and pictorial form, showing the structures of processes and their relationships. It can be used to identify problem themes: conflicts, an absence of communication lines, shortages of supply, and so on. Through debate within the organi-

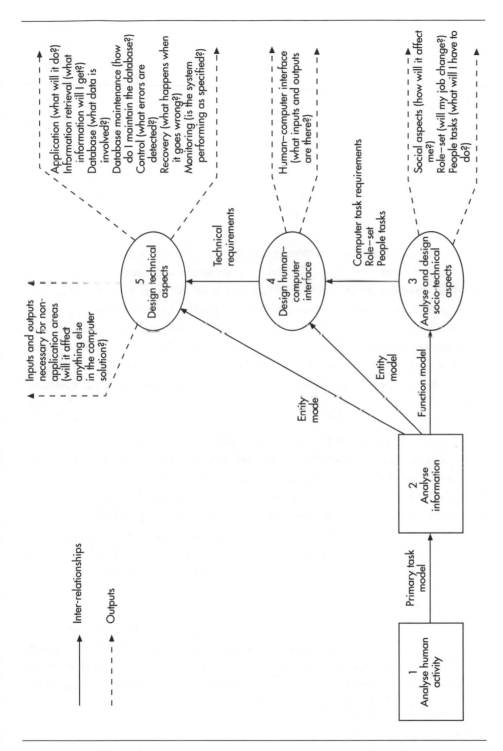

Figure 5.4   The Multiview approach

zation, it is possible to identify relevant systems which may relieve problem themes. The root definition describes the major relevant system requiring attention. The root definition is then analysed to ensure that all necessary elements have been identified and included: that is, the **O**wner of the system, the **A**ctors involved, the **C**lient, the **T**ransformation that takes place, the **E**nvironment in which it takes place, and the world view (or **W**eltanschauung) assumed in our root definition. Changing the order, this check-list is called the CATWOE criteria. The activities necessary in the system defined in the root definition are also identified and compared to the representation of the 'real world' in the rich picture. In some cases the output of this stage is an improved human activity system and the information systems development process stops at that point (Checkland and Scholes, 1990).

2. Analysis of information (sometimes called information modelling)
The purpose of this stage is to analyse the entities and functions of the systems described, independent of any consideration of how the application will eventually develop. By using functional decomposition, it is possible to break down progressively the main function (clear in a well-formed root definition) into subfunctions, and, by using data flow diagrams, the sequence of events and data flows are analysed. In developing an entity model, the problem solver identifies and names entities (anything we want to keep records about); relationships between entities; and attributes describing entities.

3. Analysis and design of socio-technical aspects
The task at this stage is two-fold: (1) to produce a design from an analysis of people and their needs and the working environment and (2) to place this in context with the organizational structure, computers, and the necessary work tasks. Thus, social and technical objectives are set and alternatives specified and compared so that the best socio-technical solution can be selected and the corresponding computer tasks, role sets and people tasks can be defined. The emphasis at this stage is not on development, but on a statement of alternatives according to social and technical considerations.

4. Design of the human–computer interface
Decisions are made at this stage on the technical design of the human–computer interface—for example, batch or on-line and menu, command or form-driven. Specific conversations and interactions are then designed. The users are expected to be the major contributors of this stage. The technical requirements to fulfil these human–computer interfaces can then be designed.

5. Design of technical aspects
Using the entity model (from stage 2) and the technical requirements (from stage 4), a

more technical view can be taken by the analyst because human considerations are already integrated with the forthcoming technical considerations. This technical design includes the application subsystems and the 'non-application subsystems'. These are the information retrieval requirements subsystem, the control subsystem, the database, the database maintenance subsystem, the recovery subsystem and the maintenance sub-system.

The five stages incorporate five different views appropriate to the progressive develop-ment of an analysis and design project, covering all aspects required to answer the vital questions of users. These five views are necessary to form a system that is complete in both technical and human terms. The outputs of the methodology are shown as dot-ted arrows in Figure 5.4.

Because it is a multiview approach, it covers computer-related questions and also mat-ters relating to people and business functions. It is part issue-related and part task-related. The distinction between issue and task is important because it is too easy to concentrate on tasks when computerizing, and to overlook important issues in need of resolution. Too often issues are ignored in the rush to 'computerize'. But, you cannot solve a problem until you know what the problem is! Issue-related aspects, in particu-lar those occurring at stage 1 of Multiview, are concerned with debating definitions of system requirements in the broadest sense, that is, 'What real-world problems is the sys-tem to solve?' Conversely, task-related aspects, in particular stages 2–5, work towards forming the system that has been defined with appropriate emphasis on complete tech-nical and human views. The system, once created, is not just a computer system; it helps people do their jobs.

REFLECTIONS FROM THE EXPERIENCE OF USING MULTIVIEW

The lessons arising from using Multivew in information systems projects include the following:

- *A methodology takes time to learn*   There is a wide range and large number of techniques and tools available. Describing them all would result in an information systems development methodology that is long, complex and therefore difficult to learn and to master. Multiview is, perhaps, even more complex for two main reasons: (1) it combines 'hard' and 'soft' techniques and tools; and (2) it is a contingent approach and so does not follow a rigid step-by-step description with specific techniques and tools to be used at each stage with well-defined deliverables to be produced following each stage.

- *The waterfall model is inappropriate for describing information systems development in practice* This approach, as evidenced by the field work, does not, in practice, exhibit the step-by-step, top-down nature of conventional models and none of the applications has exactly followed the framework as espoused in the main text (Avison and Wood-Harper, 1990). The users of the approach will almost certainly find that they will carry out a series of iterations that are not shown in the framework. Further, in some of the real-world cases undertaken, certain phases of the approach were omitted and others were carried out in a sequence different from that expected.

- *The framework is not a 'guarantor of truth'* Images within the views of the approach are interpreted and selected depending on context. For example, in two cases described in the 1990 text, the social options of the socio-technical phase were either omitted or not fully explored. The appropriateness of using some techniques also varied.

- *The political dimension is important* The manipulation of power—that is, the political dimension—is important in real-world situations. This transcends the rationale of any methodology. In most cases decisions were made in light of considerations beyond those implied by Multiview. For example, in one application computer equipment was purchased before needs analysis had been undertaken fully. The reason concerned a fund of money in the organization that would not be available after a particular date (the 'year end').

- *Responsible participation is contingent* A high level of responsible participation is a positive ingredient of successful information systems development. Nevertheless, our experience suggests that the role of the facilitator is frequently that of 'confidence booster' rather than that of adviser or applications developer, as usually described in texts. The role of the facilitators proved crucial in most applications on both the people and the technical aspects of information systems development. However, participation is not always possible; for example, it depends on the organization's structure and the attitudes of the people concerned.

- *In certain situations the approach gives insufficient guidance* In several cases, when using Multiview, it was difficult to identify all the major stakeholders or further detail was needed to use the techniques described in a real situation. Textbooks and manuals supporting methodologies give general guidance, but each problem situation is unique. The approach is interpreted by user/analysts. People view each situation differently depending on their education, culture and experience. Users of Multiview (and of conventional methodologies) interpret the approach and the problem situation uniquely. There is no such thing as a 'typical situation', 'typical user' or 'typical analyst'.

These lessons are discussed fully in Avison and Wood–Harper (1990).

The framework shown as Figure 5.4 describes how the Multiview approach transfers relevant 'thinking about the content of the situation' to the 'content of the situation'. The following broad reflections are implied from the lessons and can be related to the diagram.

Reflection 1 · The Multiview framework is in a continuing state of evolution

This reflection is not an attack on Multiview in isolation—all information systems development methodologies have limitations. Information systems is a comparatively new discipline, the diversity of approaches is caused to some extent by the background and cultures of their authors and none is all-inclusive. Moreover, methodologies address a moving target in that the technology, along with techniques and tools supporting it, develop relentlessly. As such, Multiview is part of a process of improving information systems practice by reflecting on limitations and adapting to change.

Reflection 2: Developing an information system is contingent

Developing an information system is contingent on the information systems development approach, the problem situation and the information systems development team. The team of users and analysts affect the perception of the situation and they interpret the methodology. The variety of possible interpretations reflects differences in backgrounds and experiences. In some of the applications not all stages of Multiview were used because of the situation. It is possible to imagine cases in which it is deemed inappropriate to develop a computer-based information system. The framework was adapted accordingly in one case. In others, the different analysts interpreted the 'same situation' differently. In any situation in which an information system might be appropriate, there are factors such as culture, language and education that have to be taken into consideration. Frequently particular techniques and tools are not appropriate to the problem situation. The systems analyst has to choose from a 'tool box' those techniques and tools appropriate for each situation, but within the framework of an approach such as Multiview (Avison et al., 1988). Without such a framework, the information systems are likely to be idiosyncratic, difficult to maintain, and therefore of variable value.

Reflection 3: Defining an information system can be considered as a social process

The process (as shown in Figure 5.1 and based on the action research cases) can be examined within different aspects relevant to information systems development. These three aspects are: the role of the systems analyst and the paradigm of assumptions constructed in practice; the political nature of the change process; and how methodologies are interpreted. We shall look at each of these in more detail in the next section.

THE SYSTEMS ANALYST'S ROLE AND THE PARADIGM OF ASSUMPTIONS CONSTRUCTED IN PRACTICE

This theory can be explained using a 2 by 2 matrix, and represents an extension of the work of Burrell and Morgan (1979) and Kling (1987). The first dimension comprises assumptions about the nature of information systems definition, ranging from objective to subjective. The second dimension relates to assumptions about the degree of change to the information situation. This ranges from regulatory to radical. These dimensions yield four quadrants or paradigms in which the following beliefs or assumptions can be located:

- *Ontological*—about the nature of reality
- *Information situation*—about the behaviour of humans in the information situation
- *Epistemological*—about how knowledge is acquired
- *Methodological*—beliefs in the appropriate devices, acquiring knowledge about and intervening in the information situation.

These four paradigms are seen in Figure 5.5. In the functionalist perspective, the information system consists of interactions that function independently of outside manipulation. The analyst assumes that the situation can be readily understood; indeed there is an assumption of rational behaviour by the actors that makes understanding easier. The systems are well controlled, can be well understood and can be formally defined.

In the interpretive perspective, it is assumed that the analyst is subjective and interprets the problem situation. The analyst hopes to understand the intentions of the actors in the situation. Participation and involvement are, perhaps, the best ways to obtain detailed information about the problem situation, and later to be able to predict and to control it.

In the radical structuralist view, the situation will appear to have a formal existence but require radical change due to, for example, contradictory and conflicting elements. The systems analyst is assumed to be an agent for change and social progress, emancipating people from their socio-economic structures.

Finally, in the radical humanist view, the situation is seen as external and complex. There is an emphasis on participation to enable a rapport between the actors, leading to emancipation at all levels, including the socio-economic and psychological.

The view taken of the role and the effect of the systems analyst on the problem situation will depend on the perspective: it might be as a 'technical expert' imposing good

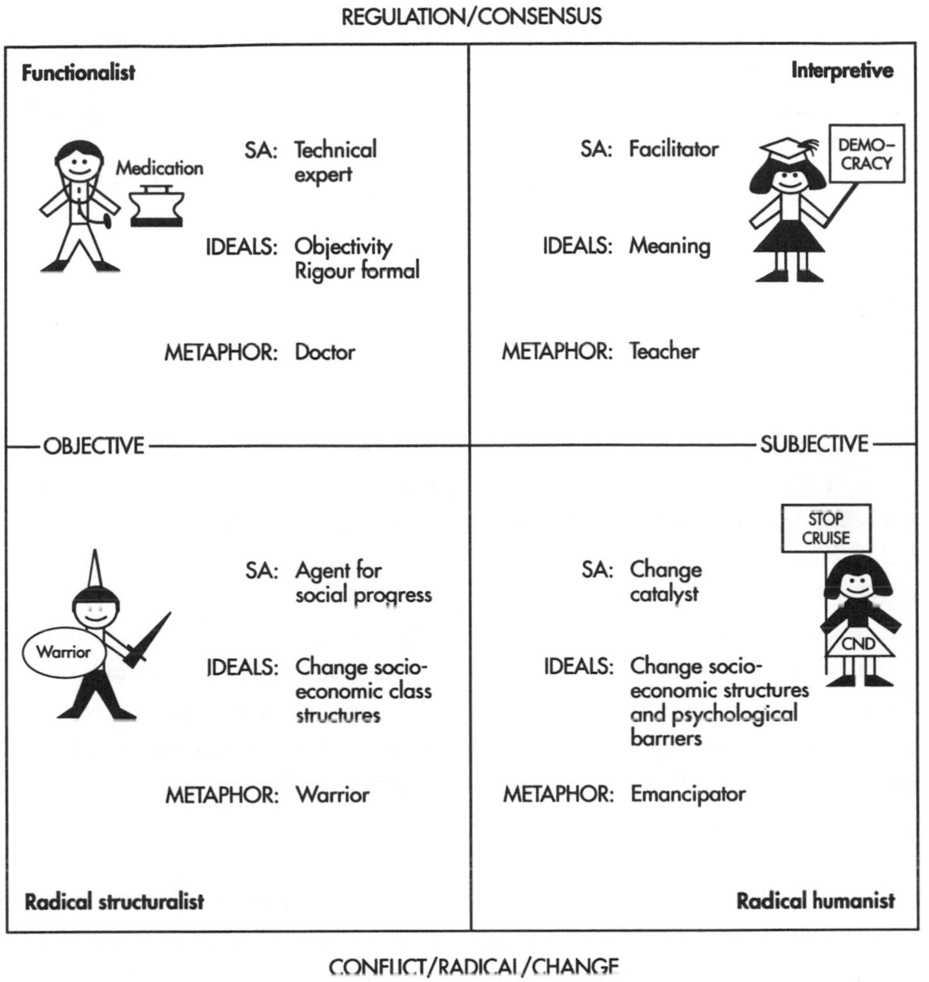
REGULATION/CONSENSUS
Functionalist
Medication
SA: Technical expert
IDEALS: Objectivity Rigour formal
METAPHOR: Doctor
Interpretive
SA: Facilitator
DEMO-CRACY
IDEALS: Meaning
METAPHOR: Teacher
OBJECTIVE
SUBJECTIVE
Warrior
SA: Agent for social progress
IDEALS: Change socio-economic class structures
METAPHOR: Warrior
STOP CRUISE
SA: Change catalyst
CND
IDEALS: Change socio-economic structures and psychological barriers
METAPHOR: Emancipator
Radical structuralist
Radical humanist
CONFLICT/RADICAL/CHANGE

Figure 5.5 Roles, ideals and metaphors assumed when developing an information system

practices on the situation; or as 'facilitator' helping the users achieve their goals; or as an 'agent for social progress' imposing radical change on the situation; or finally as 'change analyst', encouraging the users to effect major change.

THE POLITICAL NATURE OF THE CHANGE PROCESS

Kling and Scacchi (1982) identified four perspectives from which problem solvers may view the content of the information situation in which information technology is embedded. The importance of these perspectives for the information systems definition is that different strategies should be adopted based on the perspective embraced.

The first is the formal rational perspective, which emphasizes the formal organizational structure and procedures. With this perspective, we see the extreme of reductionist thought. The second perspective, the structural perspective, includes considerations of the situation's formal subunits and recognizes that communication must occur between them. The third perspective is the interactionist viewpoint which recognizes that the pieces of the information resource are neither independent nor formally defined. The social groups of interest cross intra-organizational and inter-organizational boundaries and are possibly in a constant state of flux. The process of change is founded on negotiation. The fourth perspective, organizational politics, assumes that interactions in the organization are based on the political machinations and resulting manifestations of power.

These four perspectives are embodied in two models relevant to the situation formulated by Kling (1987). The first two views represent the situation as found in the discrete-entity model. The last two views are embedded in the web model. The discrete-entity model, unlike the web model, bounds a situation. Whereas the discrete-entity model relies on formal group structures, the web model allows this to be expanded to as many factors as may be affecting the situation. This introduces subjectivity into the process, but allows a richer representation of the situation to be reached. Thus the web model includes the social organization, factors external to the formal and social organization, the interaction of all resources involved with the system, internal as well as external, and the historical background that prepares the stage.

The above models are useful in explaining the results from our fieldwork, which tends to support the web model, particularly in the political dimension, as every situation is essentially political (Wood–Harper and Corder, 1988).

THE INTERPRETATION OF METHODOLOGIES

Defining an information system can be thought of as metaphorical activity with, for example, the Multiview framework as a non-prescriptive description of a real-world process. The essence of a metaphor is understanding and experiencing one kind of thing in terms of another and, in this context, the 'methodology' is a useful, epistemological device for the process of defining an information system (Lakoff and Johnson, 1980). This means that there is support from the fieldwork that the Multiview approach is a metaphor that is interpreted and developed in the situation. Consequently, the Multiview approach can be regarded as an 'open theory' and an 'ideal type' and, in each case, people close the theory in action (Checkland, 1983; Wood–Harper, 1985).

HOW MULTIVIEW IS USED IN PRACTICE

The above discussion on Multiview can be viewed as an understanding of it in use. In general, in any practice, two different perspectives can be applied: instrumental problem solving and reflection–in–action (Schön, 1983).

From the instrumental problem-solving view, action is seen as the application of technical rationale. This means that systems analysts accept a given methodology and apply it in practice. In doing so, they use theoretical knowledge to perform specific tasks and use the tools and techniques in a prescribed manner. From this perspective, practice can be considered to be the application of knowledge as a result of research work, and generally it is seen as different from research. Consequently, practice applies research-based theories, methodologies and techniques and the research community develops these. In this view, practice is separate from theory.

In contrast to this view, our fieldwork supports Schön's reflection–in–action perspective. Here the assumption is that different practical contexts are unique and complex.

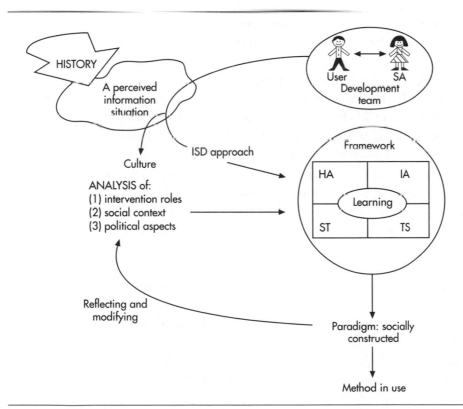

Figure 5.6   An attempt to depict Multivew in use in terms of SSM nomenclature (adapted from Checkland and Scholes, 1990)

The systems analyst and the user must be aware of this and the situation, thereby adjust-ing (1) the methodology, (2) his or her role and paradigm of assumptions, and (3) his or her reading of the political situation. This is illustrated in Figure 5.6.

Based on the above experience in applying Multiview to the fieldwork, it can be con-cluded that research and practice are intrinsically related. Therefore, developing an information system in practice can be considered to be a research act in which the approach to information systems development is interpreted. This change process can be thought of as a social process having technical and cultural aspects and its focus will vary with the situation and the social context based, in this case, on the learning para-digm of soft systems methodology. (Mumford *et al.*, 1985.)

Acknowledgements
We wish to express our thanks to Heather Watson for her very helpful comments on an earlier draft of this chapter.

REFERENCES

Avison, D. E. (1990) 'A contingency approach to information systems development', PhD Thesis, Aston University, Birmingham.

Avison, D. E. and Fitzgerald, G. (1988) *Information Systems Development: Methodologies, Techniques and Tools*, Blackwell, Oxford.

Avison, D. E. and Wood-Harper, A. T. (1986) 'Multiview – an exploration in infor-mation systems development', *Australian Computer Journal*, **18** (4).

Avison, D. E. and Wood-Harper, A. T. (1990) *Multiview: An Exploration in Information Systems Development*, Blackwell, Oxford.

Avison, D. and Wood-Harper, A. T. (1991) 'Information systems development research: an exploration of ideas in action', *Computer Journal*, **34** (2).

Avison, D. E., Fitzgerald, G. and Wood-Harper, A. T. (1988) 'Information systems development: a tool-kit is not enough', *Computer Journal*, **31** (4).

Benyon, D. and Skidmore, S. (1987) 'Towards a tool-kit for the systems analyst', *Computer Journal*, **30** (1) 29–38.

Boland, R. and Hirschheim, R. A. (1987) *Critical Issues in Information Systems Research*, Wiley, Chichester.

Burrell, G. and Morgan, G. (1979) *Sociological Paradigms and Organisational Analysis*, Heinemann, London.

Checkland, P. B. (1983) 'O.R. and the systems movement: mappings and conflicts', *Journal of Operations Research Society*, **34** (8), 661–75.

Checkland, P. B. (1984) 'Rethinking a systems approach', in *Rethinking the Process of Operational Research and Systems Analysis* (R. Tomlinson and I. Kiss, eds), Pergamon, Oxford.

Checkland P B. and Scholes, J. (1990) *Soft Systems Methodology in Action*, Wiley, Chichester.

Davies, L. J. and Wood-Harper, A. T. (1989) 'Information systems development: theoretical frameworks', *Journal of Applied Systems Analysis*, **16,** 61–74.

De Marco, T. (1979) *Structured Analysis and System Specification*, Prentice-Hall, Englewood Cliffs.

Gane, C. P. and Sarson, T. (1979) *Structured Systems Analysis: Tools and Techniques*, Prentice-Hall, Englewood Cliffs.

Kling, R. K. (1987) 'Defining the boundaries of computing across complex organisations', in *Critical Issues in Information Systems Research* (R. Boland and R. A. Hirschheim, eds), Wiley, Chichester.

Kling, R. K. and Scacchi, W. (1982) 'The web of computing: computing technology as social organization', *Advances in Computers*, **21** 1–90.

Lakoff, G. and Johnson, M. (1980) *'Metaphors We Live By'*, The University of Chicago Press, Chicago.

Land, F. F. and Hirschheim, R. (1983) 'Participative systems design: rationale, tools and techniques', *Journal of Applied Systems Analysis*, **10,** 91–108.

Mumford, E. (1981) 'Participative systems design: structure and method', *Systems Objectives and Solutions*, **1** (1).

Mumford, E., Hirschheim, R., Fitzgerald, G. and Wood-Harper, A.T. (eds) (1985) *Research Methods in Information Systems*, North-Holland, Amsterdam.

Rock-Evans, R. (1981) *Data Analysis*, IPC Press, London.

Schön, D. (1983) *The Reflective Practitioner*, Basic Books, New York.

Tomlinson, R. and Kiss, I. (eds) (1984) *Rethinking the Process of Operational Research and Systems Analysis*, Pergamon, Oxford.

Wood-Harper, A. T. (1985) 'Information research methods: using action research', in *Research Methods in Information Systems* (E. Mumford, R. Hirschheim, G. Fitzgerald and A. T. Wood-Harper, eds), North-Holland, Amsterdam.

Wood-Harper, A. T. (1989) 'Comparison of information systems definition methodologies: an action research–multiview perspective'. PhD Thesis, University of East Anglia, Norwich.

Wood-Harper, A. T. and Corder, S. W. (1988) 'Information resource management: towards a web-based methodology for end-user computing', *Journal of Applied Systems Analysis*, **15**.

Wood-Harper, A. T., Anthill, L. and Avison, D. E. (1985) *Information Systems Definition: the Multiview Approach*, Blackwell, Oxford.

6

EMPOWERING THE CLIENT: THE RELEVANCE OF SSM AND INTERPRETIVISM TO CLIENT-LED DESIGN

Frank Stowell

Department of Computing and Information Systems, University of Paisley

INTRODUCTION

As an antidote to the successful but somewhat narrow rationalistic approach to problem solving there has emerged a conscious desire in many information system (IS) researchers and practitioners to change the way in which they think about information technology (IT) provision and the way in which they approach organizational problems. Of particular importance to the change in thinking about IS development is 'systems thinking' and in particular that dimension of systems thinking called soft systems. Partially in an attempt to avoid failures in computer system installation and partially to discover design methods that can exploit advances in technology, soft systems thinking is increasingly used in IS development (e.g. Wilson, 1984; Stowell, 1985, 1991; Stowell and West, 1992, 1994b; Miles, 1985, 1992; Avison and Wood–Harper, 1986, 1990; Lewis, 1993). This chapter is concerned with one such development, referred to as client-led design (CLD) (Stowell and West, 1994b).

CLD is intended to empower the clients (stakeholders or users) and enable them to exercise full control over the provision of technology to support their information systems. The notion of CLD is based upon the interpretative paradigm and uses a variety of systems-based ideas as a means of facilitating problem appreciation as a precursor to the specification of technology that might be used to aid the effectiveness of the clients information system. The influence of the work of Checkland upon the thinking that lies behind CLD will be considered, as will the value of CLD in demystifying technology for the client.

IT AND THE BUSINESS ORGANIZATION

There is little doubt about the relationship between the success or failure of business in the market economy and the wealth of a nation. The relationship between the two seems to be pronounced at every level of business endeavour, whether competing in world, national or local markets. The role of technology in the success of business is also relevant. This is not a recent phenomenon; although the technology might be new, the motivating factor is not. Competition between businesses throughout the twentieth century has been a continuous struggle as each business strives to protect its market sector by keeping one step ahead of competition (Stowell, 1993) and technology has played an important part in this.

The importance of successful trading and effective business in creating vast national wealth can be seen from a review of the literature. In the post-war years we see the increase in national wealth of countries such as Germany, Japan and Singapore and the relative decline in global economic dominance of the UK and, to some extent, the USA. Businesses that have improved their production efficiency and the quality of their product to obtain a position of pre-eminence are also characterized by their ready use of new ideas, both in management techniques and in the use of technology. The ability of a business to survive over a number of years is usually characterized by the readiness of that business to incorporate technological innovation. In this respect there are some similarities between the nineteenth and twentieth centuries. The availability of machine power in the nineteenth century improved productivity, spawned new skills, made others redundant and initiated significant social change. There is a similar pattern to be found in the latter part of the twentieth century as newer technologies replace the old. As a generalization, the 'technology' of the nineteenth century relieved the need for physical power, and the technologies of the twentieth century are supplementing (and in some cases replacing) mental skills.

Perhaps the most pronounced difference between early nineteenth- and late twentieth-century industrialization is the speed at which the technology is incorporated and the wider ramifications it has upon society as a whole. For example, at the macro level the impact of IT affects not just those within industry but the population in general. One of the more obvious changes is the ratio between the employed and unemployed sections of the population. There are many reasons for the change in ratio but there is little doubt that IT has made an impact (Forrester, 1985). Employment levels have ramifications for government policy and upon the general view of the population about work versus leisure time. Moreover, the way in which IT enables the formation and management of business has allowed many companies to become international, with their headquarters based within their own nation and a major part of their business operations based overseas. This development, although not new, is easily facilitated by IT and has an impact upon both management and government policies. For an example, many businesses, despite their national origins, implement policies by which contracts can be awarded to the overseas subsidiary that offers the best business deal, irrespective of the impact on employment that such a decision may have in the home country.

At an individual level, during the past decade or so there has been a decline in the need for some skills and the emergence of a new set of specialist domains to cater for the demands made upon this late-twentieth-century technical phenomenon. This kind of change is not dissimilar to that experienced by the workforce during the nineteenth century as one industry grew because of technological innovation which, in turn, effectively led to the demise of another, e.g. railway and canal transportation. In the late twentieth century IT has spawned new ways of working, new skills and enabled business to operate in a hitherto unimaginable fashion. Microprocessors have had a significant impact upon human communication and the way in which individuals and groups develop and operate their information systems. This suggests that there is a requirement for a new set of analytical skills and specialist knowledge to address these new demands. Skills needed by the information systems analyst (ISA) include a combination of knowledge of technology, business and human information systems.

INDUSTRY AND TECHNOLOGY

Hitherto the responsibility for the IT design process has been primarily that of the technologist and, consequently, despite the attempts to involve the 'user' in the IT definition (e.g. information engineering), the 'user' does become marginalized because of the predisposition of the technologist to be concerned with things technical. Most of the IT design methods developed over recent years have been more concerned with the specification of the technology than with the information system itself (Stowell, 1991), partially because of the way in which the use of computing has evolved and partly to address operational needs.

Increasingly the user, who may be better referred to as the 'client' to underline the importance of his or her position to the success of a project, is prepared to purchase hardware and associated software without the aid of a computer specialist. The tendency towards independent action is not limited to private individuals or to small business enterprises but includes managers within large companies. Managers are no longer ignorant of the potential assistance of computers and are aware of the lack of business knowledge of many of the computer specialists. Many business managers seem to prefer to identify their own computing needs which they can relate to personal experience of their business problem. Often, it is only when the extent of the technological support is considered by the company management to be company-wide that specialist aid is enlisted. This apparent trend towards 'do-it-yourself' computing may have a number of origins: for example, it may reflect that management now have a level of IT expertise that safely enables them to purchase and install technology; that technology has become flexible and simple enough for anyone to install; or it may relate to a lack of confidence in IT specialists.

The idea that computing for business requires mainly technical specialist knowledge appears to be viewed with scepticism by some business managers. There would seem to be a growing belief that the incorporation of computing power is more likely to be successful if undertaken by a person with knowledge of the problem than by a person with knowledge of the system. Common practice seems to reinforce that idea: since individuals can purchase quite sophisticated technology for domestic use with very little aid from a technical expert, why cannot the same principle apply to the purchase of business IT? Perhaps such an argument is superficial, but it does underline the point that the general public have an increasing familiarization with quite sophisticated technology each day, whereas many computing specialists have relatively little managerial experience or knowledge of business.

It seems clear that the method by which we develop technology-based information systems, and the manner in which we use them, will have a significant effect upon the way the systems behave and also upon the actions of those who access the data held. An examination of the methods by which we define the technology reveals that the methods themselves are either *ad hoc*, developed by an individual to meet a particular need, or are attempts to install rigour (as an antidote to the *ad hoc* approach) and owe their origins to scientific rationalism rather than from a recognition of the complexity of human decision making.

One lesson that seems to have been learned in the 1900s about information technology and its importance upon decision making is that the methods of information systems definition and design used in the 1970s and 1980s are inadequate for modern needs (Methie, 1980). Numerous examples exist to show that while a technology-supported information system provides fast processing and fast response, it often fails to provide the flexibility of a human communication system, sometimes with serious consequences (e.g. The London Ambulance Emergency Service failure in 1992). The paradox is that while many managers consider themselves computer literate, there is often still a deference to a computer output as far as decision support aid is concerned. While the technology can process data quickly and reliably, an unquestioning acceptance of displayed results by a human operator may have unfortunate consequences.

DESIGN METHODS

Attempts by analysts to undertake a reappraisal of the IT design process have met with only partial success primarily because changes have been attempted at the practical level alone and the philosophical underpinning of the entire domain has been ignored. Why is this? The prime reason appears to be that the methods employed for the design and development of computer systems relate to what Winograd and Flores call the 'rationalistic tradition' (Winograd and Flores, 1986) and to what Hirschheim describes as the 'positivist' view (Hirschheim, 1985). Winograd and Flores refer to the 'tradition of rationalism and logical empiricism' as the underlying philosophy from which computing has been developed. Such a development should not be seen as surprising; in fact it represents a historical development since, as Winograd and Flores explain, we are taught from an early age that the rationalistic tradition, with the prestige and success it has received through scientific method, has become synonymous with 'what it means to think and be intelligent' (p. 16). In order to break free from the predominance of positivistic thinking, there must be a significant shift in the way we think about the world, but we are trapped by the omnipotence of the contemporary. MacIntyre (1993) points out the paradox of our moral experience in that while we are taught to see ourselves as autonomous we become involved and manipulated by ourselves. In order to pass on the principles of our own autonomy, we have little alternative. We seek to preserve 'the incoherence of our attitudes as our experience arises from the incoherent conceptual scheme which we have inherited' (p. 68). Why is this important to information systems? It would seem that the way in which we think about information systems requires a different mind-set to the way we think about computing, and to do that we need to consider the intellectual basis upon which the discipline is based. As far as information systems definition is concerned, it would seem that unless we address this issue we are in danger of continuing to think about IT in more or less the same way as we have for the past 20 years.

INFORMATION TECHNOLOGY

Is there really a difference between IT and IS? Information technology enables a large volume of data to be processed quickly, accessed easily and presented authoritatively. A mass of data is available to a variety of users who need no qualification to manipulate it outside that of being able to gain access. Easy-to-use software enables any user of IT to access and manipulate vast quantities of data and present them in such a way as to create the impression of the data being unquestionable fact. IT has enabled communication between human groups to take place more rapidly than ever before and provides the opportunity to act swiftly. However, this facility may not always be advantageous. The data that is manipulated is often without context and may arrive too quickly. The speed and 'authority' with which the data is presented may seem to have an urgency that may force hasty decisions and effectively make the decision-taking system behave as a positive feedback system.

The speed and volume of available data means that it is not always possible for a decision taker to be able to deal with the intricacy of the data itself or to be fully aware of its source or integrity. The decision taker may be put into a position of unconsciously influencing the behaviour of the wider dimensions of a problem situation in a way that may be counter-productive. Consider the effect IT has had upon the celerity of stock-market transactions and the knock-on effect that the sheer speed of these transactions have had upon national economies over the past decade. The increased use of IT in stock market transactions has, at times, made the market behave in unexpected ways. There have been instances where precipitate action has created, on the global economic system, undesirable effects of a magnitude that had not been previously contemplated by either the designer or the user of the information technology.

A computer is a tool which facilitates improvements to human information systems, intrinsically through the speed and accuracy with which data is processed. This is no different to a telephone system providing the means of voice communication between remotely located individuals or groups. Neither computer nor telephone can be accurately defined as an information system, but each is an important technical component supporting one. IT, then, can be considered as a generic name for the technology that is used to aid and improve human decision making.

Before the advent of computers, other forms of technology were used to support decision making within and between business enterprises to facilitate management control—for example, lampson tubes, telephones and telex have been successful technological methods of supporting inter- and intra-departmental communication in many businesses. However, the advances in data manipulation provided by the computer scientist has provided an aid to communication that is more powerful than anything previously available. By the sheer speed of this development, the loci of the problem has shifted from technology to the more difficult area of information system provision. Consequently, the role of IT is now subordinate to the definition and requirements of the information system.

The enthusiasm of some managers about the potential data-processing power of computers increased as machines became more powerful, smaller, cheaper and easier to use. This continuing enthusiasm has been fuelled by the development of business computers and the variety of software that provides specific business applications. The success of the computer games market is being exploited for the more serious business software market. Software houses and IT manufacturers are studying the speed at which individuals learn to use their games software, and from these lessons they aim to make business software equally as easy to use. This has interesting ramifications for the computing professional. First, will this mean the demise of some aspects of computing specialism? and second, is this further evidence of the clear shift towards the development of more ways of facilitating client control over technology? It would seem that just as the admiration of telex, Fax and electric typewriters has diminished, so too is the acclaim of the computer as a wondrous machine. As far as business is concerned, it is simply a management tool, and the quicker it earns its keep the better.

As technology has become more transparent to those that seek to harness it, so the nature of the specific technological requirements has become more complex. The technology often provides support for other activities, and while this may seem obvious it has often not been the case where computing is concerned. At the practical and philosophical levels there would then seem to be many reasons for the modern IT professional to concentrate upon the process of understanding company information systems as a precursor to making sensible suggestions about the way in which IT may be used.

INFORMATION SYSTEMS

If IT refers to the technology that can be used to support human decision making, then what is human decision making? In order to consider that we need to think about the process of human decision making itself which seems, at an elementary level, to be concerned with selecting a course of action from a variety of alternatives. It seems reasonable to assume that the process is enhanced by the amount of information available to aid the decision taker in his or her task. The operative word here is 'information' as distinct from 'data' It is the conversion of the data *plus* the context in which the process takes place that seems to translate what are little more than stimuli into information. The information itself is, of course, personal although there are times when there is a common interest in the data—e.g. a railway timetable. If technology is to be harnessed to help in the decision-making process, and if the technology is concerned with the processing of data, then the IT specialist needs to understand the information system that the client is using in order to support it through the data-processing capabilities of the technology.

There seems to be no agreed definition of information or information system within the literature, and so the following are offered as working definitions:

- *Information is the result of a process in which an individual or group assign meaning to some stimuli, for example data.* [This result is a personal interpretation and description that relates to our perceived world.]

> *Information is data to which meaning has been attributed in a particular context and an information system, in principle, serves the decision-making process to enable consequent actions to take place.* (Stowell and West, 1994a)

The argument has been made that there is a difference between information system and information technology—a fundamental shift from 'thinking about an organization in which technology will make its procedures more efficient' to 'thinking about an organization in terms of the Information Systems which make it up'. The recognition of this change in thinking may have both philosophical and practical ramifications for information systems definition.

OBJECTIVISM, SUBJECTIVISM AND INFORMATION SYSTEMS DEFINITION

The sense of the argument made in this chapter is that the changes to which business organizations are subjected, both from outside influences and from the complexities arising out of interaction between human groups within, suggest that an understanding of these changes would be best achieved by the *involvement* of the analyst in the problem situation (Stowell, 1990, West, 1991, Stowell and West, 1994a). Clearly it is not possible to predetermine methods of IS definition for every organizational eventuality since each organization will have a different culture and be subjected to a different set of circumstances, but from the argument made so far there would seem to be the need to provide the client with control over the whole development process. This suggests (a) the employment of methods of analysis which both clients and analysts can use, (b) that there is a clear relationship between the technology and the information system that can be shown diagrammatically. While these two requirements may appear to be easily satisfied it is necessary to make a change in thinking if a lapse into previous mistakes is to be avoided. One way of addressing the change is offered in this chapter as a framework to aid the thinking about the organizational analysis and information systems. The framework itself is proposed as a means of empowering a client or clients to exercise control over the whole information systems definition process.

It has been argued that in order to understand the way an enterprise works requires experience of its operation from within. Philosophically, the methods of analysis and design employed need to be based upon the notion of subjectivity rather then objectivity, and this presupposes the adoption of the interpretive paradigm in which recognition of the real world 'as "it is" is considered at a level of subjective experience' (Burrell and Morgan, 1979). Explanation is sought from the perspective of the observed rather than the observer, and social reality is considered to be a function of an individual's self-consciousness plus assumptions, together with the shared meanings and beliefs between individuals and groups.

Neither the method of investigation employed in organizational analysis nor the method of IS definition should be constrained by the need to support a proposition about 'The Organization' empirically, or by the need to validate logically a given organizational theory. Moreover, the definition of the technology should be related to the way in which it can support the information system as its prime function, rather than the other way round. The information systems analyst (ISA) should not be prevented from interacting with those involved by the techniques used since that experience can be employed to help describe the situation and may make an important contribution to the solution of the problem. The difficulty for the ISA lies in the selection of an appropriate method of investigation and an IS definition that it suited to the complexities of a business organization.

It may be that interpretivist systems provide a useful basis upon which to consider the method of IS definition. For Checkland, systems thinking is underpinned by what might be described as 'weak' phenomenology (Mingers, 1984) in which systems thinking is a process of inquiry through which useful changes to improve human endeavours might be contemplated. Interpretivist systems are characterized by the assumption that the perceived 'real-world' is perplexing and any method employed in an attempt to understand it should be systemic. In *Soft Systems Methodology in Action* (Checkland and Scholes, 1990) the authors propose a developed version of SSM, 'ideal type' mode 2, in which the seven-stage model of the 1980s is relegated to that of a practical vehicle of problem expression while the real systems thinking is carried out through the essence of systems thought brought about through the understanding of the problem via a hermeneutic/phenomenological mode of inquiry supported by SSM.

In many respects SSM, 'ideal type' mode 2, is the clearest example of interpretive systems that exists in a practical form. The arguments are put forward by the critics of SSM—who claim that it endorses the status quo and condemn it as being a tool for management—are less sustainable given this development. Checkland addresses the difficulties of radical change and the effect of organizational power through the methodology itself, without losing the essential interpretivist nature of the methodology. Stowell has proposed that the ideas that inspire SSM mode 2 can be extended further into what he refers to as client-led design (CLD). This proposal is made for three reasons: (a) in order to capitalize on the thinking that underpins SSM mode 2; (b) to bypass the conceptual model/data-flow diagram debate (e.g. Mingers, 1990; Prior, 1990; Doyle and Wood, 1991); and (c) to enable interpretive systems thinking to be the intellectual basis from which a range of tools/methods useful to the IS design process are selected.

CLIENT-LED DESIGN

Client-led design is an attempt to operationalize through interpretivist systems think-ing the idea that the information systems design process is orchestrated not by the prac-titioner but by the clients (Stowell, 1991); what is meant by design here is the whole process of information systems development, from information systems definition through specification to IS maintenance. One of the aims of CLD is to demystify tech-nology for the clients so it is important that the methods used in the design process are easily understood by the clients in order that they may exercise control over the whole process. The prime role of the practitioner is that of teacher in which a variety of sys-temic ideas are used to facilitate discussion. The client-led approach seeks to enable the process of inquiry to be conducted systemically without ascribing to the existence of purposeful human activity systems other than as a means of initiating a debate around perceived reality.

Stowell and West (1994b) have suggested two major areas of weakness in the process of information systems design: (a) the lack of problem appreciation by the analyst and client, and (b) the failure to give the client the lead in the design of the technology supported information system. They propose that one way of addressing this is to re-define the information systems definition process and CLD is offered as the underlying principle upon which to base the process.

DEFINITION OF CLD

The framework through which CLD is described should be thought of in terms of the hermeneutic circle (Dilthey, 1961), in that each phase of the framework contributes to an appreciation of the problem situation. As the participant's understanding of the sit-uation increases this may in turn affect a previous or following phase of the design process necessitating a return and review of past decisions: in this sense the cycle of learning is 'never-ending'. Clearly there will be a time when all parties will consider that enough has been learned about one phase and move on to the next, but this will always be in the recognition that no phase is ever totally complete.

The client-led information systems design approach is described through five phases of development, but these should not be seen as mapping onto any proclaimed 'real world' stages or activities as is the case of the traditional, and questionable, 'systems life cycle'. It is emphasized that the proposed five phases are intended as a framework to support the practical application of tools and techniques that enable client-led design to take place. It is *not* a formal method with a check-list of actions within a discrete set of steps embedded within clearly defined and structured stages. CLD is a framework for thinking which the clients, the team, or stakeholders, may find useful in helping them to undertake and manage the design process, and as such can be seen as a set of phases that appear to be relevant to the development of technology-supported information systems. As a framework for thinking it should be seen by all involved as supporting an iterative process and the starting point may be at any stage of the framework that is appropriate to the needs of the team. Within the framework a method or part of a method might be used if it is appropriate to the problem and the concept upon which CLD is based, namely interpretivist systems thinking.

Methods that may be employed include soft systems methodology, object-oriented design, information engineering or specific tools such as brainstorming, root definitions, data flow diagrams (Stowell and West, 1994b). The important thing for the designer to remember is that the design process needs to embrace all stages before action is taken to install the technology. Moreover, the framework itself should be seen as representing a never-ending cycle of learning in the tradition of action research. In the case of the technological input to the information systems design process, action itself should be taken at a point at which all parties agree that action is appropriate. Figure 6.1 illustrates the iterative nature of the framework for client-led design.

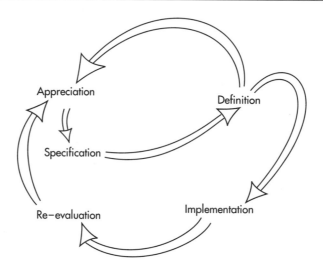

Figure 6.1   Diagram showing the cycle of events involved in client-led design (Stowell and West, 1994b)

The diagram provides a pictorial representation of the client-led design process. CLD is a series of phases with the phases themselves being vehicles for 'packages' of ideas that will aid the process of expressing the information system requirement right through to the fulfilment of that expressed need. Within the framework represented by the CLD phases the practitioner and client will use ideas and methods that are appropriate to the problem situation but, and this is most important, with respect to the philosophy upon which client-led design is based. The phases of design should not be used as if they were stages of a technique. Each phase is intended to enable the clients to express their needs and to enable them to reflect upon the relationship of each expression to each part of the process as a whole, and so the phases become an iterative cycle of events in which the clients define and agree to technology being implemented, updated, extended and replaced in a time-scale appropriate to their needs.

The phases of CLD are described briefly below, including the general actions that one would expect to take place within each of its evolutionary phases. A full account of the approach can be found in Stowell and West (1994b), *Client-Led Design of Information Systems: A Systemic Approach*.

Phase I

Phase I is the most important part of the framework in which the clients and the information systems analyst (ISA) gain an *appreciation* of the problem situation and of each other's perception of the problem. Appreciation describes the learning processes expressed by Vickers (1983) and by Checkland (1981). Appreciation involves both judgements of value and judgements of reality, and is described by Vickers as a system that manifests itself in 'the exercise through time of mutually related judgements of reality and value' (Vickers, 1983, p. 67). Vickers refers to this process as a system because each attribute appears to be part of the overall method used by human beings to make sense of what is observed. Appreciative judgements reflect the view held by an individual of a situation at a given point in time. 'Value' and 'reality' are not static but develop with each situational encounter. So, too, the ISA's and the client's preconception of a situation is modified by the knowledge that they gain from their observations as an attempt is made to appreciate what is taking place. The development of the appreciative system is both enabling and inhibiting but is essentially the 'inner history of an individual, an organisation and a society' (Vickers, 1983, p. 69). The idea of the appreciative system is elaborated upon in Phase I by utilizing appropriate systems tools as enabling methods to increasing client/ISA awareness through participation.

Vickers suggests that individuals learn not only new valuations through experience but also increase their skill in valuing; and they learn these things by the activity of 'appreciation' (Vickers, 1983). This process is summarized by Checkland (1981, p. 263):

> Vickers ... argues that our human experience develops within us
> 'readiness to notice particular aspects of our situation, to discriminate

them in particular ways and to measure them against particular standards of comparison, which have been built up in similar ways'. These readinesses are organised into 'an appreciative system' which creates for all of us, individually and socially, our appreciated world. The appreciative settings condition new experience, but are modified by the new experience; such circular relations Vickers takes to be the common facts of social life, but we fail to see this clearly, he argues, because of the concentration in our science-based culture on linear causal chains and on the notion of goal-seeking.

The main objective of the first part of CLD is for the participants to gain an understanding of the problem situation and each others' view of it, and of the information systems that enable the decision-making systems to operate.

The success of this first phase of CLD is important to the outcome of the project. This is particularly the case if it is a 'green field' project and the participants are unknown to each other. Phase I, in such instances, is the foundation upon which the project will be built. It is important that the ISA ensures that the client-set (that is, those clients directly affected by the problem situation) is representative of those involved in the problem situation and that the procedures adopted as part of the learning process are not intimidating to junior members of the group. It may not be relevant or useful to use the traditional model of 'representative personnel' (e.g. managers, union representatives and staff), since the participants should be representatives from those members of staff who can contribute to the overall appreciation of the group about the problem situation. Ideally, this would include all members of staff, but clearly this may not be possible in some cases. The closer the ISA can get to representing all views and ensuring that all involved are acquainted with those views, then the fewer difficulties are likely to be encountered at later stages in the project. As a general rule-of-thumb, the ISA is urged to spend at least one quarter of the total project time on Phase I, the 'appreciation' phase of the project.

It is important that all those that are involved in Phase I should be dedicated to gaining an appreciation of the problem; that is a tacit agreement between the participants about the nature of the problem situation. This does not mean an *agreement* about the *cause* of the problem but an *acceptance* of a *description* of the problem. The second important task for the client-set is an expression of the component parts of the defined problem. If this phase has an objective as such, it is that the clients should describe the problem in such a way that no member of the enterprise could add to or subtract from the description in a useful way.

Phase II

The time at which the project moves on to the next phase is dependent upon a number of things, not least the magnitude of the problem. It should become apparent to the participants when they have reached a point at which they can usefully proceed to Phase II, e.g. they will have expressed the problem situation as well as they can and agreed upon it. Their next task is to change the emphasis from describing the problem towards a description of the information system(s) that seem to underpin the 'systems' involved in the problem itself. The description of the information system can be facilitated by a number of useful modelling methods (some examples are provided in Stowell and West, 1994b). The ISA needs to aid the clients in the selection of modelling methods that seem appropriate to them and to this phase. The choice of method should be one that serves the expression of the information system as defined by the clients and should not be selected on the merit of its implications for representing or meeting the technical requirements of the information system. Clearly the kind of modelling that is used should be one that can be understood by the whole group. There will be instances where quite 'technical' models can be used and others where the models are less technical.

The model produced should be used (a) as a means of representing the information system(s), (b) as a means of communication among all those involved, and (c) as a means of validating that the information system(s) identified is suited to the needs of the clients (e.g. by 'walking' through the model). This is an important area if we are to take the opportunity to consider whether the methods currently in use are the most appropriate. If the opportunity is not taken to widen the thinking about possible alternatives to addressing the requirements of the information system at this stage, the result of the analysis would be little more than a translation of current procedures into more efficient procedures, including any problems inherent in the current procedures—a situation not unknown in IT projects.

Phase II of the project development provides an opportunity for the clients to consider information dissemination, storage and 'value'. At this stage the clients should be encouraged to question how the information will be generated and by whom, who will use it and for what purpose, where the information will be stored and the value of the stored information. In this phase, the need to think about the problem situation as a whole is vital. If changes are to be made to current procedures in order to address perceived problems, then the team needs to be certain that making a change in one area will not merely move the 'problem' to another, or create further unanticipated problems. Once again the use of appropriate systems tools and diagrams can aid this awareness. It has been found possible to use a rudimentary form of structured data flow diagram, providing the diagram is used formally as a vehicle for recording the information system and the variety of interactions and interfaces that the clients describe within it.

Phase III

This is the phase that is most familiar to the computer systems analyst. The outcome of Phase III is the production of a technical specification that will support part or all of the information system(s) defined in Phase II. The ISA will call upon his or her technical knowledge to fulfil this part of the project, but it is important that the clients are able to relate to and comment in a meaningful way upon the specification. It is at this stage that specific technology is advised by the ISA. It is of benefit if the model used in Phase II is one that can be developed into a technical specification. For example, the structure diagram that might have been used in Phase II might be an appropriate tool to lead into the technical specification of Phase III. If it has been used in the right way, i.e. initially as a vehicle for communication rather than as a vehicle for a technical specification, then the clients may find little difficulty in continuing with its development. It is important to maintain the relationship between Phase II and Phase III through the methods used to represent the information system in order that the clients can continue to exercise control over the design process. However, it is not merely compatibility of methods and models that make this move from Phase II to Phase III possible but the continued central role of the clients. The active involvement of the clients at this phase will help to assure them that their requirements are not being modified without their full knowledge and approval by any technological necessity. Where incompatibility exists between technology and the clients' requirements it should be easily recognized and dealt with by the clients, with the ISA, among others, acting as expert consultant.

The clients should be urged to consider questions about the relationship of the technology to the information system specified in Phase II in terms of (a) what the technology will achieve and, perhaps equally importantly, what the technology will not achieve; (b) what effect the technology will have on the working practices; and (c) what training will be required for all affected by the technology—not only those who will be using the technology but also those who may be involved in its output. As with the previous phases, the outcome of the phase is an increased awareness by all involved about the planned changes, and whether or not they are obtainable. By the end of this phase the clients should have a clear understanding of the technological ramifications of the proposals.

Phase IV

If the previous phases have been conducted correctly then this phase should present fewer problems than projects developed using a technically-based approach. This is the implementation stage and, if the design process has been undertaken correctly, should be dominated by the clients. The programme for the installation and operation of the IT-supported information system should be determined by the clients, as should the training activities for staff. Clearly, the ISA will provide expert advice to aid the clients in the formulation of the implementation programme but the decisions about the actions and resources required to support the programme and details relating to how the IT-supported information system is to be made operational is the responsibility of the clients. There are many ways in which the clients can be aided to attain this role, which to some degree will be determined by the particular installation. The clients should be concerned with the probable effects that the operation of the IT-supported information system might have upon the operation of the enterprise and upon the working practices of the staff at the time of changeover. Contingency plans in the event of failure should be formulated and discussed with the staff involved before the changeover takes place. Matters of project coordination and control appropriate to the successful conclusion of this phase should be embraced and the methods by which these activities are achieved should be those with which the clients feel most comfortable and which they feel will be culturally feasible. By this stage of the project the new information system should be assured by the clients and the role of the ISA primarily is one of expert adviser. The ISA will continue to have the traditional role of managing the technical aspects of the implementation, which is combined with that of client adviser on matters relating to the information system as a whole.

Phase V

Following implementation, the clients should gather together a group of 'experts' (i.e. those who work within the enterprise as well as IT experts) to evaluate the operation of the IT supported information system. Rather than functioning as an investigation into the IT-based system, the meetings should be seen as positive contributions to the on-going process of improving the way the enterprise operates through the employment of IT. The agenda of the meetings, ideally, should include discussions about the company's strategic plans, and the installation of IT should not be considered by company management as something that happens every few years but as part of an on-going process of business improvement. It is worth remembering that IT support is only a part of the information system and the clients need to continue to review the situation in order to keep aware of the changes that will take place as time passes. It may be that the CLD process of design might be one means of enabling the enterprise to keep abreast of the effects of environmental change.

IMPLICATIONS OF CLD FOR IS REQUIREMENT

The argument for CLD is based upon the belief that the successful understanding and definition of an information system may be constrained and misdirected by the practice of placing the technological development of the information system at the centre of the analysis and design process. What is offered instead is a holistic approach to the process of information systems design which places at its centre an understanding of the *information system*. At this level of appreciation (the development of which is described within Phase I) there is no need to concern oneself with the technical aspects of the definition. The understanding that is gained through acquiring an appreciation of organizational culture, the information required, how it is used, who it is used by, the form in which it is used, how is it processed, and who shares it will make a fundamental contribution to the satisfactory design and introduction of appropriate technologies. The answers to these questions need to be appreciated not from the ISA's perspective alone but by all those within the organization who are likely to be affected by the project. In this instance, those directly affected by the possibility of a technologically-based information system are referred to as clients rather than users or stakeholders.

The information systems definition is described in the form of an induction process in which a number of elements are drawn into the design as the problem/opportunity awareness of the clients and ISA increases. The problem is explored from several points of view, and, through discussions with the clients, the information systems are identified and appropriate technology is eventually considered. To aid those involved in the project to gain a wide perspective of the situation and at the same time maintain credibility, it is important that advantage is taken of the experience of all the employees involved. The client group should include members from management and staff who can contribute to the development of the information system—that is to say, those who have a vested interest in the finished design. There is little point in excluding staff who are opposed to the project since their views may help avoid future problems and their involvement might help to overcome their objections. The technical specification of hardware and software should begin only after Phases I and II have been satisfactorily undertaken, which means that there is a firm basis upon which to proceed. These two phases are important in helping all the clients to gain an appreciation of the problem, decide what their information system should look like and then define this requirement in such a way that it can be readily translated into a form from which technological support can be identified. Without a shared acceptance of *what* needs to be done, the *how* it is to be done is valueless.

Naturally the opportunity provided for staff to express opinions will, at first, produce a myriad of views and many of these may be at odds with each other. This may seem to complicate the information system's design process beyond what is required since what we are ultimately seeking is some formalized, clearly defined way of working. However, it is this process of unravelling the situation, eliciting opinions, identifying and agreeing the problems that exist which is the key to the whole information systems design activity. In many information systems design methodologies, the amount of time spent, first, in defining the problem and, second, in identifying the information system, is small compared to the time spent on the technical specification. Yet the production of the technical specification can only progress from an initial agreed understanding of the problem situation, and to ignore this fact seems to be short-sighted. The increasing use of sophisticated application generator tools, computer-assisted methods of IS systems design and the overall pressure upon consultants and upon IS design teams to show rapid results encourages a lack of attention to the activities in Phase I. This problem is exacerbated by the undue reliance upon the technically-oriented models that are often at the heart of these tools. The importance of the appreciation stage, fundamentally Phases I and II of CLD, is that these phases provide the foundation for the project. While the time spent on them might at first appear to be extravagant, in the longer term the investment is worth while and makes very little difference to the overall time spent on the project. This is particularly the case when 'maintenance' of faults is considered as part of the total time spent on the project.

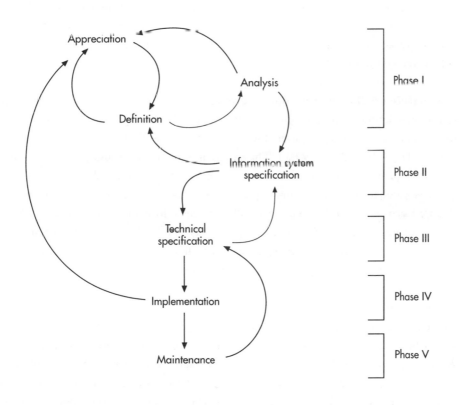

Figure 6.2   Diagram showing the activities involved in each phase of CLD (Stowell and West, 1994b)

It is worth repeating that CLD is not a methodology but a way of thinking about information systems definition. Here the emphasis is placed on (a) the early stages of appreciating the situation under investigation, (b) the complete involvement of those working in the situation and, (c) the role of the practitioner as a 'facilitator'. The process of learning and appreciation as described through CLD suggests a different set of activities in the process of information systems development from those carried out as part of a technology-based project, which most of the current design methods promote. The new emphasis and its relationship shown through the activities involved are illustrated in Figure 6.2.

CLD AND SOFT SYSTEMS

The expression of SSM ideal type 'mode 2' (Checkland and Scholes, 1990) is perhaps similar to the ideas embedded in CLD (Stowell and West, 1994a). The difference is that SSM is a methodology and CLD is statement of intent. CLD offers a platform for discussion between clients and analyst about information systems and about the technology that might be used to support information systems. The implementation of the policy of CLD involves the use of a variety of tools and methods appropriate to the task of information systems definition. CLD embraces a range of 'systemic' tools, diagrams and ideas that can be harnessed in order to help facilitate discussions about information system requirements.

The practice of CLD owes its roots to experience of the use of SSM, first as a method of problem definition and then in the exploration of SSM as a potentially useful method of information systems definition (Stowell, 1985; Stowell et al., 1990; Stowell and West, 1992, 1993, 1994a, 1994b). The experiences gained from using SSM in IS definition has provided some useful lessons, notably its strengths in aiding discussion and facilitating debate about problems/opportunities. Some difficulties have arisen when (a) the approach has been directed specifically towards information system definition and (b) the results, usually in the form of a conceptual model, have been translated into a technical specification of some kind, e.g. data flow diagram (Doyle–Wood, 1991; Probert, 1992) since SSM itself is not an information systems design methodology.

In addition to its many practical benefits SSM has also provided a stimulating debate about organizational inquiry (e.g. Jackson, 1993) and it was this kind of debate that provided the basis for a reconsideration of information systems definition (Stowell, 1991). The result of this was, first, to find a way of bringing the apparent problem of client dissatisfaction to the fore and, second, to try to find a practical means of addressing this problem. The result is client-led design, which is intended to support the use of systems-based ideas within the context of interpretivist systems and with respect to information systems. In the same sense that SSM mode 2 does not need the seven-stage methodology (Checkland and Scholes, 1990) neither does CLD need SSM as such. SSM might be useful as part of the process of appreciation in Phase I of CLD but so too might other systems ideas, e.g. system boundary. The important ingredient is the thinking behind the approach.

The key to CLD lies in the adoption of interpretivist systems thinking. The importance of Phase I in CLD has been stressed already but the appreciation that is gained is not limited to an appreciation of the problem situation but includes an understanding of the framework and thinking surrounding CLD. Once the paradigm has become absorbed into the analyst's thinking, then the framework can truly facilitate organizational inter- action within the phases. Each phase indicating which aspect of the process is being dealt with and its relationship with the remaining activities. Client-led design is an expression of a particular philosophy of information systems definition by which the clients are enabled to express their information system needs unfiltered by the need to satisfy organizational theory or technology.

REFERENCES

Avison, D. and Wood-Harper, A. T. (1986) 'Multiview—an exploration in informa- tion systems development', *Australian Computer Journal*, **18**, (4).

Avison, D. and Wood-Harper, A. T. (1990) *Multiview*, Blackwell, Oxford.

Burrell, G. and Morgan, G. (1979) *Sociological Paradigms and Organisational Analysis*, Heinemann, London.

Checkland, P. B. (1981) *Systems Thinking, Systems Practice*, Wiley, Chichester.

Checkland, P. B. and Scholes, J. (1990) *Soft Systems Methodology in Action*, Wiley, Chichester.

Dilthey, W. (1961) *Pattern and Meaning in History* (H. P. Rickman, ed.), Harper and Row, New York.

Doyle, K. and Wood, R. W. G. (1991) 'Systems thinking, systems practice: dangerous liaisons', *Systemist*, **13** (1), 28–30.

Forrester (1985) *The Information Technology Revolution*, Blackwell, Oxford.

Hirschheim, R. A. (1985) 'Information systems epistemology: a historical perspective', in *Research Methods in Information Systems* (E. Mumford, R. A. Hirschheim, F. Fitzgerald and A. T. Wood-Harper, eds), Elsevier, Amsterdam, 13–15.

Jackson, M. C. (1993) *Systems Methodology for the Management Sciences*, Plenum, New York.

Lewis, P. (1993) 'Linking soft systems methodology with data focussed information systems development', *Systemist*, **14** (3), 168–79.

MacIntyre, A. (1993) *After Virtue* (2nd edn), Duckworth, Guildford.

Methie, L. B. (1980) 'System requirements analysis-methods and models', in *The Information Systems Environment* (H. C. Liveas, F. F. Land, T. J. Lincoln and K. Supper, eds), *Proceedings of the IDIPTET 8.2, Working Conference on Information Systems Environment, Bonn, West Germany* 1979, North-Holland, Amsterdam, 173–85.

Miles, R. K. (1985) 'Computer systems analysis: the constraint of the hard systems paradigm', *Journal of Applied Systems Analysis*, **12**, 55–65.

Miles, R. K. (1992) 'A footnote to future expectations', *Systemist*, **14** (3), August.

Mingers, J. (1984) 'Subjectivism and soft systems methodology—a critique', *Journal of Applied Systems Analysis*, **11**, 85–103.

Mingers, J. (1990) 'The what/how distinction and conceptual models: a reappraisal', *Journal of Applied Systems Analysis*, **17**, 21–8.

Prior, R. (1990) 'Deriving data flow diagrams from "soft systems" conceptual models', *Systemist*, **12** (2), 65–75.

Probert, S. (1992) 'Soft systems methodology and the discipline of information systems', *Systemist*, **14** (4), 220–6.

Stowell, F. A. (1985) 'Experiences with SSM and data analysis', *Information Technology Training*, 48–50.

Stowell, F. A. (1990) 'Systems analysis and the design of information systems'. Paper presented at the *8th International Congress of Cybernetics and Systems*, City University, New York City, 116–19.

Stowell, F. A. (1991) 'Towards client-led development of information systems', *Journal of Applied Systems Analysis*, **1** (1), 173–89.

Stowell, F. A. (1993) 'Information Systems and Systems Science', in *Systems Science: Addressing Global Issues*, (F. A. Stowell, D. West, J. G. Howell, eds) Plenum, New York, 19–24.

Stowell, F. A. and West, D. (1992) 'SSM as a vehicle for client-led design of information systems utilizing ideal type "mode 2" ', *Systemist*, **14** (3), 99–106.

Stowell, F. A. and West, D. (1994a) 'Client-led design of information systems: an application of "ideal type" mode 2 soft systems methodology', *Information Systems Journal*.

Stowell, F. A. and West, D. (1994b) *Client-Led Design: A Systemic Approach to Information Systems Definition*, McGraw-Hill, Maidenhead.

Stowell, F. A., Prior, R., Holland, P. and Muller, P. (1990) 'Applications of SSM in information systems design: some reflections', *Journal of Applied Systems Analysis*, **17**, 63–9.

Vickers, G. (1983) *Human Systems are Different*, Harper Row, London.

West, D. (1991) 'Knowledge elicitation as an inquiring system: towards a "subjective" knowledge elicitation methodology', *Journal of Information Systems*, **2**, 31–44.

Wilson, B. (1984) *Systems: Concepts, Methodologies and Applications*, Wiley, Chichester.

Winograd, T. and Flores, F. (1986) *Understanding Computers and Cognition: A New Foundation for Design*, Ablex, Norwood, N.J.

Wood-Harper, A. T., Antill, L. and Avison, D. E. (1985) *Information Systems Definition: The Multiview Approach*, Blackwell, Oxford.

7

THE APPRECIATIVE INQUIRY METHOD: A SYSTEMIC APPROACH TO INFORMATION SYSTEMS REQUIREMENTS ANALYSIS

Daune West

Department of Computing and Information Systems, University of Paisley

INTRODUCTION

The purpose of this chapter is to describe the appreciative inquiry method (AIM) and illustrate its application by means of practical examples. AIM represents an attempt to provide information systems designers with a method of 'finding out' about a domain of interest that is capable of addressing some of the criticisms levelled at other 'fact-finding' processes. In particular, the method is being developed in a response to the need to be able to elicit and record the less structured, difficult-to-describe and 'tacit' aspects of any domain (those areas that are often embedded within someone's understanding of the context of the domain). With traditional methods of fact-finding and analysis (especially those which focus upon the flow of data within a domain early on in the analysis process), this type of contextual appreciation is lacking.

The intention with AIM, then, is to provide a comprehensive method of inquiry, using appropriate tools and techniques, to facilitate both information systems analyst and client(s) in the identification and definition of their problem domain, paying particular attention to the use of information within that domain. The method has been developed out of 'interpretive' systems thinking and draws upon the work of Vickers and Checkland for its intellectual basis and practical tools (West, 1992). In this chapter emphasis will be placed upon the method and process of inquiry rather than upon the subsequent phase of producing a specification for use in a computer-based information system. However, the link between problem appreciation and technical specification will be discussed at the end of the chapter.

BACKGROUND TO THE APPRECIATIVE INQUIRY METHOD

Work on AIM began as an attempt to alleviate some of the problems associated with current approaches to the process of eliciting human expertise when building knowledge-bases for computer-based expert systems. The 'traditional' knowledge elicitation (KE) methods used were those that had either come out of computer systems analysis (e.g. structured and unstructured interview) or had been 'borrowed' from other areas such as psychology and artificial intelligence (e.g. repertory grids, protocol analysis, induction). Researchers have attempted to make the choice of appropriate method less problematic by identifying knowledge 'categories' and assigning methods to each (e.g. Gammack and Young, 1985; Welbank, 1987; Cordingley, 1989). Classification of domain or problem 'type' also provided practitioners with another means of choosing the best elicitation tool (e.g. Breuker and Wielinga, 1987). This classificatory activity has resulted in a somewhat *ad hoc* approach to knowledge elicitation with the practitioner being armed with a 'toolbox' of useful approaches (see Neale, 1988, for a thorough description of KE techniques). Further complications in the process of 'finding out'—such as the problems associated with the less easily structured and definable domains, the difficulties associated with the roles of expert, user, and elicitor (e.g. bias, misunderstanding, resentment, lack of common language, fear, time constraints), not to mention the problems of using particular fact-finding techniques (e.g. imposition of a particular structure, avoiding leading questions, difficulty of application)—have resulted in the elicitation process being considered as the most difficult but crucial stage of knowledge-based system development.

The practical result of these difficulties of knowledge elicitation has been that the application of knowledge-based systems has been limited to those domains in which action and decision making is more or less determinable (i.e. domains characterized by a complex but logical path of reasoning). Areas in which decision making relies not only upon the 'facts' and 'rules' of such logic but also upon less easily reducible explanations of behaviour have been less successful as potential areas for the application of some computer-based decision support aid. The level of decision making applicable to this level of complexity is of a strategic nature or relies upon such difficult-to-quantify aspects as 'experience' and 'intuition'.

The difficulty of accessing this qualitative or subjective aspect of human expertise leads us to another problematic area of knowledge elicitation and 'fact-finding' in general. Many researchers and practitioners concerned with knowledge elicitation recognize that human expertise consists of more than just domain 'facts' and the 'rules' which govern the use of these 'facts': they refer also to the experiental, intuitive, heuristic and tacit nature of human expertise—in fact, all the qualities of decision making that go towards making others consider an individual to be outstanding in his or her field (e.g. Basden, 1983; Feigenbaum, 1984; Hart, 1985; LaFrance, 1987; d'Agapeyeff, 1988; Bell and Hardiman, 1989; Stowell and West, 1990). The result is that knowledge elicitation has been referred to as both a 'science' in terms of its precision and systematic attention to detail and as an 'art' on account of its need to address inexplicable, subjective elements. However, a close look at the methods that are used in KE shows that they are inappropriate to eliciting this 'subjectivity'. It would seem that KE is a good example of the point made by Winograd and Flores (1986, p. 17) about the influence of the 'rationalistic orientation' upon researchers and practitioners in computer science and psychology:

> In moments of careful reflection they [researchers] acknowledge the importance of phenomena that are not subject to the rationalistic style of analysis, but in their day-to-day work they proceed as though everything were. In generating theories and in building programs, they operate in a style that is fully consistent with the naive tradition and avoid areas in which it breaks down.

Some researchers have attempted to address this problem by introducing tools and techniques to elicit the more subjective aspects of domain expertise (Gregory, 1986; Johnson and Johnson, 1987; Bell and Hardiman, 1989). However, the result is not completely satisfactory since the demands of *practice* force their proposed approaches back into the nomothetic tradition of fact-finding approaches (West, 1990).

One argument to explain this is that the theoretical basis of any action needs to be firmly established in order to maintain consistency between the theory of that action and the practical application of tools and techniques emanating from that theory. Therefore, since most fact-finding techniques commonly used in knowledge elicitation or information systems requirements analysis have been developed out of the 'scientific' or 'rationalist' tradition (Winograd and Flores, 1986), it is unlikely that they can be adapted to fulfil a type of inquiry that has quite a different starting point in terms of philosophical orientation.

Throughout the development of AIM, care has been taken to try to ensure that its underlying theory and practical tools relate to a stated perspective about 'inquiry', namely, the mode of inquiry that can be described as characteristic of the ideas that Burrell and Morgan locate within the 'interpretive' paradigm (Burrell and Morgan, 1979). The method represents an attempt to operationalize Vickers' notion of appreciation and hence the overall process is concerned with learning, as opposed to extracting, the rules by which decisions are made within the domain. The difference between this approach and a functionalist approach is important: as opposed to seeking to *elicit* expertise, with AIM the primary focus is upon *learning* about the whole domain *out of which* may come the elicitation of information about decision making within the domain. This change in emphasis from 'elicitation' to 'learning' and 'appreciation' as a process prior to elicitation' is illustrated in Figure 7.1.

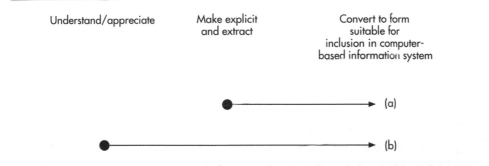

Figure 7.1 (a) Conventional elicitation (e.g. using structured interviews and (b) emphasis in the use of AIM upon learning and appreciation

Central to Vickers' work is the notion of a continual cycle of learning (by individual or group) as a result of being in the world and taking part in what Vickers (1965) refers to as the 'two-stranded rope; the history of events and the history of ideas'. The components of this learning cycle may be broken down into three main activities (Figure 7.2): perceiving, judging and acting (Checkland and Casar, 1986, p. 4).

This process, according to Vickers, is constrained by what he calls 'readinesses of the mind' to perceive. Such readinesses may be seen as the result of the previous history of the appreciative cycle and represent what Vickers described as the 'appreciative "setting"' (1965, p. 54). The description of decision making and action taking, as des-

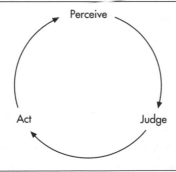

Figure 7.2 The appreciative process as a result of the cycle of perceiving, judging and acting

cribed by Vickers, is an internal and personal affair and as such encompasses the subjectivity and experiential aspects that we might assign to human expertise. Although Vickers was not concerned with locating his ideas within the history of social theory, it is not difficult to equate his work on appreciation to the arguments and propositions of phenomenology and hermeneutics and, of course, to the 'soft systems' movement.

While Vickers' work on 'appreciation' and the 'appreciative system' forms the basis of the theoretical foundation of AIM, soft systems methodology (SSM) provides many of the practical tools of the method. Checkland describes SSM as 'an inquiring system which orchestrates and articulates the process of appreciation' (Checkland and Casar, 1986, p. 10) and, therefore, its practical models (together with their interrelationship) which support this inquiring system provide a useful source of 'tools' for our fact-finding method. It is important to emphasize here that AIM is *not* intended to be a re-packaged SSM. Although AIM borrows systems models from SSM it does not share the same objectives; where SSM provides the process for bringing about change, AIM is intended solely as a means of finding out what is considered to be the case in a given situation. With AIM some change may be brought about, but this is more likely to involve a greater understanding of what was known/unknown rather than a radical rethinking of the situation. It seems unlikely, too, that any change in using AIM would be of an attitudinal nature. Any structural or procedural change that is brought about is likely to be in terms of the way in which individuals *view* the processes in the domain and restructure their ways of *thinking* about their activities when formalizing their understanding.

THE APPRECIATIVE INQUIRY METHOD
OVERVIEW

As a way of explaining AIM it is useful to break down the method into three phases, which correspond to the three different activities undertaken by the 'client'. The first phase involves the client producing a systems map. In the second phase the various map elements are translated into carefully described 'activities'. Each description will be of some purposeful activity which is identified by considering the transformation brought about by the corresponding map element. To achieve this movement from map element to system description, the analyst seeks answers to questions which are developed out of the 'CATWOE' elements of SSM. Having described the activity through CATWOE, the analyst uses this information to develop a careful description of the 'system' identified, resulting in a root definition. The analyst then develops a conceptual model from the root definition. The third phase involves the analyst returning to the client to 'check' the validity of the conceptual model in representing the client's view of the domain and to further the learning process by using the model as an agenda for dis-

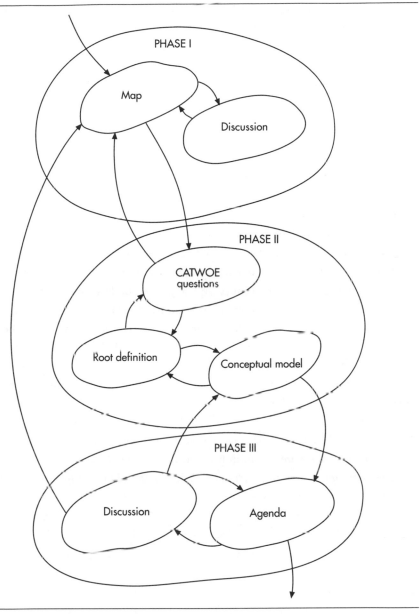

Figure 7.3 Overview of the different phases of AIM and their interrelationship

cussing the domain. However, the result of checking the model may involve a reiter-
ation of the process to either correct an imperfect interpretation on the part of the analyst or to re-explore the client's own understanding. In addition to iteration of the
method it is important that any of the phases may be used at any time. For example, it
may be appropriate to pass through several levels of resolution at the systems map stage

before embarking upon the CATWOE questions. Figure 7.3 gives an overview of AIM, illustrating the different activities involved and the relationship between each phase of the method.

The remainder of this section deals with each phase of the method in detail and gives practical examples as a means of illustration.

PHASE I: THE SYSTEMS MAP

In the first phase of AIM, the client draws a picture of his or her understanding of the domain of interest. The tool used to help to achieve this is the systems map, a diagrammatic representation based on the Venn diagram convention, which is illustrated in Figure 7.4. The map consists of a central 'bubble' (x) in which is written a concise statement of the domain of interest. For example, the area of concern might be 'Reason for management training' (West, 1991). The wording of this initial statement should be carefully considered in order to avoid making the boundary of investigation too tight. However, as the process continues and a greater understanding of the domain is reached, it may be necessary to rephrase this initial statement and, thereby, redefine the area of interest. Having agreed the central statement as a starting point the client is shown how the map can be built up by adding further 'bubbles' (y) around the central element. These bubbles represent elements or aspects of the situation that are relevant to the central statement. Influencing factors can be included by adding a second row of bubbles (z).

Although when explaining the map convention to clients no instructions other than those described above are given, in practice clients have developed their own conventions as a way of representing their view of the domain. For example, the 'bubbles' may

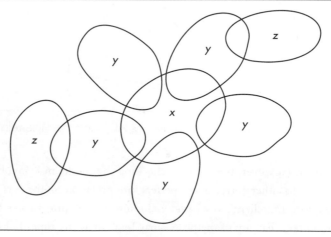

Figure 7.4   The convention of the systems map

be ordered in sequence of the client's view of their importance to the domain or may
be clustered to illustrate distinct groups; they may be overlapped to show influence or
even conflict; different coloured pens may be used to signify group responsibilities, or
even to represent a three-dimensional view of the situation (West, 1991). In Figure 7.5
a client's map is reproduced as a practical illustration of its use.

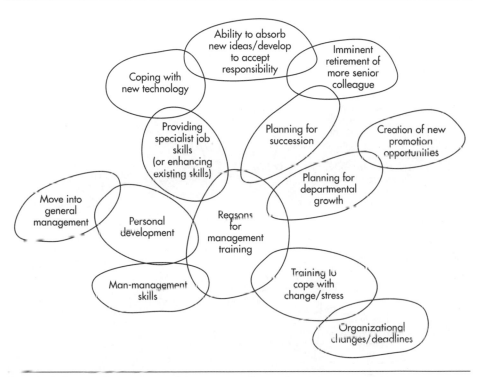

Figure 7.5   A client's map of the reasons for management training

A significant advantage of the systems map is its simplicity. It takes only a few minutes
to demonstrate and explain its use and a surprisingly detailed map can be produced by
a client in about 20 minutes. Apart from describing the way in which the map works,
the analyst plays a minimal role in this phase. When the map has been produced by the
client, it is used as a discussion document between client and analyst. The aim at this
stage is for the client to 'teach' the analyst about the domain by describing the map elements while also checking for any repetitions or similarities that might merit the merging of elements. At this stage it is useful to identify any jargon and, perhaps more
importantly, to check that the 'bubbles' represent activities at roughly the same level of
resolution. If this is not the case then it may be necessary to either cluster the more

detailed elements under another heading or redraw the map so that all elements are considered at the same level of detail. In addition to the analyst being taught about the domain, there is an opportunity for the client to learn about his or her own perception and understanding of the domain. It is likely that in discussing the map the client may amend the first attempt by adding elements previously omitted. Even at this early stage

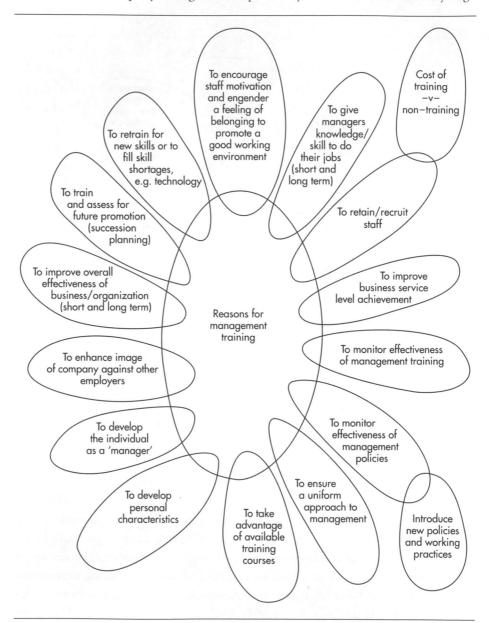

Figure 7.6   The composite map developed out of 10 clients' view of the reasons for management training

it may be necessary to reconsider the boundary of the domain as proposed at the out-set of the study, and even re-name the central element to represent this change in direction.

Experience has shown that the systems map appears to offer the client a relatively quick and simple means of expressing and requesting his or her view of a given domain in a form that can be communicated to others readily. The ease with which the map can be developed is particularly valuable at the start of any project in that it is unlikely to incommode the client by the length of time it takes to produce or by its complexity. It also has useful in-built mechanisms for limiting the amount of detail that can be included owing to the number of elements that can be crowded around the central element. This somewhat unsophisticated means of limiting the detail included in this first session helps to encourage a 'birds-eye view', or panorama, of the domain—exactly what is required when trying to establish the boundary of the domain and its relevant components.

The systems map has also been used as a method of gathering and sharing ideas between a number of clients. In this situation each client produces a map which are then collected and used to produce a 'composite map' that should include all the different elements named, and, where appropriate, group similar or related elements under one heading (see Figure 7.6).

This composite map may be taken back to the individual clients and used to help widen their thinking about the domain. Alternatively it can be used as a discussion document in a group meeting. A potential problem for the analyst in this latter scenario is the need to prevent any individual imposing his or her view on the group (e.g. through the authority of a senior position within the organization, or through forcefulness of character). As shown in Figure 7.7, discussion with the client(s) may enable large composite maps to be subdivided into smaller maps to make them easier to discuss as well as helping to identify any useful groupings or 'themes'.

Summary of aims of Phase I
The aims of using the systems map as a practical way of beginning the appreciation and elicitation process are as follows:

(1) to avoid focusing on any particular aspect of the problem situation too soon (i.e. getting 'bogged down' in detail), and, instead, encouraging a wide view of the problem domain
(2) to allow the clients to express their view of the domain without interference from the analyst

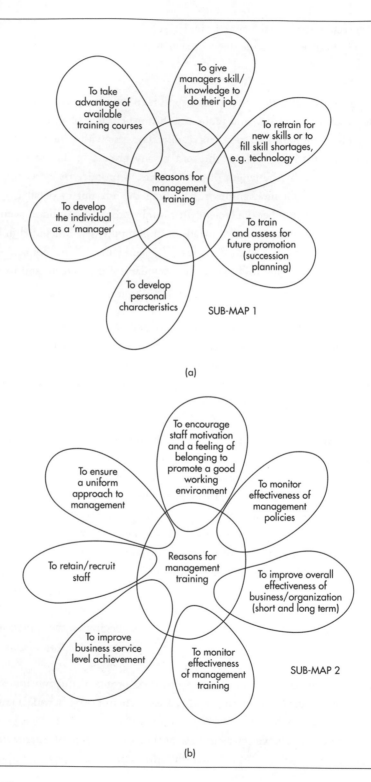

To take
advantage of
available
training courses

To give
managers skill/
knowledge to
do their job

To retrain for
new skills or to
fill skill shortages,
e.g. technology

Reasons for
management
training

To develop
the individual
as a 'manager'

To train
and assess for
future promotion
(succession
planning)

To develop
personal
characteristics

SUB-MAP 1

(a)

To encourage
staff motivation
and a feeling of
belonging to
promote a good
working
environment

To ensure
a uniform
approach to
management

To monitor
effectiveness of
management
policies

To retain/recruit
staff

Reasons for
management
training

To improve overall
effectiveness of
business/organization
(short and long term)

To improve
business service
level achievement

To monitor
effectiveness
of management
training

SUB-MAP 2

(b)

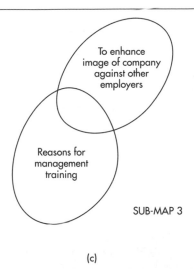

SUB-MAP 3

(c)

Figure 7.7   A client's break-down of the composite map into three sub-maps

(3) to support the clients by offering a framework that allows the expression and rep-resentation of this view without imposing a rigid framework upon the thought processes

(4) to avoid, as far as possible, the considerations of any future technological applica-tion influencing the fact-finding process

(5) to provide a task which is quick and simple so as to (a) reduce a client's potential concern at facing a difficult process and (b) to help establish rapport between client and analyst

(6) to enable the analyst to break the problem domain into 'subsystems' for further dis-cussion and investigation.

PHASE II: DESCRIBING THE MAP ELEMENTS AS PURPOSEFUL ACTIVITY

The second phase of AIM focuses upon the process of translating the map elements into descriptions of purposeful activity. The rationale behind this is that in redefining each map element as an activity we can then model the logical components of the activity and use this model as a way of asking further questions about the domain. This approach has been shown to be particularly useful in areas that involve the more 'con-ceptual' and difficult to verbalize area of a domain (e.g. when discussing the importance of an organization's 'image' to its employees and customers).

In Phase II the method adopts 'tools' from SSM in order to bring about this translation of map element into a description of some purposeful activity. The client is asked to describe each map element in relation to questions, posed by the analyst, that are derived from the so-called CATWOE 'test' of SSM. The most important requirement of this phase is for the analyst to establish the 'transformation' (T) that the map element represents. Experience has shown that the client's first attempts at identifying the 'T' can be difficult, but confidence and an understanding of what is required comes with practice. It is useful if the analyst facilitates this specification process by recording the client's comments so that the client can review what he or she has said. Diagrams and quick sketches can also be valuable as they can offer a visual explanation of the nature of the question being asked. For example, when asking the client to describe what the process involved in the element is, it is useful to use an input–output diagram, along the lines of:

Such a diagram has proved a useful way of eliciting the inputs and outputs of the process and this, in turn, helps in the naming of the transformation process involved.

Once the 'T' has been identified then the other CATWOE components can be sought by the analyst asking such questions as:

- Given the problem you have identified here, who would you say the process affects (either for good or for bad)? (C)
- Who are involved in carrying out this process? (A)
- Who is in charge, or responsible for the overall process? Who could stop it? (O)
- What constraints do you think there are on this activity being carried out? (E)

The worldview (W), or perspective, from which the transformation is meaningful can be supplied in one of several ways. For example, it may be elicited by such a question as:

- Why is *this* activity, important? Why does it need to be done in this way?

Alternatively, it may be elicited in conversation between the analyst and client, or even supplied by the analyst as a result of their joint interpretation of the situation. An argument for this latter approach is that naming the 'W' is a useful way of 'testing' the analyst's interpretation of what the client has explained.

Smyth and Checkland (1976) developed the notion of CATWOE as a way of testing a root definition for completeness, but in AIM it is used to ensure that enough information is provided in order to develop a description of some purposeful activity (Checkland and Scholes, 1990, pp. 23–27). By using CATWOE in this way the analyst is able to explore the activity implicit in the map element without asking context-dependent questions. The questions used are designed to supply the information necessary to describe any purposeful human activity and neither presuppose a given answer nor depend upon the analyst's understanding of the domain.

Once the CATWOE questions have been answered, the analyst may use these answers to construct a root definition that relates to the map element. The following is a root definition derived from the client's description of sub-map 1 in Figure 7.7:

> *A management-owned system to train unit head managers to address the needs of the business and the company while maintaining good day-to-day customer service.*

It is especially useful that this process of developing the root definition may be undertaken away from the domain and client since it alleviates the pressures upon both parties and also means that a relatively short amount of time is needed for the participation of the client—a factor that is easily overlooked in planning a project, but is useful in practice. Furthermore, used in this way the client is not required to have any understanding of the construction of a root definition or of the origins and theoretical underpinnings of SSM. The next step of converting the activity descriptions (root definitions) into activity models is also undertaken by the analyst away from the domain, using the convention of the conceptual model of SSM. The aim at this stage is to identify the activities and the relationship between activities that are necessary to enact the purposeful activity described in the root definition. Figure 7.8 shows the conceptual model that was developed out of the root definition presented above. The conceptual model is then used as the basis of a more focused discussion about the domain between client and analyst at the next meeting (Phase III). The focusing-in on the domain is achieved by the fact that the questions arising from the conceptual model are context-dependent upon the activity modelled and so provide a valuable process of moving from modelling the client's view without imposing any structure other than the notion of it being possible (and useful) to describe purposeful human activity systemically. The origins of the conceptual model can be traced back directly to the client's own description of the domain and, although produced by the analyst, it offers a valuable way of allowing the analyst to 'teachback' the interpretation of what has been said by the client.

Summary of aims of Phase II

The aims of using the CATWOE–root definition–conceptual model stages of SSM to help specify the elements of the map produced by the client at Phase I are as follows:

(1) To enable the appreciation and elicitation process to focus upon the activities identified in the map and thereby encourage the analyst to acquire as full an understanding of these activities as possible.

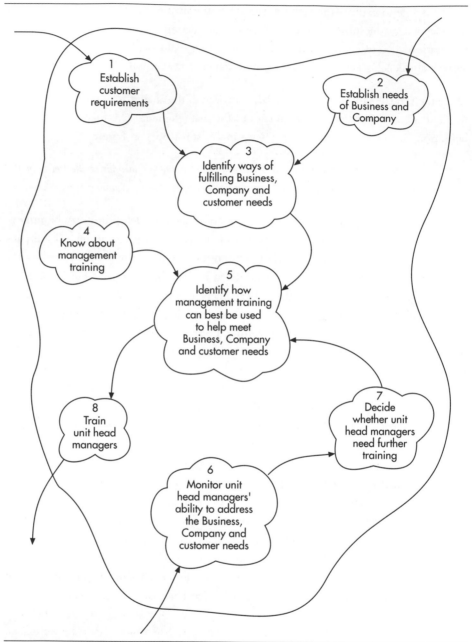

Figure 7.8   An example of the operational activities of a conceptual model
developed out of the root definition on p. 153

(2) To provide a means of structuring the activities of each element of the map so that
their relationships to each other can be inspected (and potentially the relationships
between different elements of the map).

Activity number	Description	Present in real world?	Comments
1.	Establish customer requirements		
2.	Establish needs of Business and Company		
3.	Identify needs of fulfilling Business, Company and customer needs		
4.	Know about management training		
5.	Identify how management training can best be used to help meet Business, Company and customer needs		
6.	Monitor Unit Head's ability to address Business, Company and customer needs		

Figure 7.9   An example agenda for discussion based upon the conceptual model in Figure 7.8

(3) To achieve (1) and (2) above in such a way as to alleviate (as far as possible) the potential influence of a future technological application in the domain affecting the appreciation and elicitation process.

(4) To make explicit the perspective of the client so as to enable the analyst to understand the foundations of his or her thoughts about the domain (and hence offer a way of enabling the client to reflect upon his or her own thinking).

(5) To provide a means of investigating the more subjective elements of human expertise.

(6) To model the client's descriptions of the domain in a context-independent way but which eventually enables context-dependent questions to be asked about the domain.

PHASE III

In Phase III the analyst returns to the client with the conceptual model which is used as discussion documents. It has proved useful for the analyst to draw up an agenda for discussion which is based upon the conceptual model, and use this to direct questions about the domain (West, 1991). Figure 7.9 illustrates an example agenda. As the domain 'unfolds' it is possible to start linking the conceptual models together to provide a wider view. Even at this stage new areas may need to be explored and the appropriate phase of the method should be used to facilitate this.

Summary of the aims of Phase III

The aims of Phase III centre around the wish to continue the logical modelling of the client's description of the domain and to use these models as a way of helping the client to reflect upon his or her views, approaches and opinions, as well as furthering debate between client and analyst.

THE APPRECIATIVE INQUIRY METHOD, INFORMATION SYSTEMS REQUIREMENTS ANALYSIS AND CURRENT WORK

As it continues to be developed AIM has shown itself to be a powerful method of inquiry, with the added benefit that it results in a well-documented process of exploration and appreciation which is logically defensible and can be 'validated' by the client. However, the rich context that can be elicited using the method provides us with other problems if we are to use the method as a practical way of establishing information systems requirements prior to the development of some computer-based information system. Because of the difficulty of moving from the information collected when using AIM to the use of this information in some computer-based information system, the method is currently being translated into a computer software package written in Supercard for use on an Apple Macintosh (West *et al.*, 1994). The exercise is offering not only a potential computer-based 'front-end' package for use in the development of computer-based decision support aids and knowledge-based systems, but is also offering new ways of looking at AIM itself. For example, it seems possible that the Supercard package may enable the analyst to make greater use of pictures and graphic representations as a way of carrying out the process, such as when establishing the components of the purposeful activity in Phase II using the 'CATWOE questions'. One way of achieving this may be to use a development of Checkland and Scholes's pictorial representation of purposeful activity (Checkland and Scholes, 1990, p. 6) as a way of presenting the idea of some activity with the package prompting for appropriate parts of the picture to be supplied, or named, by the client. An important benefit of Supercard (hypertext software) is that it allows the input of text, or graphics, by the client which can then be manipulated and exported to any other part of the program (or method). This offers a useful way of moving 'ideas' between the phases of AIM as well as providing a potentially dynamic inquiring process.

Current use of AIM is highlighting future application areas and, in particular, is drawing attention to a potentially different approach to the use of the computer as a decision support aid. First, it offers a structured way of widening different participants' appreciation of a problem situation, and thereby offers the potential for more informed decision making. Second, it may offer a way of searching through collected material (held in different media such as text, pictures, sound, video, and animated sequences) in hypermedia decision-support systems, illustrating the contextual setting of any information and, therefore, prompting an awareness of the implications of the results of any decision making.

REFERENCES

Basden, A. (1983) 'On the application of expert systems', *International Journal of Man–Machine Studies*, **19**, 461–77.

Bell, J. and Hardiman, R. J. (1989) 'The third role – the naturalistic knowledge engineer', in *Knowledge Elicitation: Principles, Techniques and Applications* (D. Diaper, ed.), Horwood, Chichester, 49–85.

Breuker, J. and Wielinga, B. (1987) 'Knowledge acquisition as modelling expertise: the KADS methodology', in *Proceedings of the First European Workshop on Knowledge Acquisition for Knowledge-Based Systems*, Reading University Press, Reading. Section B1.

Burrell, G. and Morgan, G. (1979) *Sociological Paradigms and Organisational Analysis*, Gower, Aldershot.

Checkland, P. B. and Casar, A. (1986) 'Vickers' concept of an appreciative system: a systemic account', *Journal of Applied Systems Analysis*, **13**, 3–17.

Checkland, P. B. and Scholes, J. (1990) *Soft Systems Methodology in Action*, Wiley, Chichester.

Cordingley, E. S. (1989) 'Knowledge elicitation techniques for knowledge-based systems', in *Knowledge Elicitation: Principles, Techniques and Applications* (D. Diaper, ed.), Horwood, Chichester, 89–175.

d'Agapeyeff, A. (1988) 'The nature of expertise and its elicitation for business expert systems: a commentary', *The Knowledge Engineering Review*, **3** (2), 147–58.

Feigenbaum, E. A. (1984) 'Knowledge engineering: the applied side', in *Intelligent Systems: The Unprecedented Opportunity* (J. E. Hayes and D. Michie, eds), Edinburgh University Press, Edinburgh, 37–55.

Gammack, J. G. and Young, R. M. (1985) 'Psychological techniques for eliciting expert knowledge', in *Research and Development in Expert Systems* (M. Bramer, ed.), Cambridge University Press, Cambridge, 105–12.

Gregory, D. (1986) 'Delimiting expert systems', *IEEE Transactions on Systems, Man and Cybernetics*, SCM-16, Nov./Dec., 834–43.

Hart, A. (1985) 'Knowledge elicitation: issues and methods', *Computer-Aided Design*, **17** (9), 455–62.

Johnson, L. and Johnson, N. E. (1987) 'Knowledge elicitation involving teachback interviewing', in *Knowledge Acquisition for Expert Systems: A Practical Handbook* (A. L. Kidd, ed.), Plenum, New York, 91–108.

LaFrance, M. (1987) 'The knowledge acquisition grid: a method for training knowledge engineers', *International Journal of Man-Machine Studies*, **26,** 245–55.

Neale, I. M. (1988) 'First generation expert systems: a review of knowledge acquisition methodologies', *The Knowledge Engineering Review*, **3** (2), 105–45.

Smyth, D. S. and Checkland, P. B. (1976) 'Using a systems approach: the structure of root definitions', *Journal of Applied Systems Analysis*, **5** (1), 75–83.

Stowell, F. A. and West, D. (1990) 'The contribution of systems ideas during the process of knowledge elicitation', in *Systems Prospects: The Next Ten Years of Systems Research* (R. L. Flood, M. C. Jackson and P. Keys, eds), Plenum Press, New York, 329–34.

Vickers, G. (1965) *The Art of Judgement: A Study of Policy Making*, Chapman and Hall, London.

Welbank, M. (1987) 'Knowledge acquisition: a survey and British Telecom experience', in *Proceedings of the First European Workshop on Knowledge Acquisition for Knowledge-Based Systems*, Reading University Press, Reading, Section C6.

West, D. (1990) ' "Appreciation", "expertise" and knowledge elicitation: the relevance of Vickers' ideas to the design of expert systems', *Journal of Applied Systems Analysis*, **17**, 71–8.

West, D. (1991) 'Towards a subjective knowledge elicitation methodology for the development of expert systems', PhD Thesis, Portsmouth Polytechnic (unpublished).

West, D. (1992) 'Knowledge elicitation as an inquiring system: towards a "subjective" knowledge elicitation methodology', *Journal of Information Systems*, **2**, 31–44.

West, D., Stansfield, M. H. and Stowell, F. A. (1994) 'Using computer-based technology to support a subjective method of inquiry', *Systems Practice*, **7** (2) 183–204.

Winograd, T. and Flores, F. (1986) *Understanding Computers and Cognition: A New Foundation for Design*, Ablex, Norwood, N.J.

8

MODELLING SUBJECTIVE REQUIREMENTS OBJECTIVELY

John Gammack

Department of Computing and Information Systems, University of Paisley

INTRODUCTION

This chapter describes an approach to constructively modelling users' requirements, and computing with the implications of particular models to support querying and decision making in current contexts. The approach attempts to reconcile the 'hard' computing that is possible from objectivized databases representing an organization's business, or other historically recorded evidence, with the 'soft' or subjective interpretations, judgements, theoretical constructions and appreciation of local situations which characterize human activity systems.

The first part of the chapter outlines some of the thinking behind this kind of system and links it to some concepts of information systems design and object orientation. The remainder of the chapter illustrates the reconciliation of subjective and objective aspects through detailing a prototype demonstrator designed and implemented in an object-oriented language providing examples of the modelling environment in use. We begin, however, with some background, identifying some of the dimensions along which IS provision can be categorized, the nature of these dimensions, and the possibility of unifying some of the analytic opposites which characterize information systems debates.

SUBJECTIVITY AND OBJECTIVITY IN INFORMATION SYSTEMS DESIGN

A schism, or at least a tension, is apparent in much of the literature on information systems, which seems symptomatic of a deeper malaise. This schism may be characterized as dividing 'hard' and 'soft' systems approaches (Checkland, 1981), and variously emphasizing interpretivism vs functionalism (see Burrell and Morgan, 1979), distinguishing 'rationalistic' vs 'hermeneutic' viewpoints (elaborated by Winograd and Flores, 1986) and adopting (philosophical) realism vs idealism, explained in an IS relevant manner by D. Gregory (1987). In another milieu, Pirsig (1976) gives a profound treatment of the related distinction between romantic and classic views, which can lead to symptoms such as technophobia or deeply felt anti-emotionalism. The distinctions have a certain family resemblance, if not an actual identity, and in their characteristic bipolar form represent dissociated extremes which sometimes reflect philosophically fundamental incompatibilities. Although these distinctions may be used as analytic conveniences for structuring discussion, such epistemological and ontological differences, recognized or not, underlie any approach to IS provision, and frame its meaningful context.

In this chapter a key dimension is characterized as lying between 'subjective' and 'objective', and is intended to capture both the softer, judgemental and interpretational aspects of meaning assignment which is sometimes held to differentiate information from data in human activity systems, and the harder, 'factual' data which is more amenable to unproblematic coding and acceptance. Without any commitment to humanist or species-chauvinistic values, the phrasing of this distinction adopts the vocabulary of the human-centred 'school' traditionally strong in Europe and described in Gill (1991a, 1991b). In our approach to IS provision there is an ontological continuum between the extremes, and the formal representations in the technical system of IS are uniform in kind: a point to which I shall return towards the end of the chapter.

Within the literature on IS provision, certain distinctions serve to reify some contemporary bias, and can become dated or normalized into standard philosophical dilemmas. In this chapter we take the position that distinctions are arbitrary analytic conveniences, making oppositions from some unbroughtforth, but shared context, and if not serving a corrective or explanatory function, often produce essentially futile dispute among partisans. Proponents of one approach rather than another may find their own comfortable position on one or other side of an opposition; they may utilize a rhetoric or vocabulary to which they are partial, and perhaps human knowledge increases concerning the contingencies and circumstances in which particular approaches may be favoured. It would be easy to lapse into a form of 'neat vs scruffy' stereotyping (as happened in the AI community) to reflect the varying emphases on formalism required by the traditional computing scientists, and on less tangible, social and cognitive processes dear to the socially oriented investigators. Both have qualities from which the other can learn and grow, and promoting a dialogue is surely helpful. But dialogue is one thing and unity is another. While there are numerous approaches to IS provision, to avoid bias and incompleteness, there remains a need for theoretical integration through some overarching conciliatory framework. But is such an integration possible?

Notwithstanding philosophical 'theories of everything', in the IS world (where the proof of thinking is generally constrained by a requirement to be applied in physically located practice) there are to date few explicit attempts to reconcile the ontologies that different systems approaches span. Indeed, if such reconciliation was shown to be *in principle* impossible, as soon as we all recognized this (and why) we could give up and go home. Pessimists and logicians may argue that when fundamental ontologies conflict, a hard/soft consistency is out of the question: optimists and synthesists may keep trying anyway, and succeed or die in the attempt, and unbiased and non–naive realists may find another way altogether. The situation is compounded when the agendas differ: if one IS practitioner is primarily interested in thinking about shifting the perspective from 'what is' to 'what might be', feasible or not in physical practice, and another is labouring under the assumption that something is to be done to 'what is', through applying a method that gets results regardless of 'what might be', a meeting of minds may be a distant hope (especially when the one seems resigned to an unending learning cycle, and the other believes in a terminating teleological purpose!).

Against this background, there remain to date few attempts to deal practically with the ambiguity of stance implied and the possibility of information systems provision which avoids some partisan commitment. Later in this chapter, I detail the approach I have taken, which admits both that information systems involve human activity, and that objectivity would be a fine thing, but first I briefly indicate some of the approaches currently being taken in IS development to reconciliation.

From the earlier days of systems thinking, when a unified science was dreamed of, there have been detectable shifts towards pluralism, complementarity and contingency in systems practice often bound up with an appropriate pragmatism concerning effective interventions by judicious methodological choice (see Jackson and Keys, 1984, Oliga 1988). While the principles of systems thinking may offer guidance in the selection of appropriate methodologies and methods, this is different from reconciling analytically conflicting ontological assumptions within a single methodology, and some would contend that this is logically impossible

Nonetheless, perhaps the single methodology most committed to reconciliation of ontologies in IS is Keith Sawyer's OPIUM (Organizational Performance Improvement and Understanding Methodology). In OPIUM, there is a commitment to going from the soft interpretive, judgemental, subjective stages to the hard specific goals and defined activities required in implementing a strategy. In traditional terminology, the methodology embraces functionalist values and methods, while at the same time recognizing and honouring the multiple views and interpretations of stakeholders in the organization (Sawyer, 1990). Having been used to date in over 200 organizations, and now with a suite of supporting and integrated software models, OPIUM is finding favour in the marketplace (Sawyer, 1993, personal communication).

OPIUM, from the start, was designed in recognition of the hard/soft schism, and although there are several methodologies that are participative, or include elements of both extremes, these still tend to polarize towards the softer conceptual analysis side or the more technically exacting design aspect. An obvious strategy would seem to involve the use of an interpretive methodology for the conceptual part, then a functionalist one for the design part, but would this be ontologically consistent? For some time there has been a significant debate on the linking of SSM to detailed IS design, and the possibility of this is critical to an effective reconciliation between hard and soft. Stowell (1985) was one of the first to recognize the value to organizations in going from a soft systems analysis to the requirements of a hard, data-oriented system through involvement of the users in design. He also noted that instead of the analyst imposing a particular technology, through SSM modelling activity coupled with a structured system design technique (in particular DFDs) the technical specification could follow on, using the model as reference. However, the detailed linking between SSM and detailed design of computerized systems has not yet been achieved (Checkland and Scholes, 1990).

The particular aspect of current interest concerns the relation of SSM towards technically specific constructs (such as DFDs) which can be handed over to a programmer, and various authors, notably Miles (1988), have made contributions which focus on a distinction between *grafting* and *embedding*. The proponents of embedding would suggest that SSM can contain the tools and techniques of other methodologies to realize the design and implementation stages that follow analysis, whereas the alternative view would suggest that SSM is a front end analysis technique which then gives way to some other methodology to realize the hard system. If this was to prevail, there would be the prospect of an ontological clash: the dangerous liaisons of Wood and Doyle (1991).

The debate continues, and may resolve itself practically through effective exemplars of embedding (or grafting!), and may theoretically transmute into some standard philosophical issue, or a more general paradox of theory vs practice. As the saying goes: 'There is no difference between theory and practice in theory, but there is all the difference in practice.'

Another angle on the issue of hard vs soft comes from Beeby (1993) who takes the view that although the different approaches to systems may be incommensurable, that does not stop effective information provision—a position elaborated in Crowe *et al.* (forthcoming). This has numerous precedents in other domains of intellectual inquiry, such as biology (see Beeby 1993; Kampis, 1991), and in the fractionation of psychology (Watts, 1992), which has been undergoing a paradigm crisis between (for instance) natural-science and hermeneutic approaches for some time. Anderson (1987), manoeuvring in apparent reaction to the threatening growth of neural networks as a challenger paradigm to the high-level symbolic information processing orthodoxy, positioned the two contenders as having dominion at different levels, each with their own proper domain of inquiry, a detente which allows established cognitive science to carry on in familiar terms. Systems wisdom tells us that properties at emergent levels are meaningless or unrecognizable at lower ones, and if behaviour at an algorithmic level is incommensurable with that at an implementational one, it may be practically possible to conduct an analysis on one level, then switch to a theoretically incompatible ontology for the implementation, without encountering any real problem. This was my experience in a number of expert system developments for which I did the knowledge elicitation. Theoretically I believed the purist view that knowledge acquisition was impossible (cf. Winograd and Flores, 1986, pp. 98–9). But practically I just went out and did it! What's more—it worked, just as many practitioners could have told me it would. I had no illusions that what I had elicited was knowledge: it certainly was not, but severing my clean ideal from hands-dirty practice allowed me to have my cake and eat it. This stance attunes with Probert's (1992) contribution to the debate on linking SSM and IS design: use aspects of SSM along new methodological lines, and accept that was is being done is not SSM *per se*. Both the 'meaning assignment' and the 'evidenced data' aspects apply, but to different aspects of the same thing, and the point here is that information provision needs must contain both aspects.

Apart from the above 'head-on' approaches to integrating interpretive aspects with hard technologies, and explicitly participative approaches such as ETHICS (Mumford and Weir, 1979), a number of other approaches to IS provision aim to reconcile the two. However, perhaps stemming from an unredeemed positivism, while they do acknowledge the importance of the user's views and his or her interpretation in systems development, they deny the effective dynamism of this interpretation by seeking to reduce the user to a few parameters, objectivized and static, and often ignore the user after the very early stages of analysis. Such lip service merely adds complexity and the germs of obsolescence, resistance and irrelevance to an information system development. What is required is some dynamic way in which the user's world and interpretations can be made an active part of ongoing IS design and use. One possible approach to this is detailed below under 'The IDIOMS approach'.

The above review has picked up some trends from the IS development literature. From another, more software-oriented computing science camp, the white knight of object orientation comes pricking on the plain. Superficially at least, some of its incarnations have an affinity with the models and definitions of SSM and exploring these linkages may be fruitful.

Object orientation is a philosophy of computing which offers several simple but powerful concepts which show promise for computer-based IS developments, and although the technological concepts have been 'pushed' for some time now, a user pull is beginning to emerge. Various object-oriented versions of the language C, such as Borland's and Microsoft's C++ have become increasingly popular, and in the UK a user-based pressure group has been formed to assess the use of object orientation as a mainstream IT development approach. In a recent survey of 150 users more than 60 per cent were planning to invest in object technology (*Computing* 10/12/92), with most experienced users giving reasons such as reduction of development time and maintenance costs. However the uptake of object-oriented methods is laced with an eclectic pragmatism: as consultant Chris Wallace pointed out recently (quoted in Peltu, 1993) 'object technologists are (accepting) the need to live with other ideas and techniques (and can) coexist'. Wallace also notes that while learners of a technology are more comfortable following a well-defined process, experienced designers prefer to improvise solutions guided by their instinctive judgements.

Although object orientation involves a number of refined and optional ideas which distinguish its various flavours, there are a few basic ones which these approaches usually share. In the next section I wish to outline the key concepts of the object-oriented philosophy that were adopted, purely on the grounds of their practical utility, in the system I describe later.

KEY CONCEPTS OF THE OBJECT-ORIENTED APPROACH

A basic feature of the object-oriented approach is *encapsulation*—namely, the idea that data and the operations performed on it are combined together (encapsulated) into *objects*. This encapsulation is supported by *information hiding*, so that it serves to control the way in which data is accessed and used. The object defines a visible interface which declares to the client objects that use it what operations on the hidden data are recognized. This computational structure has affinities with the pragmatic and utilitarian imperative of most information systems, in that the data often exists only in a purposive context, its interpretation is governed by quite strict semantics, and in the phenomenal world of linguistic changes, its meaning (a point from Wittgenstein) is given by its use.

A related property of object-oriented systems is messaging, which is used in communication between objects. Objects send and receive messages. A message may contain data, or be a request to perform an action. An object can receive a message and act upon it, with different objects capable of acting differently to the same message as the details of the action to be performed are encapsulated in the receiving object. The messaging concept has supported widespread reusability in hardware where standards have been developed for interconnecting components, allowing loose coupling between them, and therefore reuse (Ledbetter and Cox, 1985). This has not been the case with software even with 'standard' utility libraries, and software reusability has been a massive problem for the industry. Ledbetter and Cox (1985) observe that hardware reuse benefits from the fact that standard functions are easy to identify owing to their close mapping into the real-world model of hardware systems, and if software reusability is to become a reality languages must support a more direct mapping from the model of the real world functions to the implementation.

This, however, makes assumptions and begs questions about what a model of the real-world function is, and its correspondence to the operational information system. SSM emphasizes the development of a conceptual model as a key stage of analysis. However, as Gregory (1993) points out, there is no guarantee that the conceptual model will correspond to anything that can actually exist in the physical world, and although SSM practitioners are often more interested in changing persons' perspectives than in affecting the physical world, it remains the case that SSM is insufficient for IS developments where such a correspondence is required. Gregory suggests a solution to this, which involves, first, ensuring that the terms of the model refer to objects or events in the world, and that the relations between those should have the same logical form as pertain in the world. He extends SS models to include connectives representing relations of sufficiency, and this produces an exhaustive logico-linguistic model that can represent any state expressible in first-order logic. Without further extension, however, to higher order or modal logics, this is still insufficient to express absolutely any state of affairs (for example, first-order logic cannot completely express all the theorems of arithmetic) but these ideals give a useful theoretical background to the models that are produced later.

These two concepts, of encapsulated objects and messaging, suffice for a system to be called object-based; other concepts which characterize the approach involve the groupings of objects (hierarchically) into classes, and the inheritance between classes. These concepts are less relevant to the present system. The key notion of information hiding was alluded to above. This captures the idea that people do not need to see the gory detail of how something is done in order to use it effectively. This applies, of course, not only to the objects in a software system but to the interface the system presents to the user. One of the reasons for the attractiveness of object-oriented approaches is that they lend themselves to the effective design of such interfaces (for example, Jacobson *et al.*, 1992, describe an object-oriented method centred around analysing cases of how the software is used and using this to derive a major part of the object-oriented structure). To avoid misunderstandings, there should be a set of relatively transparent principles that even a naive end user can apply. We distinguish two types of user in our system—the application developer, who may be of any arbitrary level of sophistication, and the naive end user, who may be almost computer illiterate—and describe how some concepts of information hiding were implemented in IDIOMS.

Before we leave object orientation, however, one major feature of the approach must be clarified. Object-oriented approaches have been largely data driven, implying an empiricist value. The term 'data driven' is used here to suggest that the nature of the objects formed are predicated upon properties of the data itself, which connotes a philosophy of natural kinds, self-evidencing and produced through observation and natural constraint. This would be an oversimplification, both of object orientation and of the approach we took. Wegner (1987) explores the classification paradigm of object-oriented approaches in some detail, and relates it both to the objective/subjective dichotomy and to the nature of computational reality. Characterizing both aspects in the context of building software systems, and identifying the need for integration of design and implementation, he notes that object orientation can provide the integration required. In our approach, we view the development of a (business) application primarily as a conceptual act. Certainly an application program can be generated from a database, using the categories extant in that database, with the semantics rooted in the culture and history of the company and beyond. Even though (for example) an employee database has categorical commitments to fields such as name, salary and national insurance number, these have generally unproblematic referents and have been found historically useful, therefore why would anyone not wish to use them?

The answer to that rhetorical question goes without saying! People would not wish to use them because they had no use for them! Or because those individuals had a more useful classification. Or because they wished to amend their view of the employees in a particular manner, using private or publicly known categories. Or because they had changed their perspective on what the company was about and wished only to retain essential historical information, and to supply new categories of information to the record. All of these reasons reference use to the purposive context of information, and make the cognitive act of categorization contingent on that purpose.

The data–driven approach informs, but does not determine the forward thinking that human analysis and contextual awareness can bring to application development. Models of memory in the field of cognitive psychology have recently begun to indicate an integration between these elements in forming categories to deal with the presenting world. Barsalou (1986, 1987) has posited a model in which the long-term memory (through which humans' access to their past experience is mediated) interacts with recent uses of the category and with demands of the current situation in a dynamic fashion. Out of this interaction comes a category which is adapted to action in the current moment. This may often be the category that has always been used before, but not necessarily. Maybe it has always been used because it has always been useful before, or maybe it has been used before because no one thought of a better category. The advantage of allowing for creative thinking to go into category formation is that it frees objectivity from a deterministic process governed only by tradition. SSM, by allowing conceptual models to become free from the confines of the physical and purely empirical, provides an exemplary stance for the liberation of IS provision.

The point of our approach is that the historically useful practices and traditions of the past should be learned from, and the principles extracted and made relevant to current concerns. But the systems they give rise to are not to be hidebound by that past, and that empirical and historical data should be balanced against critical new insights, perspective shifts, innovations, and potential new realities. Where the subjective meets the objective, the phenomenal meets the noumenal and SSM meets object orientation.

But the overriding advantage of the object-oriented approach compared to traditional IS provision lies in its potential for reuse. In a world where bespoke software is expensive, problematic to maintain and support, and in any case may be outdated and unadaptable as business processes become redefined, or as they spontaneously form, dissolve and reform, there is an attraction to a system that can provide IT support to keep up with change. Object orientation can promise reuse of software components for the rapid redevelopment of applications, and this is a factor that has attracted various users.

One advantage seen by users of object-based methods is the flexibility in changing interfaces in application development. With libraries of object templates available, it is much easier for application developers to customize objects for particular users than to develop everything from scratch. It is this flexibility that will be illustrated in the application development examples given later.

Although it is tempting to criticize some of these features of object orientation as over-simplistic for human activity systems, in keeping with the imperative to 'produce something that does significant work' it is more relevant to consider where they do prove useful for practical IS developments. To this end some practical concerns of classification which impact on development must be addressed.

In the formalized modelling of a domain—'the knowledge representation'—the classification constitutes the object, and if that object is to be reified in a shared world another being must predictably be able to manipulate its representation. If the scientific representation of the physical world is lawful, this predictability can be guaranteed by correspondence, as a history of physical manipulations shows—leading us to rely upon not falling through the floor for instance when we step on it confidently (although such hubris may not always be warranted if the physical realm is ultimately uncertain!). In the social and phenomenological domains, the signifiers typically used must have a sedimented meaning which allows predictable behaviour to ensue—but these too can change, and their interpretations can be substantially affected by situational factors in their decoding. The relative success of physical sciences can be attributed to the universality and history in the ontology of human experience of external material, and its shared long-term stability. It is not the purpose of this chapter to explore whether the physical world is real, predictable, and discoverable. The issue is not even whether we learn a classification of objects that the world possesses innately, or whether we negotiate a reference system that allows us to approximate communication. Instead, we presume (a) that objects CAN be identified in a way that (tautologously) can be deemed useful by users of those objects, (b) that such objects can have a purely subjective function to their originator, without a public conception, and (c) that some objects can have an essentially public status, robust against aberrant interpretations. We also presume (a) that these classifications can erode and change; (b) that the rate of change (or apparent stability) is some function of their utility and amount of use; (c) that these objects can be modelled if not actually reified using linguistic tokens (for practical purposes); and (d) rather than divert attention towards the ontological and epistemological status of objects, whether defensible or not, the following position can be taken, and can at least be agreed with in some community of like minds.

The position is that the *raison d'être* of information systems is to support some form of praxis. Notwithstanding inquiry and metaphysical philosophizing surrounding their design, an instantiated IS will result from some tacit or explicit stance, and from definite decisions and constraints that are inevitably informed by practical considerations. This applies also to the choice of representational objects in the system, which will be justified on the grounds that they 'work' or 'don't work'. This judgement, however, is taken to be in the eye of the beholder, and the evaluation, validation and success or failure of an IS is viewed as a subjective judgement. In this sense, any 'below the line' thinking is in a realm unavailable to the material world of practical decisions; and given that those who commission and fund an IS development usually require practical results, some utilitarian values, for better or worse, are likely to prevail.

THE IDIOMS APPROACH

Against this backdrop, the remainder of this chapter describes the implementation of an information system for management: an application development environment which allows the managerial end-user to design, test and generate instantiated decision support systems for business applications.

The project in which the (demonstrator) system was developed was code named IDIOMS—Intelligent Decision-making In Online Management Systems—but the acronym also carries an appropriate semantic message. An idiom is a particular form of expression characteristic of an individual or culture, and the IDIOMS development environment allows the terminology of the application to reflect the idiomatisms of the user. Allowing such subjectivity to enter into the fabric of an IS does more than locally customize an off-the-shelf application; it reflects the idiosyncratic manner in which individuals carve up their experience of phenomena and the classifications they impose on their particular world. To the extent to which these classifications correspond either to the natural kinds of that world or to commonly understood concepts, the interpretation of terms will be unproblematic. Before elaborating this point further, let us examine, through two detailed simulated runs of application development, the IDIOMS environment. Following the presentation of these, several aspects of this approach to IS provision will be described.

The first run shows a series of screendumps which demonstrate the entirely subjective development of an application. This is to demonstrate how the user can supply a set of

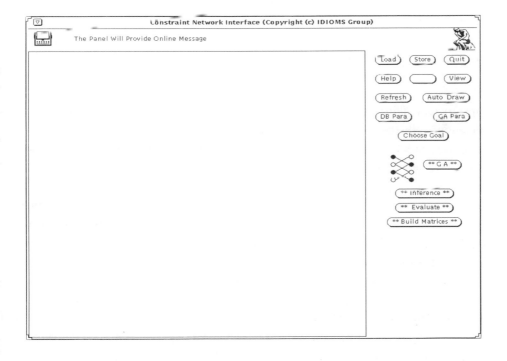

Figure 8.1   Initial screen showing main window buttons

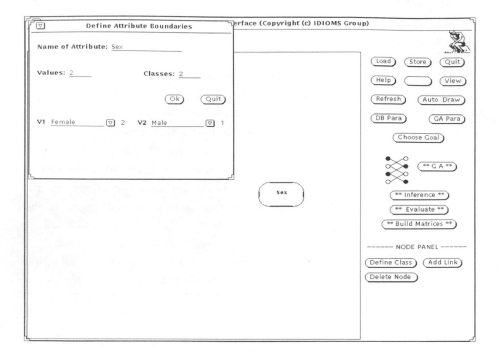

Figure 8.2   First (discrete) category (attribute) specified in model

categories specifying a particular area of interest, the options open to him, her (or, more interestingly, them) in tailoring these categories, and the sort of simple inferential questions that can be asked once a model has been built through mouse-based interaction with the graphical user interface.

Our walk through a 'subjective' application development begins with the initial window that the user sees on the screen after calling the program. It contains a number of buttons and a work area (Figure 8.1). By clicking in this area a rounded box (or NODE) appears, into which the user can type a class (model attribute) label, and a new panel appears with relevant buttons. Clicking the 'define class' button causes a window to appear asking whether the attribute is nominal (i.e. discrete categories) or continuous, and a subsequent window to pop up in which the user can specify details of this class (Figure 8.2). The difference between classes and groups will be made clear later.

A similar process causes a second attribute to be defined, this time a continuous variable of AGE ranging between 16 and 80, using integer precision and containing up to

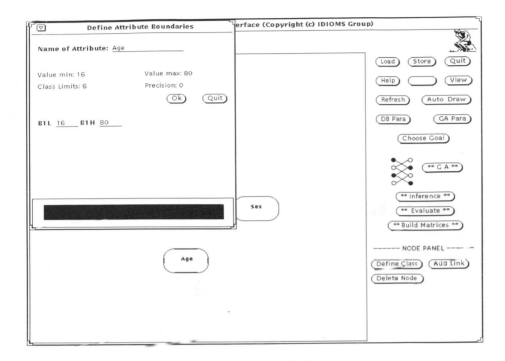

Figure 8.3   Continuous category showing initial boundaries

four subclasses or intervals on that range (Figure 8.3). By using the slider, or typing at appropriate points, the user can classify this variable into a series of upper and lower boundaries, perhaps in this case representing four ages of adults an insurance company might wish to distinguish as forming particular target groups (Figure 8.4). If these are not sensitive enough for the purpose, the user can increase (or decrease) the number of classes, and slide boundaries either graphically or by typing: both displays, being coupled, will update (Figure 8.5).

The final class in this model is nominal, and consists of some given names of people. For some models the class 'Jim' may equate to the class 'James' so these can be identified as a single group (Figure 8.6). This is up to the user, and will depend on the purpose of the model.

Next, the user decides which attributes are to be linked by selecting a pair and then using the appropriate button and associated menus and windows invoked from the link panel. Figure 8.7 shows that some specified relationship or constraint exists between the

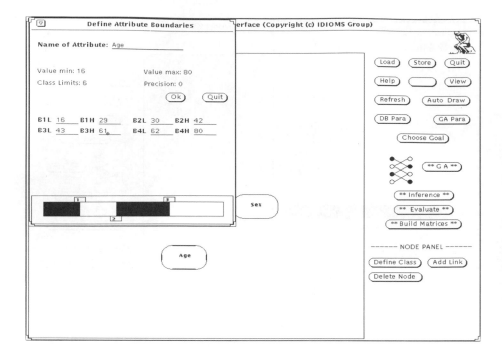

Figure 8.4   Adjustment of interval boundaries

classes name and sex, and age and sex: this relationship is to be detailed by a matrix on that link. Here one instance of Sue (Class 3 of Name) has co-occurred with Class 2 of sex (Male), 20 per cent of the population surveyed, and entered accordingly. The user may have been thinking of the Johnny Cash song 'A boy named Sue' and perhaps wanting to build a model to test hypotheses about names that can apply to either sex. Figure 8.8 completes the model with example data on the constraint between age and sex: exactly 1 member of the female population falling into each rage range, and all the male population falling into the lowest age bracket. The numbers in each row add up to 1, and represent likelihood ratios rather than probabilities. These figures are only illustrative and the user is charged with ensuring any objective and consistent basis for inputting them. Although mathematical checking utilities are easily introduced, this lack of control gives the user freedom to run various what-if models on hypothetical figures.

Once the model has been built the user can ask questions from it by inputting the known value of a category, and finding out how it is statistically related to another

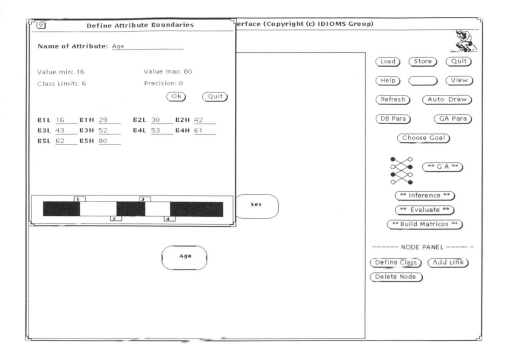

Figure 8.5   Increasing sensitivity of category

category of interest. In a version of this contrived model, the user might discover that, given someone called Hilary, he or she had an overall 50 per cent chance of being female, from the sample, but that if they were in the upper age range he or she had more chance of being male, and in the lower, of being female. Knowing that a male is called Hilary allows a more or less confident prediction that he is older.

This type of model may have applicability in identifying a fictitious name and profile for an average customer to be used in marketing campaigns, but this example is really only to show some of the model-building utilities available to a user without a database, or only with subjective data from his or her own experience. The application is built around a survey, which means that it has no database underlying it but relies on figures supplied by the user. Although this implies manual typing when data is not electronically available it would be straightforward to import spreadsheets, or generate the matrices from original survey forms.

This first application development shows how the users can build up a model, in their

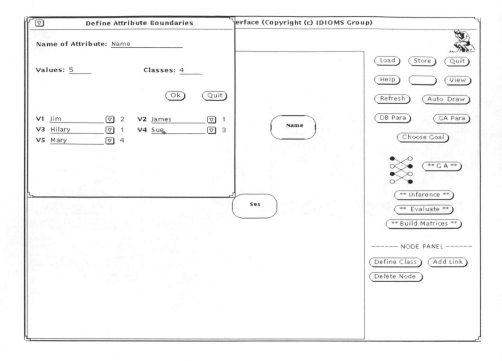

Figure 8.6   Final (nominal) category showing groupings

own terms, and at their own level of granularity to answer questions in the knowledge domain for which they have a certain amount of empirical observations, and perhaps some theories of their own that have no such base. The second run of the program, however, illustrates a more realistic use of the tool and develops an application automatically from a database of observations—in this case the agaricus–lepiota data (Fisher, 1936), itemizing a set of mushrooms and their properties, and which is often used for benchmarking machine learning systems.

Figure 8.9 shows a sample of the database, each record of which contains the values of 23 attributes of mushrooms, along with a 'session file' which specifies the interpretation of the database. In this application we are interested in the nominal attribute 'edibility' distinguishing poisonous from edible mushrooms, and the first field of each record contains a 'p' or an 'e' accordingly.

Again the user begins with the initial screen, from which he or she selects the button to load the database, causing the specified attributes automatically to be drawn on

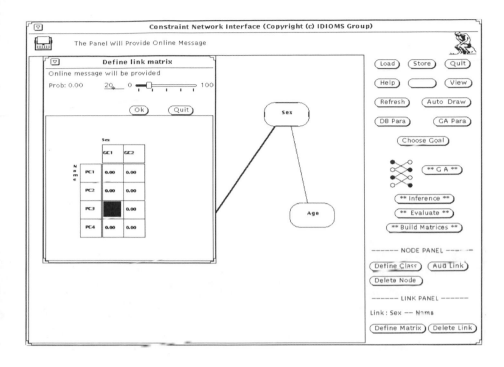

Figure 8.7   Linked categories showing association matrix development

the screen. Using the mouse to redraw the configuration, the user has visually isolated the attribute of particular interest. This identification has been highlighted in Figure 8.10 by selecting the 'choose goal' button. Figure 8.10 also shows two other user choices. Firstly, several attributes have been deselected, marked by the absence of a black dot in the corner. This may be because we have no data for those attributes, or they have not been found to be useful predictors in the past. Secondly, a function window has appeared containing buttons for the user control of genetic algorithm (GA) parameters. The detailed operation of this need not concern us here: essentially this is an optimization technique that will search the database to find the best categories for discrimination. This is described more fully in Cui *et al.* (1993), and in Fogarty *et al.* (1992). The GA is started, its operation marked by a flashing DNA icon, and when it terminates it has drawn links from the predictor attributes to the goal attribute, completing the matrices attached to those links with optimized figures and, when appropriate, indicating combinations of attributes containing category values which together constitute a good prediction, indicated by a square junction between links (Figure 8.11).

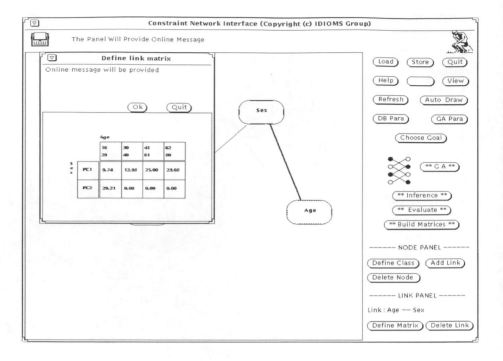

Figure 8.8   Completed association matrix for highlighted link

Figure 8.12 shows a closer examination of a highlighted link, where the difference between classes and groups is again brought out. For the attribute of stalk colour above ring, the nine colours identified fall into five groups, such that there is no predictive advantage gained by distinguishing (say) pink from red. These may be treated as statistically equivalent in the matter of predicting edibility. Figure 8.12 also illustrates the matrix attaching to this attribute pair, and shows for instance that, according to this database, no 'gray' mushrooms are poisonous, and although there are relatively few cinnamon mushrooms, they are all poisonous.

The default model is now built, and is ready for some test queries that will demonstrate its predictive power. Pressing the inference button produces the display shown in Figure 8.13, which displays an alphabetical menu of the attributes and two thermometers associated with the categories of the goal variable. By default 48 per cent are poisonous and 52 per cent edible: the numbers in the original database. Adding information, however, alters the probability of these predictions, so that noting a stalk colour of 'red', and detailing two other attributes, increases the likelihood of the mush-

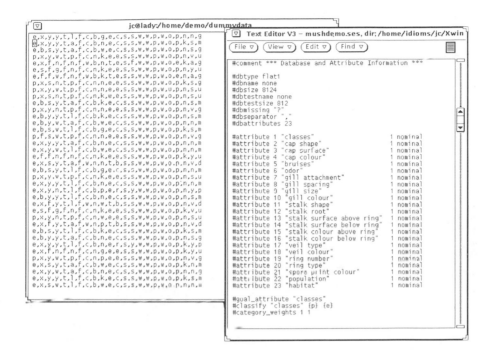

Figure 8.9   Database and associated descriptive session file

room being edible. This value is also recorded in the category's visual display. The value can be typed at the prompt, or selected from a pull-down menu as preferred. Changing information predictor attribute strengthens the chances that the mushroom is poisonous (Figure 8.14). Although the user has had the opportunity to affect this model, this example provides essentially a fully automated model of the database contents for use in decision support. Although not described here, it is possible either to use machine induction techniques on the raw data, or to translate the matrices formed after optimizing and optional user adjustment to generate an expert system embodying the decision model. Such an expert system naturally contains the certainty factors known empirically, in a consistent and calibrated fashion (Oates and Gammack, 1992).

These applications cover two extremes of the type of model that can be built in the IDIOMS environment, from 'fully subjective' to 'fully objective'. In a realistic application, however, one would expect a hybrid model, where perhaps a database supplies the initial configuration and set of categories, and an experienced and contextually aware manager experiments with various models on known data sets, dropping

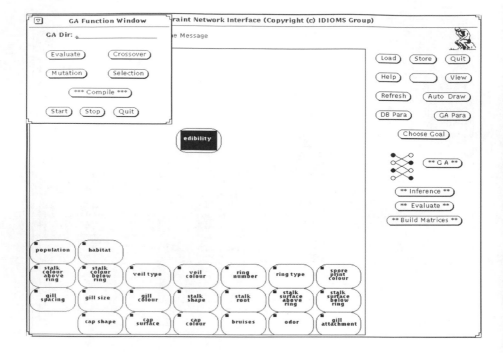

Figure 8.10   Selected model categories showing goal attribute prior to running the genetic algorithm

categories, altering their resolution and (using some of the utilities described in the first example) adding new categories of information to optimize the predictive power of the models, before committing a particular configuration into a decision support situation through an application generator.

FEATURES OF IDIOMS

IDIOMS has been tested in various banking application areas, and is currently being developed for exploitation as a commercial product. These runs of IDIOMS have not, however, detailed the key concepts for general IS provision of this kind: this final section describes some of these concepts away from the specific application context.

Firstly, IDIOMS uses an object-oriented GUI developed and running under the X-windows system. One of the key concepts implemented in IDIOMS is the human centred principle of users-as-designers. One of the reasons that spreadsheets have been such a successful piece of software is that they do not overconstrain the users' space by

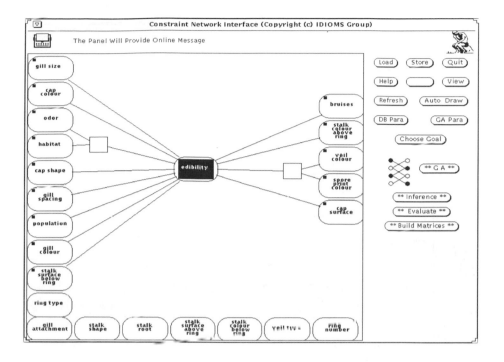

Figure 8.11   Model produced by GA showing links from predictor (or co-predictor) variables

anticipating the uses to which they will be put. This allows users to design the type of application they require for themselves. Shifting the onus of detailed design onto the users makes for flexibility, empowerment and user-enhanceability and changes the emphasis for the supporting system designer onto the provision of relevant general-purpose utilities.

Compare this user-led 'less is more' approach with some of the alternative, computing-led approaches which require the designer to have comprehensive overviews of different models of a system, and the judgement to arbitrate among these. For instance, in 'Object-Oriented Interface Design' (IBM, 1992) the authors distinguish the user's conceptual model from the programmer's model from the designer's model, noting that as mental constructs, no two users' models are exactly alike, and the designer requires to understand both the user's and the programmer's models as well as his or her own. A sub-industry of cognitive science arose in the 1980s aiming to identify formal models of users that can influence designers, and against which designer's models can be

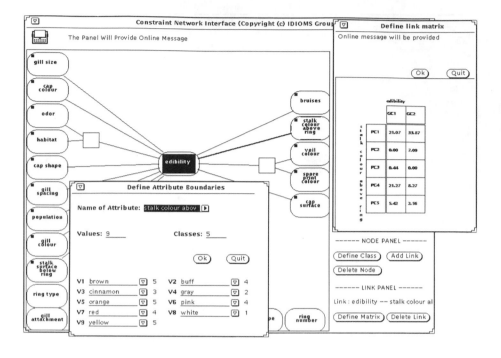

Figure 8.12   Optimized matrix for highlighted attribute showing likelihood ratios and groupings

matched (e.g. Card *et al.*, 1983). Software engineering appears to have taken little notice of research into the psychology of programming and software design (Green, 1993) and introducing such complexities may be needless.

By giving users a lot of freedom to design their own applications, the issue of the user's programming skill arises. It might be possible to adopt a sort of case-based reasoning approach whereby models, and object configurations used within models, are stored in some organized retrieval system, and adapted by subsequent users to fit new purposes. Indeed, buttons to store models, and menus to browse directories, are provided in the existing interface, although there is no necessity for an object-oriented interface to be supported by object-oriented code. With respect to the issue of reuse of code frag-ments, however, there is some concern that programmers find it easier to re-invent wheels than to find and utilize existing wheel designs (Green *et al.*, 1993) Green *et al.*'s 'cognitive browser' project aims to allow programmers to externalize what they know of the code fragments to increase easy access to these off-the-shelf objects,

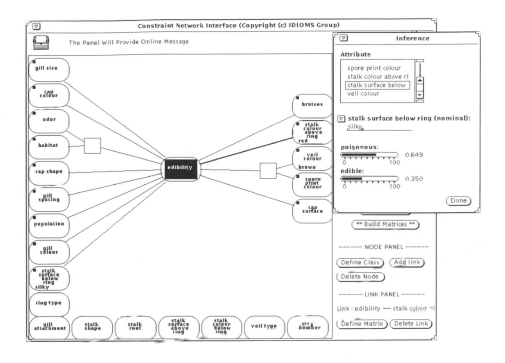

Figure 8.13   Initial (default) window of inference procedure

and the LaSSIE (Devanbu *et al.*, 1991) project provides a knowledge-based index over a library of reusable components which is attuned to the programmer's view of a large system. Another conclusion, however, is possible: that only by re-inventing the wheel does one understand it, and it is often quicker, and more apt, to invent one's own wheel. For users who prefer this style, providing the utilities to design and proto-type their own information system with a minimum of indexed code fragments may be more suitable. However, utilities allowing these to be saved and indexed at the object level may prevent a lot of hard work when objects play a part in a variety of applications.

CONCLUSION

As (for present purposes) relatively defined concepts, subjectivity and objectivity exist as extremes on a continuum where the difference between them is one of degree rather than of kind. If it is argued that the model reconciles only the external projections from one or other stance, and that the basis of each stance is fundamentally opposed, the suc-cess of such attempts is questionable. Despite the attempt to reconcile subjective with

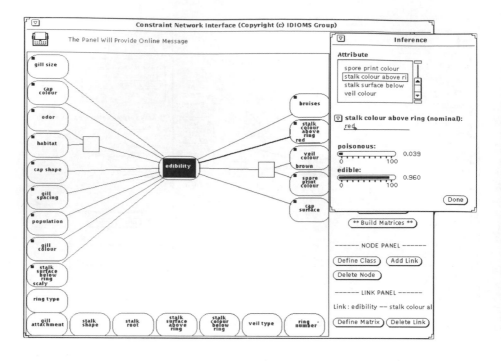

Figure 8.14   Inference about goal attribute after two pieces of information

objective, as suggested by the IDIOMS approach, only the shadows of these ideals are evident in the world of form represented in any model. Furthermore, the objectivity referred to is capped by subjective interpretation, category preselection and, in any case is contingent on previous context-bound and, probably at best, only consensual decisions. The ideal of objectivity remains elusive to IS modelling. I close with the words of the Hungarian poet Babits Mihály:

> *The Epilogue of the Lyric Poet*
> Compelled to be the hero of my verse,
> the first and last in every song I write,
> I long to shape in them the universe
> but naught beyond my self comes in my sight.
>
> There's naught but me: such thoughts I start to nurse;
> if there is, God alone can get it right.
> A blind nut in shell: this is my curse—
> to await being cracked in hateful night.

To break my magic ring I try in vain.
Only my arrow pierces it: desire—
though I know well my hopes will shrink by half. A

prison for my own self I must remain,
being subject and object, son and sire,
being, alas, both omega and alpha.

(Translated by István Tótfalusi)

Acknowledgements

I wish to thank Richard Beeby, Keith Sawyer and Frank Stowell for helpful comments on the draft manuscript. The IDIOMS project was supported by a grant from the DTI under the IED programme.

REFERENCES

Anderson, J. R. (1987) 'Methodologies for studying human knowledge', *The Behavioural and Brain Sciences*, **10** (3), 467–506.

Barsalou, L. W. (1986) 'Are there static category representations in long term memory?', *The Behavioural and Brain Sciences*, **9** (4), 651–2.

Barsalou, L. W. (1987) 'The instability of graded structure: implications for the nature of concepts', in *Concepts and Conceptual Development: Ecological and Intellectual Factors in Categorization* (U. Neisser, ed.), CUP, New York, 107–40.

Beeby, R. B. (1993) 'On the incommensurability of hard and soft approaches to information systems provision', in *Systems Science: Addressing Global Issues* (F. A. Stowell, D. West and J. G. Howell, eds), Plenum, New York, 307–12.

Burrell, G. and Morgan, G. (1979) *Sociological Paradigms and Organisational Analysis*, Heinemann, London.

Card, S. K., Moran, T. P. and Newell, A. (1983) *The Psychology of Human-Computer Interaction*, Erlbaum, Hillsdale, N.J.

Checkland, P. B. (1981) *Systems Thinking, Systems Practice*, Wiley, Chichester.

Checkland, P. B. and Scholes, J. (1990) *Soft Systems Methodology in Action*, Wiley, Chichester.

Crowe, M. K., Beeby, R. B. and Gammack, J. G. *Systems and Information*, McGraw-Hill, Maidenhead (forthcoming).

Cui, J., Fogarty, T. C. and Gammack, J. G. (1993) 'Searching databases using parallel genetic algorithms on a transputer computing surface', *Future Generation Computer Systems* **9** (1), 33–40.

Devanbu, P., Brachman, R. J., Selfridge, P. G. and Ballard, B. W. (1991) 'LaSSIE: a knowledge-based software information system', *CACM* **34** (5), 34–49.

Fisher, R. A. (1936) 'The use of multiple measurements in taxonomic problems', *Ann. Eugenics*, **7**, 179–88.

Fogarty, T. C., Ireson, N. S. and Battle, S. A. (1992) 'Developing Rule-Based Systems for Credit Card Applications from Data with the Genetic Algorithm', *Journal of Mathematics Applied in Business and Industry*, **4** (1), pp. 53–61.

Gill, K. S. (1991a) 'Summary of human centred systems research in Europe (Part 1)', *Systemist*, **13** (1), 7–27.

Gill, K. S. (1991b) 'Summary of human centred systems research in Europe (Part 2)', *Systemist*, **13** (2), 48–75.

Green, T. R. G. (1993) 'Why software engineers don't listen to what psychologists don't tell them anyway', in *User Centred Requirements for Software Engineering Environments* (D. Gilmore and R. Winder, eds), North-Holland Elsevier, Amsterdam.

Green, T. R. G., Winder, R., Gilmore, D. J. Davies, S. P., Hendry, D. and Joly, G. (1993) 'Designing a cognitive browser for object-oriented programming', *AISB Quarterly*, **81**, 17–20.

Gregory, D. (1987) 'Philosophy and practice in knowledge representation', in *Human Productivity Enhancement* (J. Zeidner, ed.), Praeger, New York.

Gregory, F. H. (1993) 'Cause, effect, efficiency and soft systems models', *Journal of the Operational Research Society*, **44** (4) 333–44.

IBM (1992) *Object Oriented Interface Design*, Que Corporation, Carmel, CA.

Jackson, M. C. and Keys, P. (1984) 'Towards a system of system methodologies', *Journal of the Operational Research Society*, **35**, 473–98.

Jacobson, I., Christerson, M., Johnsson, P. and Overgaard, G. (1992) *Object Oriented Software Engineering: A Case Driven Approach*, Addison-Wesley, Wokingham.

Kampis, G. (1991) *Self-modifying Systems in Biology and Cognitive Science: A New Framework for Dynamics, Information and Complexity*, Pergamon, Oxford.

Ledbetter, L. and Cox, B. (1985) Software-ICs, *Byte*, June, 307–15.

Miles, R. (1988) 'Combining "soft" and "hard" systems practice: grafting or embedding?', *Journal of Applied Systems Analysis*, **15**, 55–60.

Mumford, E. and Weir, M. (1979) *Computer Systems in Work Design: the ETHICS Method*, Wiley, New York.

Oates, T. H. and Gammack J. G. (1992) 'Generating knowledge for expert systems from databases'. Paper presented at *International Conference on Automation and Systems, Hefei, China*, September.

Oliga, J. (1988) 'Methodological foundations of systems methodologies', *Systems Practice*, **1** (1), 87–112.

Peltu, M. (1993) 'Modern methods for modern tools', *Infomatics Supplement*, June, 29–32.

Pirsig, R. (1976) *Zen and the Art of Motorcycle Maintenance*, Corgi, New York.

Probert, S. K. (1992) 'Soft systems methodology and the discipline of information systems', *Systemist*, **14** (4), 220–6.

Sawyer, K. (1990) 'Goals, purposes and the strategy tree', *Systemist*, **12** (4), 135–42.

Stowell, F. A. (1985) 'Experience with soft systems methodology and data analysis', *Information Technology Training*, May, 48–50.

Watts, F. A. (1992) 'Is psychology falling apart?', *The Psychologist*, **5**, 489–94.

Wegner, P. (1987) 'The object-oriented classification paradigm', in *Research Directions in Object Oriented Programming* (B. Shriver and P. Wegner, eds), MIT Press, Cambridge, Mass., 478–560.

Winograd, T. and Flores, F. (1986) *Understanding Computers and Cognition: A New Foundation for Design*, Ablex, Singapore.

Wood, J. R. G. and Doyle, K. (1991) 'Systems thinking, systems practice: dangerous liaisons', *Systemist*, **13** (1), 28–30.

9

NEW CHALLENGES AND DIRECTIONS FOR DATA ANALYSIS AND MODELLING

Paul Lewis
Management School, University of Lancaster

INTRODUCTION

Changes in the way in which information systems development is perceived and the demand for development methods that take account of social and political factors pose new challenges for data analysis and modelling. This chapter concentrates upon the nature of the challenges posed for using data analysis and modelling in the early stages of information systems development and in ill-defined problem situations. Certain weaknesses of the theory of data analysis become exposed here because, rooted in an objectivist paradigm, the possibility of multiple, equally valid views of reality is not allowed. It is suggested that an additional level of data analysis and modelling may be required—one whose concern is the cognitive categories through which the participants in a problem situation make sense of that situation and understand the nature of their own organization and its environment. The creation of such models would constitute an additional *interpretative* form of data analysis, enriching and complementing, rather than challenging, existing well-proved techniques. There is good reason to believe that the soft systems methodology might provide the basis for such an interpretative form of data analysis.

IMPORTANCE OF DATA ANALYSIS

Data analysis and modelling are well established in information systems development, and required by the most widely used development methodologies. For example, the widely favoured SSADM methodology (Cutts, 1987; Ashworth and Goodland, 1990; Downs *et al.*, 1992; Eva, 1992; Weaver, 1993) prescribes that an analysis of the data, its use and storage be achieved through logical data modelling, normalization and entity-life histories. The emphasis currently given to the subject is, however, a relatively recent phenomenon, and the same emphasis is not to be found in the recommended IS practice of the past. In a typical 1960s' approach to development such as the ARDI methodology described by Hartman *et al.* (1968) there is no prescribed consideration of data in its own right; items of data are discussed only indirectly in terms of how they might be used by programs and how they will be stored in files and records.

The key factors in bringing about this change were both technical, the availability of database management systems, and organizational, with data becoming seen as a corporate resource requiring management and, more recently, capable of being used to gain competitive advantage. Though many early attempts to employ database technology to create organization-wide management information systems failed, the attractions of a data-oriented approach to information systems development proved to be more enduring. Well-structured organizational databases offered the ability to integrate separate processing requirements, to introduce control over the data resource and promised release from the fear of changing requirements. The oft-quoted justification of the latter is that an organization's basic data requirements change relatively slowly and unless the organization moves into an entirely new line of business then the type of data required tomorrow will differ little from that required today. This placed at the top of the agenda for IS research the question of how to organize the data in the best possible way. The pioneering work of Codd (1970), regarding the normalization of relations, and Chen's (1976) exposition of entity–relationship modelling provided the basis for an extensive new literature—that concerning data analysis and modelling. This differed from previous discussions of data storage in that it emphasized a focus upon the structure of the data itself rather than the structure of files, records and physical storage structures, and separated discussion of the intrinsic structure of the data from discussion of the organization of the physical database.

The 1980s and 1990s have seen many more organizations adopting the 'database approach' and employing database technology as the basis for all of their data-processing activities. This has inevitably increased the importance of data analysis as a component of the development process. A crude indication of this is the space allocated to the subject in descriptions of methodologies for information systems development: whereas one of the original expositions of Structured Analysis and Design (De Marco, 1978) devotes little more than eight pages (roughly 2 per cent of his text) to data analysis, modelling and storage design, in Weaver's (1993) description of SSADM there are over one hundred pages (approximately 29 per cent of the text) concerned with those subjects. It seems unlikely that there will be any diminution of the importance of data analysis in the future. Indeed, recent developments such as the emergence of object-oriented databases and the consequent search for object-oriented analysis methods suggest the opposite. The question, then, of how to investigate the data components of a problem situation is likely to remain a critical issue for the field of information systems, and any discussion of new 'paradigms' of development must take account of whether current data analysis techniques are appropriate and if our understanding of the processes involved is sufficiently well defined.

NEW CHALLENGES

Despite the practical importance of the subject and its extensive literature, very little attention has been given to the process of inquiry that data analysis represents, or to the essential philosophy of that enquiry. This is becoming of increasing importance as data analysis is used earlier in the systems development process, and as thinking in the field of IS increasingly emphasizes the social nature of organizations.

CHANGED ROLES FOR DATA ANALYSIS

The techniques for data analysis and modelling were originally developed with the intent of producing better data storage mechanisms, but in the early 1970s the ANSI-SPARC three-level architecture for database systems formalized a distinction between the data models that might be provided at the internal, conceptual and external levels, and consequently between the data analysis activity producing each type of model. This 'de-coupled' the analysis of the structure of data from the detailed design of particular data storage mechanisms, making is possible to conceive of using data analysis techniques earlier in the development process. Over the years the techniques have gradually begun to be used ever earlier in the development process, until now their use is suggested at its very beginnings: analysis of the organization's data is used to create the enterprise models required by such approaches as IBM's business systems planning (BSP) and authors such as Ward *et al.* (1990) and Olle *et al.* (1991) suggest the use of data analysis in information systems planning and business analysis.

If data analysis techniques are used in such early stages of development they are being employed for different purposes than previously. Rather than being used to decide the best way of storing the data required to satisfy largely known requirements they are being used to demarcate and define the problem domain. This means that one is forced to be more critical of the system of enquiry that data analysis represents and of the constraints imposed by its underlying philosophy.

NEW THINKING IN IS

The desire to use data analysis in the early stages of development has been fuelled by new ideas that are emerging in the field of information systems. Of particular importance are those ideas which concern:

- The role of information systems with respect to the business that they serve and the need for the development of information systems to be closely linked to strategic planning of the organization.
- The complex social and political nature of human organizations, including the construction of meaning that takes place within any human situation and the interpretative and communicative action that takes place in business and information systems planning.

LINKING OF IS AND BUSINESS PLANNING

The desire for a closer alignment of the planning of information systems and the planning of the business is an inevitable consequence of recognizing the importance of information systems as a factor in strategic planning of the business. The work of such as Ives and Learmouth (1983), Wiseman and MacMillan (1984) and Porter and Millar (1985) has led to wide acceptance of the idea that information systems do not merely facilitate existing business practices but may themselves shape the business, be used to secure competitive advantage or be required through competitive necessity. They may, of course, also restrict freedom of action, for otherwise attractive business plans may be ruled out by the inability to create new, or modify existing, information systems to support them. With these considerations it has been suggested that we are now in a third era of Information Systems (IS) use, where businesses are becoming critically dependent upon their investment in information systems, and IS/IT planning

> ... has crept unerringly away from the computer room, through the
> IS department and is now clearly a process that depends on users and
> senior management involvement for success. It has become difficult
> to separate aspects of IS/IT planning from business planning. Hence,
> it is important to use the tools and techniques of business strategic
> analysis and planning to cement that relationship. More specific
> IS/IT planning approaches have to be knitted into this pattern of
> business strategic management.   (Ward et al. 1990, p. 37).

Surveys of the practice of strategic information systems planning (SISP) suggest, however, that achieving a closer linking of business and information systems planning is not simple.

> While it is invariably argued that SISP should be closely associated
> with the business planning process (if only one part of it), it is still
> too often the case that the link is tenuous at best, with the two
> processes being undertaken in isolation from each other and with
> little business planner involvement in SISP and vice versa (Galliers,
> 1991, p. 60).

A contributory factor to this may be that information systems professionals and business planners often view the organization through different mental models. In particular, a closer linking of information systems work with planning of the business requires IS practitioners and researchers to abandon the certainties that exist when IS work is envisaged merely as the satisfaction through technology of given data-processing requirements. Embracing instead the uncertainties and value-laden questions that are more familiar to the social scientists is an uncomfortable change for many information systems professionals, since the IS field has long employed somewhat outmoded, rational and positivist models of organizations and decision making.

Concern for organizational cultures

Gaining some understanding of the organization and the business that an information system is to serve has, of course, long been seen as a prerequisite for development. But if development is to be more closely allied to strategic planning then 'understanding the served business' can no longer be restricted to investigating the present business procedures (still the starting point of many development approaches and methodologies) and IS professionals must be able to comprehend and perhaps contribute to the debates about what the organization might or might not aim at, and how it might strive to achieve those objectives in the future. The need therefore arises for IS practitioners to understand the images that organizations have of themselves and their environment and, as one would expect, IS thinking is becoming increasingly influenced (some might say becoming belatedly aware of) the models of organizations used in the management and social sciences. The simple, 'hard' systems thinking model that has influenced IS thinking so strongly in the past is that organizations can be understood as goal-seeking, adaptive-regulatory mechanisms. This is now being rejected in favour of more complex systems models of human organizations as purposeful, socio-political systems in which shared meaning and symbolic relationships are maintained and modified through human discourse and interaction.

Examples of this may be found in the literature concerned with improving the 'organizational fit' of information systems, which means enhancing the degree to which information systems are not only technically efficient but also appropriate to the power structures and culture of the organization that is to use them. The conclusions of Markus and Robey (1983) or Pliskin et al. (1993)—that care must be taken to ensure that an information system 'fits' its organizational context of use and that their designers should be aware of the *organizational culture* including actual and perceived power relationships—are still relatively novel to the field of IS: the reader may care to try to name one IS methodology that includes such considerations.

More general management literature has, however, long discussed the importance of cultures, the way in which they become enshrined and reflected by language and the extent to which they guide both management thinking and the observable structures and actions of the organization. For example, Pettigrew (1979, pp. 574–5) points out that:

> Symbol construction serves as a vehicle for group and organisational conception. As a group or organisation at birth represents its situation to itself and to the outside world it emphasises, distorts, and ignores and thereby attaches names and values to its structure, activities, purposes, and even the physical fabric around it. The symbols that arise out of these processes—the organisation's vocabulary, the design of the organisation's buildings, the beliefs about the use and distribution of power and privilege, the rituals and myths which legitimate those distributions—have significant functional consequences for the organisation.

An information system developer who makes no attempt to understand the culture and symbol construction, present and historical, within a problem situation would be at a loss to understand the context of a new information system. In failing to empathize with the way in which potential users understand their world they might easily design information systems that breach particular, perfectly rational in their own terms, norms or taboos.

Pfeffer (1981) argues that organizations can be legitimately understood not only in terms of a functional purpose (the manufacture of cars, the sale of products and services) but also as both political arenas in which power is exercised and as

> ... social systems populated by individuals who come to the system with norms, values, and expectations and with the necessity of developing understandings of the world around them so there can be enough predictability for them to take some action. (p. 4)

Pfeffer concludes that gaining an understanding of organizations therefore requires two distinct levels of analysis. The first is concerned with the organizational actions and decisions that have observable, substantive outcomes such as inventory levels or the average time taken to satisfy an order. The second is concerned with understanding how such organizational activities are perceived, interpreted and legitimated. Information systems development techniques have traditionally concentrated upon the former, identifying task responsibilities, charting the flow of materials, data, etc. An important consequence of the new thinking about information systems is that analysis, including data analysis, should also attend to the latter.

How this might be done is not obvious, for Lewis (1992, 1993b) points out that the literature is remarkably bereft of attempts to ally data analysis with any sociological paradigm. The available theory of data analysis provides no justification for its recommended activities in terms of the nature of social reality or how human beings make sense of their world. Our understanding of data analysis is seriously impoverished by these omissions, and they also lead to some very practical problems.

DATA ANALYSIS AS AN OBJECTIVIST APPROACH

Conventional data modelling has been described as both scientific (Wood-Harper and Fitzgerald, 1982) and objectivist (Klein and Hirschheim, 1987), through *in practice* data analysis may contain a large degree of subjectivity and data models may be neither 'neutral' nor value free (Lewis, 1993b). Descriptions of the process in the literature do, however, support the contention that conventional data analysis and modelling are rooted in an objectivist paradigm, having ontological assumptions that are realist and epistemological assumptions that are positivist. The consequent assumption that data structures, entities or objects exist, independently of the observer, in the real-world is most evident when data modelling is employed in the design of data storage mechanism. For example, Hughes (1991) says that '*For database applications an entity is something about which descriptive information is to be stored, which is capable of independent existence and can be uniquely identified*' (p. 4) while Date (1990) argues that '*By definition, any database contains representatives of certain real-world entities*' (p. 596). The same assumptions may also be found when data modelling is used earlier in development; for example, in SSADM there is assumed to be always an underlying, generic data structure to any problem situation (see Cutts, 1987, p. 23; Ashworth and Goodland, 1990, p. 10). With the assumptions that an objective reality exists only waiting to be described, and that data models should uncover and describe that reality, the starting point for data modelling is an identification of real-world things or events, and once a data model has been created it is checked by comparison to known application requirements. A single, independently existing, objective reality is therefore relied upon as the source of knowledge for creating and validating data models. Underlying much of the newer thinking about information systems, however, is a recognition of the social and political construction of meaning that takes place within any human situation and the interpretative and communicative action that takes place in business and information systems planning: that there is, in effect, no single, independently existing reality but instead multiple perceived realities that are socially constructed.

The mismatch between such ideas and the objectivism of data analysis is most pronounced when data analysis is used in the early stages of development. Here are to be found few well-defined technical problems but many social and political issues. To not allow for the possibility of multiple, equally valid views of reality leaves data analysis open to manipulation, for data models may easily become infused with political meanings, or be distorted so as to legitimize or invalidate a particular view of the organization and its purposes.

PROBLEM OF IDENTIFYING ENTITIES

In addition to possible political naïveté, the absence of any clear declaration of the models of social reality and human sense-making within which the process of data analysis may be understood also presents data analysis with methodological difficulties. The assumption that an objective real-world is to be represented in a data model leaves one with the problem of deciding which parts of that world should be included in, and which omitted from, the model. The directives of various authors to identify those things that are of relevance and importance to the organization only raise further questions concerning how to determine relevance. The generalized suggestions for how to identify the entities and objects given in the literature, while practically useful, are drawn from the 'craft knowledge' of experienced practitioners and not the consequence of any theory of how human beings make sense of their world or inquire into problematical situations. Guidance may be provided by the results of discussions with probable users, investing the contents of existing data stores, studying written problems statements or by intuition and experience; in the last resort, however, data analysts are forced to make subjective choices of what are relevant entities or objects.

Ontological or epistemological devices

The ill-defined philosophy of data analysis has also led to a certain confusion as to the status of 'entities' or 'objects' and whether these are ontological labels for parts of the real world or epistemological devices through which the nature of the real world may be explored. Lewis (1993h) provides a number of examples from the literature illustrating this.

Recent interest in object-oriented methods has led to re-interpretations of the nature of data analysis and at least some recognition that a data model might be an epistemological device. Odell (1992), for example, emphasizes that:

> Object-oriented (O-O) analysis should *not* model reality—rather it should model the way reality is understood by people. The understanding and knowledge of people is the essential component in developing systems'. (p. 45)

Regrettably, the literature conceding object-oriented analysis is beginning to display some of the same conceptual confusions of its predecessors and the same lack of concern for its essential philosophy. De Champeaux and Faure (1992) compare a number of different approaches to object–oriented analysis, but the terms of comparison are limited to discussion of technical details such as whether the influence of reuse (desirable from an implementation perspective) affects the definition of classes, the diagramming conventions used and whether or not the different approaches allow multiple inheritance. More fundamental questions of ontology and epistemology are, significantly, not considered at all. This may not be too serious when object orientation is applied at the implementation level (in database design and programming) for the problem domain is then well defined. To define object as '*a named representation of a real-world entity*' (McFadden and Hoffer, 1991, p. 189) or state that '*Any real-world entity is an object, with which is associated a system-wide unique identifier*' (Kim, 1990, p. 13) is unlikely to affect the results of the analysis unduly. But if object orientation is applied in less well-defined situations then the assumption of one-to-one correspondences existing between the objects in the data model and parts of an external reality is more dangerous and blinkering. McGinnes (1992) expresses the dangers well:

> The idea that object-oriented systems are a 'natural' representation of the world is a seductive but dangerous over-simplification. In reality, the fact that the object model seems so close to reality makes it far easier to misuse it than other modelling technniques which do not purport to represent the world so directly. (p. 13)

Whether working with object–oriented ideas or more established forms of data modelling, the danger that arises from not being clear whether core concepts such as 'entity' or 'objects' are epistemological or ontological devices is that one is forced to fall back upon 'common sense', example-led definitions. Lewis (1993b) exemplifies this by reference to a definition of an abstract object as

> a non-value object in the real world. An abstract object can be, for example, a tangible item (such as a person, a table, a country), or an event (such as an offering of a course by an instructor), or an idea (such as a course) (Rishe, 1988, p.5).

Lewis questions whether 'a country' is ever a tangible item in the real–world or merely a perception shared by many individuals. He asks us (pp. 179–80) to

> ... consider, for example, the aspirations of many Middle Eastern and East European citizens for regional independence. Did there exist a real-world thing called Slovenia in December 1991 when some inhabitants of Yugoslavia had declared its independent existence? Did it exist in January 1992 when the European Community (but not the

United Nations or the government of Yugoslavia) recognised its existence? The answers, of course, depend on how we define 'a country', and this is socially and politically decided: it is not an absolute characteristic of something existing in an independent 'real-world'.

These theoretical problems can give rise to very real organizational costs. A chastening experience of the author was to spend many hours designing a database only to find that the structure of the database would not meet certain processing requirements. The root of the problem was that despite many discussions with one particular set of users we had not realized that their concept of a 'customer' was subtly different to ours. Their concept of 'customer' was any outside body with whom they traded, and in just a few cases this described what we would have called 'suppliers'. The databases had to be redesigned and reloaded.

The conundrum of the cassowary

A rather more developed example of the difficulties that the somewhat unclear theory of data analysis (in particular the lack of any underlying model of human sense-making) might cause is given by Lewis (1994) which offers a rendition in IS terms of a classification problem suggested by Law and Lodge (1984). This concerns the hypothetical predicament faced by a data analyst charged with the remit of producing a conceptual data model of the flora and fauna of New Guinea. It would be reasonable to expect that the abstracted classes of the data model would perhaps include such things as 'Bird' with subclasses including 'Parrot', 'Mammal' with subclasses including 'Pig', and so forth. The theory of data analysis allows that our data analyst might find it difficult to create a data model unless the problem domain is further defined. For, unless the data analyst has some idea of who will use the information system based upon the data model, he or she will have no guidance as to what might, or might not, be considered as a 'relevant' thing to be included in the model. The theory of data analysis also allows for users to have different interests and data-processing requirements, so that each might require his or her own 'user view' or external schema. The classes in these, however, are merely a selected subset of the classes in the larger conceptual data model, and it is expected that those classes are understood in the same way as in the conceptual data model and in every other user-view.

The theory of data analysis does *not* recognize that users might perceive the situation in fundamentally different ways, so the anthropological study of Bulmer (1967) suggests that our data analyst may encounter a particular problem concerning the flightless creature called, in the West, the cassowary. The Karam people that reside in the New Guinea habitat of the cassowary have their own name for this creature, but our data analyst could no doubt accommodate this in the form of an alias in the data dictionary. Unfortunately, Europeans and the Karam also perceive and classify the creature in very different ways. Europeans, seeing similarities with creatures such as emus and ostriches, classify the cassowary as a type of 'bird'. The Karam people, however, do not include the cassowary in their class of 'yakt', which covers flying birds and bats, placing it instead in an alternative taxon, that of 'kobtiy'. This is in no sense a perverse or foolish decision, for the Karam recognize as important a different set of similarities by which to classify the cassowary, and their classification is perfectly respectable in terms of its coherence and its usefulness to them.

Whose view, then, of the cassowary is to be used by the data analyst? Should the conceptual data model show 'cassowary' to be a subclass of 'bird' or not? If we accept the view exemplified by Batini *et al.*'s (1992) declaration that 'Data models are vehicles for describing reality. Designers use data models to build schemes, which are representations of reality' (p. 15), then of whose 'reality' is the data model to be a representation? Clearly, the data model that our data analyst produces will be very different, depending upon whether he or she adopts the perspective of the Western visitor or the indigenous inhabitant. The generic classes of which the cassowary and other creatures are considered subtypes will differ, the attributes associated with particular classes would vary, and one data model could contain a whole range of classes that the other would not consider to be 'things of interest', for the reason that certain types of creature have religious significances to the Karam that are unrecognized by the Westerner. The data model produced in this situation will, in common with all data models at the level of abstraction, be affected by very particular cognitive categorizations, subjectively chosen or unconsciously accepted. These determine the selection of the problem domain and the way in which that problem domain is understood. This is not entirely unrecognized; practising data analysts know that in real life much more time is spent arguing about and agreeing a meaning for the entities or objects used in a data model than is spent operating the mechanics of techniques such as normalization—and more thoughtful authors recognize the subjective nature of the data models produced. For example, Kroenke (1992) points out that

> ... sometimes, when evaluating alternatives, project team members engage in discussions and arguments about which data model best represents the real world. These discussions are misguided. Databases do not model the real world, though it is a common misconception that they do.
>
> Rather, databases are models of users' models of the world (or, more to the point, of their business environment). The question to ask when evaluating alternative data models is not 'Does this design

accurately represent the real world?' but rather 'Does this design accurately represent the users' model of his or her environment?' The goal is to develop a design that fits the user's mental conception of what he or she wants to track (p. 117).

It is a serious failing of data analysis that this is only rarely acknowledged, but understandable since the theory of data analysis contains no model of human sense-making that explains it, and none of the techniques of data modelling assists by making the subjectivity explicit and open to debate.

UNDERSTANDING DATA ANALYSIS IN NEW WAYS

Let there be no misunderstanding of our admiration for conventional data analysis and its techniques; these have proved to be of immense practical utility; they have, in contrast to many fads and fashions of the IS field, been thoughtfully expanded and will certainly continue to be the mainstay of systems development. But the absence of any underlying theory of how human beings make sense of the apparently chaotic reality that they experience, and of how they organize and create knowledge of their world, is an omission that cannot be ignored for much longer.

A significant technical achievement has been made in providing database technology that attractively meets the practical needs of organizations. The challenge is now to complement that with an intellectual achievement, and to ensure that we may employ that technology in ways that are socially and politically appropriate. This, we believe, requires us to re-interpret data analysis. We must recognize that data analysis leads to models of data that reflect not, as has so far been all too readily assumed, any objective reality but a particular group's knowledge and perceptions of a problem situation. And we must find ways to investigate and model that knowledge and those perceptions—in ways that are sympathetic to the complex manner in which social realities are created. These are significant challenges, but some attempts have already been made to address the problem. These include the shift towards increasingly sophisticated forms of semantic data model, Klein and Lyytinen's (1992) call for a new understanding of data modelling and Baskerville's (1993) suggestion that prototyping be employed in data analysis to increase 'semantic consensus'. In 'semantic database prototyping' end-users and designers gain a *shared understanding* by focusing on a prototype and engaging in a social process in which '*users and designers mutually must adjust their semantics, the rules of their language, their thinking and ultimately their artifacts*' (p. 124). This provides a formal vehicle and a focus for those negotiations, about how a data model will be understood, that commonly occur in practice but that are rarely acknowledged in the literature of data analysis. However, semantic database prototyping is proposed as a method '*for permitting end-user validation of a semantic data model*' (p. 124) and is initiated '*when analysts first meet with the users and conduct a brief study of the problem domain. They produce an entity–relationship diagram'* (p. 125). This suggests that it is most appropriate to conventional single application development and does not directly address the difficulties of producing Entity Relationship (E–R) diagrams in, or the suitability of E–R diagramming conventions for, ill-defined problem situations involving a variety of potential users.

AN INTERPRETATIVE FORM OF DATA MODEL

All models are designed for a purpose and have only limited utility. A good example of this is the schematic map of London's underground railway lines and stations. This is excellent when travelling on the underground railway, but extremely misleading if one uses it as a guide to the relative physical location of the underground stations. Similarly, we suggest that the forms of data model produced by conventional data analysis, while of proven value when the problem domain is well defined, are not well suited for use in the early stages of systems development, where the future of the organization, what it may wish to achieve and how it will pursue its objectives are all to some extent undecided. In response we might choose to give no consideration to data until the development process has progressed far enough for 'the problem' to be well defined and for the likely data usages to have been identified. Alternatively, we might accept the challenge of creating new types of data model through different forms of data analysis that are more sensitive to the importance of cultural and political factors and recognize the possibility of socially created realities. Such *interpretative* level data models would be complementary to the existing forms of data model. In the same way that data models at the level of abstraction do not make redundant data models at the physical level, but serve a different purpose, so interpretative data models would complement rather than replace data models at the level of abstraction. It is in pursuing this latter possibility that we believe that soft systems methodology may play a role.

USE OF SOFT SYSTEMS METHODOLOGY

The basic premise of any interpretative form of data analysis would, by definition, be that the only knowledge one may have of the world is that which is acquired subjectively and intersubjectively. This basis in constructivism alters the way in which we regard the process and the products of data analysis. It implies that one can only ever investigate or model the nature of some part of the 'real-world' as it is understood by those who perceive it as problematical. If, then, individuals regard the same situation differently, this should not be seen as the result of erroneous observation, imperfect knowledge or an inconvenient human failing; those different perceptions constitute as 'real' a factor for analysis as any other. But rigour is still required: if an interpretative data analysis cannot produce data models that mirror an objective real-world, it must produce data models that are coherent, internally consistent and have meaning in the context of particular beliefs, values and expectations.

Any abandonment of belief in an objective reality must create a major practical problem; if there is no single 'real' problem situation 'out there', but only multiple and sometimes incompatible views of a situation, then how may these be dealt with? This problem can be most easily resolved if interpretative data analysis is used within and builds upon a methodology that has already proved to be capable of dealing with such dilemmas. The soft systems methodology (SSM) described by Checkland (1981) and Checkland and Scholes (1990) is such.

SSM is a well-proved and effective means of engendering debate and learning in complex problem situations. As is evidenced by the other chapters of this text, much attention is now being given to its role in dealing with the social aspects of information systems development (ISD). There have already been a number of suggestions that ISD should employ, in some shape or form, the soft systems methodology in association with more conventional development methodologies: examples of this include Multiview (Avison and Wood-Harper, 1990), Compact (CCTA, 1989) and some recent attempts to use SSM as a business analysis tool for SSADM (CCTA, 1993). These all use SSM as a 'front-end' means of examining a problem situation and deciding what information systems are required, before turning to traditional tools of the developer to create such information systems. SSM, however, does not currently provide for any consideration of data. This may be partly because its present techniques are process dominated and partly because questions of data have been too readily dismissed as purely technical and the concern of technical experts. This is unfortunate, for the essential philosophy of SSM is ideally suited to an interpretative form of data analysis.

Certainly, SSM appears to allow consideration of the cultural aspects of organizations that one would expect to be of importance to an interpretative form of data analysis. Pliskin et al. (1993) single out SSM as particularly suitable for studying culture in relation to information systems on the basis (p. 151) that:

> This promising methodology is sensitive to complex dimensions of
> organizations such as culture. At the same time it is highly structured
> and goal oriented. These attributes make it potentially suitable for
> further study of culture in the context of MIS implementation.

Checkland and Scholes (1990) certainly emphasize the importance of a stream of cultural inquiry, arguing that in SSM this is:

> ... equal in importance to the logic-driven thinking. That this is the
> case stems from the acceptance that although facts and logic have a
> part to play in human affairs, the *feel* of them, their felt texture,

> derives equally (or more) from the myths and meanings which
> human beings attribute to their professional (and personal) entangle-
> ments with their fellow beings. (p. 44)

In SSM the on-going analysis of the culture and politics of the situation guides both the course of an SSM study and the suitability of possible recommendations, with 'cultural feasibility' being an explicit requirement. The cultural enquiry component of SSM is not yet fully developed and little guidance is yet provided on how it may be conducted formally. SSM might also be criticized for suggesting that only a single culture need be inquired into, for Gregory (1983) points out that many organizations can be best viewed as multicultural and composed of subgroups, each with its own conceptual framework and system of meanings. Despite this, SSM appears in many other ways to be a promising basis for an interpretative data analysis. Not least of its attractions is that it employs a model of human sense-making of the sort lacked by data analysis at present, and by which much of the practice of data analysis is explicable.

Appreciation as a sense-making model

In practice data analysts already engage in a continual process of negotiation and definition of meaning, and many hours are spent in finding acceptable agreed entries for data dictionaries. The notion of 'appreciation' originating from the work of Sir Geoffrey Vickers (1965, 1968, 1970, 1983, 1984) and used in SSM provides an explanation of why this is necessary and the basis for just the kind of model of human sense-making that data analysis lacks. Lewis (1991) suggests that the idea of appreciation not only provides a basis for distinguishing between 'data' and 'information' but also has profound implications for our understanding of the nature of data analysis. A major theme of Vickers' work was that management (or as Vickers preferred to call it 'governance') is concerned with the continuing maintenance of desired relationships and avoidance of undesired relationships, both within the organization and between the organization and the external world. Maintaining or eluding relationships requires that the organization continually adapt to changing circumstances, but this adaptation is dependent upon the organization's 'appreciation' of itself and its environment. At any moment in time the organization will have a particular 'appreciative setting', which Vickers (1984) defines as a readiness to see and value things in one way rather than another. That appreciative setting will be dependent upon past experiences, the history, culture and mythology of the organization—and it will consist of standards, norms and values. These result in the organization recognizing as important or relevant only particular features of the situation, only particular actions as possible, and only particular data as meaningful.

Settings of the appreciative system not only provide meaning and allow an understanding of the world but also *restrict* understanding (Lewis, 1991). The appreciative system therefore acts as a 'cognitive filter' that recognizes certain facts about reality as meaningful data and uses these to create the observer's understanding of reality, but disallows the cognizing of those things that are not meaningful in terms of the cognitive categories of which it is composed (Figure 9.1).

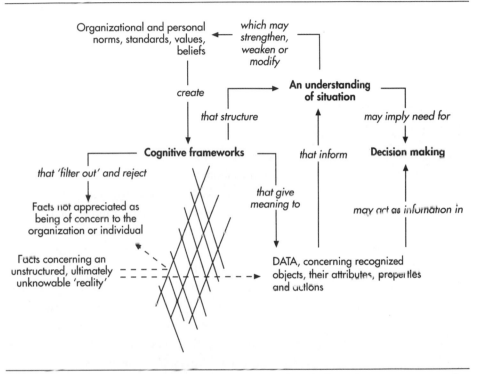

Figure 9.1   Appreciation allows and restricts understanding (from Lewis, 1993b)

SSM AS THE BASIS OF AN INTERPRETATIVE FORM OF DATA ANALYSIS

The idea of appreciation and the formal definitions of relevant systems used in SSM together provide the possibility of creating an alternative form of *interpretative* data model. Lewis (1993c) suggests how cognitive categories might provide the basic components of such a model. In SSM studies initial fact-finding and issue identification are followed by the conceptualization of a number of notional systems. Each of these is described as precisely as possible in a formal system definition, consisting of a root definition, a declaration of CATWOE components and an activity model showing the activities logically required to be undertaken by the system. These system definitions are employed in discussion, debate and learning about the problem situation.

The system definitions of SSM can, though, only be meaningfully understood by an individual if that individual is able to assign meaning to the terms used within it. One cannot, for example, understand a SSM system definition of a conceptualized patient care system without having some idea of what a 'patient' is, what a patient might do and what might be done to a patient. Each of SSM's relevant systems is then meaningful only with respect to a particular set of cognitive categories and to some assumptions about the associations that exist between those categories. Lewis (1993b) suggests that showing those categories, associations and their meanings in a new form of data model would be of value to the SSM practitioner in a number of ways; these include providing further insight into the nature of the system and establishing a clearer vocabulary for discussion and debate. More directly related to the concerns of this chapter, however, we can see that it could also be of value in providing a defensible starting point for conventional data modelling.

Just as the activity models of SSM are used as the basis for examining the things done in real-world organizations, so the categories and associations shown in a system's data model might provide guidance for thinking about implementable data storage mechanisms. The interpretative data model might, in effect, be translatable in some degree into data models of a more conventional kind. For example, the data model of a 'patient care system' might include the categories of 'doctor' and 'patient', each having a very specific agreed meaning. Part of that meaning might be defined by the allowable actions of each. A 'doctor' might by definition be capable of treating a 'patient'; a 'patient' might be understood as capable of registering with a 'doctor'; and so forth. The system's data model would therefore include action associations between the two categories. These categories and associations are relevant in terms of the explicit system definitions from which they are derived, and nothing else. Should the SSM analysis conclude that the notional 'patient care system' has some real-world equivalent, then we would expect that this would require data concerning patients, doctors and historical records of the actions that have occurred, such as treatments. The systems data model therefore provides an explicit justification for including certain things as entities or objects in a conventional form of data model.

CONCLUSION

In this chapter we have summarized arguments made in previous publications concerning the use of SSM to provide an interpretative form of data analysis. We have argued that:

- An interpretative form of data analysis is required by the wish to link information systems planning more closely with strategic planning of organizations, and by the need to give consideration to organizational cultures in information systems development.

- The underlying, objectivist philosophy and assumptions of conventional forms of data analysis make them unsuitable for use in ill-defined situations, and therefore for use in the early stages of systems development.
- The SSM concept of appreciation provides a suitable model of human sense-making for interpreting the process of data analysis and SSM is a means of inquiry that is sensitive to the complex social and political nature of organizations.
- Investigating the cognitive categories used in SSM's system definitions may provide the basis for an interpretative form of data model. This would assist in an SSM analysis and provide the starting point for later data-modelling and design work.

Much work remains to be done in refining the techniques of identifying cognitive categories, finding appropriate modelling conventions and establishing translation rules for a system's data model. However, if the title of this chapter was intended to raise awareness of the new challenges facing data analysis, then we hope we have shown that soft systems methodology may play a substantial role in meeting those challenges.

REFERENCES

Ashworth, C. and Goodland, M. (1990) *SSADM: A Practical Approach*, McGraw-Hill, Maidenhead.

Avison, D. E. and Wood-Harper, A. T., (1990) *Multiviews: An Exploration in Information System Development*, Blackwell, Oxford.

Baskerville, R. (1993) 'Semantic database prototypes', *Journal of Information Systems*, **3** (2), 119–44.

Batini, C., Ceri, S. and Navathe, S. B. (1992) *Conceptual Database Design: An Entity-Relationship Approach*, Benjamin Cummings, Redwood. CA.

Bulmer, R. (1967) 'Why the Cassowary is not a bird', *Man* (new series), **2** (1), 5–25.

CCTA (1989) 'Compact Manual', version 1.1, Central Computer and Telecommunications Agency, Norwich, Norfolk.

CCTA (1993) *Applying Soft Systems Methodology to an SSADM Feasibility Study*, HMSO, London.

Checkland, P. B. (1981) *Systems Thinking, Systems Practice*, Wiley, Chichester.

Checkland, P. B. and Scholes, J. (1990) *Soft Systems Methodology in Action*, Wiley, Chichester.

Chen, P. P-S (1976) 'The entity-relationship model: toward a unified view of data', *ACM Transactions on Database Systems*, **1** (1), 9–36.

Codd, E. F. (1970) 'A relational model of data for large shared data banks', *Communications of the ACM*, **13** (6), 377–87.

Cutts, G. (1987) *SSADM: Structured Systems Analysis and Design Methodology*, Paradigm, London.

Date, C. J. (1990) *An Introduction to Database Systems*, vol. I (5th edn), Addison-Wesley, Reading, Mass.

De Champeaux, D. and Faure, P. (1992) 'A comparative study of object-oriented analysis methods', *Journal of Object-Oriented Programming*, **5** (1), 21–33.

De Marco, T. (1978) *Structured Analysis and System Specification*, Yourdon, New York.

Downs. E., Clare, P. and Coe, I. (1992) *Structured Systems Analysis and Design Method: Application and Context* (2nd edn), Prentice-Hall, Hemel Hempstead.

Eva, M. (1992) *SSADM Version 4: A User's Guide*, McGraw-Hill, Maidenhead.

Galliers, R. D. (1991) 'Strategic information systems planning: myths, reality and guidelines for successful implementation', *European Journal of Information Systems*, **1** (1), 55–64.

Hartman, W., Matthes, H. and Proeme, A. (1968) *Information Systems Handbook*, Philips-Electrologica, Apeldooorn, Netherlands.

Hughes, J. G. (1991) *Object-Oriented Databases*, Prentice-Hall, Hemel Hempstead.

Ives, B. and Learmouth, G. P. (1983) 'The information system as a competitive weapon', *Communications of the ACM*, **27** (12), 1193–1201.

Kim, W. (1990) *Introduction to Object-Oriented Databases*, MIT Press, Cambridge, Mass.

Klein, H. K. and Hirschheim, R. (1987) 'A comparative framework of data modelling paradigms and approaches', *Computer Journal*, **30** (1), 8–15.

Klein, H. K. and Lyytinen, K. (1992) 'Towards a new understanding of data modelling', in *Software Development and Reality Construction* (C. Floyd, H. Zullighoven, R. Budde, and R. Keil-Slawik, eds), Springer-Verlag, Berlin, 203–19.

Kroenke, D. M. (1992) *Database processing: fundamentals, design, implementation*, 4 edn., Macmillan, New York.

Law, J. and Lodge, P. (1984) *Science for Social Scientists*, Macmillan, London.

Lewis, P. J. (1991) 'The decision making basis for information systems: the contribution of Vickers' concept of appreciation to a "soft" systems perspective', *European Journal of Information Systems*, **1** (1), 33–43.

Lewis, P. J. (1992) 'The feasibility and desirability of a closer linking of SSM with data-focused information systems development', *Systemist*, **14** (3), 168–79.

Lewis, P. J. (1993a) 'Data analysis and the Cassowary'. Internal Discussion Paper IDP 2/93, Department of Systems and Information Management, Lancaster University.

Lewis, P. J. (1993b) 'Linking soft systems methodology with data-focused information systems development', *Journal of Information Systems*, **3** (3), 169–86.

Lewis, P. J. (1993c) 'Identifying cognitive categories: the basis for interpretative data analysis within soft systems methodology', *International Journal of Information Management*, **13** (5), 373–86.

Lewis, P. J. (1994) *Information System Development: The use of Systems Thinking in the field of Information Systems*, Pitman, London.

McFadden, F. R. and Hoffer, J. A. (1991) *Database Management* (3rd edn), Benjamin Cummings, Redwood, CA.

McGinnes, S. (1992) 'How objective is object-oriented analysis? Paper presented at tube CAiSE '92', 4th Conference on Advanced Information Systems, Manchester, UK, May.

Markus, M. L. and Robey, D. (1983) 'The organizational validity of management information systems', *Human relations*, (36), 203–225.

Odell, J. J. (1992) 'Dynamic and multiple classification', *Journal of Object Oriented Programming*, **4** (8), 45–8.

Olle, W. T., Hagelstein, J., Macdonald, I. G., Rolland, C., Sol, H. G., Assche, van F. J. M., and Verrijn-Stuart, A. A. (1991) *Information Systems Methodologies*, Addison-Wesley, Wokingham, UK.

Pettigrew, A. M. (1979) 'On Studying Organisational Cultures' in *Administrative Science Quarterly*, **24**, 574–75.

Pfeffer, J. (1981) 'Management as symbolic action: the creation and maintenance of organisational paradigms', *Research in Organizational Behaviour*, **3**, 1–52.

Pliskin, N., Romm, T., Lee, A. S. and Weber, Y. (1993) 'Presumed versus actual organizational culture: managerial implications for implementation of information systems', *The Computer Journal*, **36** (2), 143–52.

Porter, M. E. and Millar, V. E. (1985) 'How information gives you competitive advantage', *Harvard Business Review*, **63** (4), 149–60.

Rishe, N. (1988) *Database Design Fundamentals*, Prentice-Hall, Englewood Cliffs, N.J.

Vickers, G. (1965) *The Art of Judgement*, Harper and Row, London.

Vickers, G. (1968) *Value Systems and Social Process*, Tavistock, London.

Vickers, G. (1970) *Freedom in a Rocking Boat*, Allen Lane, London.

Vickers, G. (1983) *Human Systems are Different*, Harper and Row, London.

Vickers, G. (1984) *The Vickers Papers* (Open Systems Group, ed.), Harper and Row, London.

Ward, J., Griffiths, P. and Whitmore, P. (1990) *Strategic Planning for Information Systems*, Wiley, Chichester.

Weaver, P. L. (1993) *Practical SSADM Version 4: A Complete Tutorial Guide*, Pitman, London.

Wilson, B. (1990) *Systems: Concepts, Methodologies and Applications*, Wiley, Chichester.

Wiseman, C. and MacMillan, I. C. (1984) 'Creating competitive weapons from information systems', *Journal of Business Strategy*, **5** (2), 42–9.

Wood-Harper, A. T. and Fitzgerald, G. (1982) 'A taxonomy of current approaches to systems analysis', *The Computer Journal*, **25** (1), 12–16.

INDEX